MW01090057

We Are All Armenian

EDITED BY
ARAM
MRJOIAN

We Are All Armenian

Voices from the Diaspora

University of Texas Press
Austin

Requests for permission to reproduce material from this work should be
sent to:

>Permissions
>University of Texas Press
>P.O. Box 7819
>Austin, TX 78713-7819
>utpress.utexas.edu/rp-form

♾ The paper used in this book meets the minimum requirements of ANSI/
NISO Z39.48-1992 (R1997) (Permanence of Paper).

Library of Congress Cataloging-in-Publication Data
Names: Mrjoian, Aram, editor.
Title: We are all Armenian : voices from the diaspora / edited by Aram
    Mrjoian.
Description: First edition. | Austin : University of Texas Press, 2023. |
    Includes bibliographical references.
Identifiers:
    LCCN 2022024373
    ISBN 978-1-4773-2679-4 (cloth)
    ISBN 978-1-4773-2680-0 (PDF)
    ISBN 978-1-4773-2681-7 (ePub)
Subjects: LCSH: Armenians—North America—Biography. | Armenians—
    North America—Ethnic identity. | Armenians—Social life and cus-
    toms. | Armenian diaspora. | LCGFT: Autobiographies.
Classification: LCC DS172.2 .W43 2023 | DDC 305.891/9920730922
    [B]—dc23/eng/20220601
LC record available at https://lccn.loc.gov/2022024373

doi:10.7560/326794

For the diaspora

Contents

Editor's Note

Anthologies, by their very nature, are as defined by their omissions as they are by their inclusions. No matter how comprehensive, an anthology will always be a momentary attempt, stuck in time as well as limited by space, editorial awareness, and financial constraints. This perhaps sounds cryptic, but as I set out to edit this collection, and with Armenian history in mind, I very much worried about this project's potential pitfalls and shortcomings. Diasporan Armenians cannot be pinned to a number of essays that is any smaller than the total diasporan population, and even that is problematic, only a brief and glancing representation of each person and community at a singular moment. This is to say the Armenian diaspora is both hyperlocal and intersectionally global. There is no such thing as a monolithic ethnic identity: to imagine so is harmful, marginalizing, and dangerous. To create a hierarchy or checklist of one's right to their ethnicity is an act of violence.

One of the notable themes that arises throughout these essays is the writers' not feeling Armenian enough. Many of these contributors share the sense of being pushed out and othered from both inside and outside their communities. Indeed, this is another sensation I had when I signed up to edit these works. I believed then, and still believe now, in my abilities as an editor, but I've never been able to quash the self-damaging notion that I am living behind a facade of an ethnic identity I have little claim to. My name, yes, is Armenian. My heritage, yes, is Armenian. But I don't speak the language. I don't attend the church. I've never spent much time in Armenian communities. I've never traveled back to the land of my ancestors. I am still constantly learning the basics of diasporan Armenian culture, feeling simultaneously distant from and near to this part of who I am. I guess I should not have been surprised, then, to read this same notion expressed more eloquently from many of the writers whose works are included in this collection. The false but unshakeable idea that one is not the right kind of Armenian or not Armenian enough is an inherent and inexorable part of the legacy of genocide, displacement, cultural erasure, and ethnic ambiguity.

The Armenian diaspora must also grapple with its own prejudices and forms of erasure. While there's no wrong way to be Armenian, it is damaging and hypocritical to demand recognition of one's ethnicity, one's history, and one's oppression without also recognizing the systems in which one is complicit in oppression as well as the ways one can cause harm and marginalize and erase others. Despite widely unified calls in diasporan Armenian communities for acknowledgment of the Armenian Genocide and continuing injustices, many members within these communities have maintained exclusionary practices, particularly around dating and marriage, and have at times attempted to omit queer, multiethnic, and multiracial Armenians from the diaspora. This is another tragic and malicious form of violence. Fear, privilege, and power can all spark exclusionary thinking. I worry that in feeling nationless, some seek other kinds of borders.

This collection is intentionally inclusive of work by those who have faced historical marginalization in diasporan Armenian communities. Scout Tufankjian, who traveled the world for her work of photojournalism, *There Is Only the Earth: Images from the Armenian Diaspora Project*, writes,

> I had grown up thinking that there was a tiny box you needed to squeeze into to be a good Armenian, a box that I did not fit in, but my travels showed me that there is a place for all of us within this huge Armenian family, whether we are half Armenians, gay Armenians, Black Armenians, arty Armenians, atheist Armenians, non-Armenian-speaking Armenians, or good old-fashioned 100 percent Armenian AYF/AGBU-belonging/ churchgoing/future-engineer Armenians. We are all Armenian. All of us have a role to play in the future of our community.

For many diasporan Armenians, home is also a complicated concept, and the binaries of borders present a confounding lack of definition for Armenians around the world. Where does one consider home when home is both everywhere and somewhere else? What happens when one's home is destroyed, contested, stolen, and denied?

Diasporan Armenian writers—and particularly Armenian-American writers—bear the burden of having to repeat their history over and over because it remains widely forgotten and unacknowledged. For more than a century, Turkey has leveraged geopolitical power, military force, propaganda, and terroristic violence in an attempt to eliminate the undeniable proof of their ongoing wrongdoing. Tragically, this strategy has been effective in obfuscating the history of the Ottoman Empire's genocidal legacy and makes it difficult for Armenians worldwide to find closure or address more recent acts of terror.

I have heard Armenians echo the phrase "never again," referring to the massacres that took so many of their ancestors. Those two direct words, in their axiomatic clarity, must extend to all humanity. Our respect for human rights needs be universal, inclusive, and unflinching. But right now, we must once again shout this phrase as we witness widespread fascism and violent intolerance return in contemporary iterations.

In my own personal essays, I've often argued that writers from the Armenian diaspora—across genres spanning fiction, nonfiction, poetry, and criticism—are weighed down by the incessant need to educate their audience and fight the systemic rewriting and erasing of their history with their words. The Armenian writer is often forced to lay a foundation of knowledge before getting to the story they would like to tell. Working with the writers included in these pages has helped me better see the innovative, diverse, and expansive range of narratives and research being produced by diasporan Armenians today. For their trust in me, I will always be grateful.

Aram Mrjoian

We Are All Armenian

Introduction

ON APRIL 24, 2021, Joe Biden became the first sitting US president to release a statement formally acknowledging the Armenian Genocide. The brief note quickly summarized the well-documented massacres, death marches, deportations, and legacy of displacement, events unfamiliar to many Americans. Concluding, Biden noted, "The American people honor all those Armenians who perished in the genocide that began 106 years ago today."

April 24, the date annually recognized as Armenian Genocide Remembrance Day, symbolically marks the beginning of one of the twentieth century's largest atrocities: the systemic plunder, torture, and murder of approximately one and a half million Armenians living in the Ottoman Empire during the years 1915–1923. On that date in 1915, hundreds of Armenian intellectuals, artists, activists, and other community leaders were arrested and soon killed. The mass violence and deportations that followed were a calculated, organized, and state-endorsed plan executed under the direction of the Ottoman Empire's highest leadership. Surviving Armenians in the region were displaced, exiled, Islamized, or forced into hiding.

At the time, the Armenian Genocide received extensive media coverage; 145 articles appeared in the *New York Times* in 1915 alone. An editorial in the October 14, 1915, issue of *The Nation* states, "A series of misdeeds like those in Armenia are the concern of the whole world," and ties this tragedy abroad to the lynching of African Americans. From 1915 to 1929, the Committee on Armenian Atrocities raised more than $116 million in aid. Famously, Teddy Roosevelt refused to join the committee because he instead advocated for war against Turkey and found it hypocritical to "solicit permission to help the survivors." After finding support in Congress, President Woodrow Wilson designated October 21 and 22 as days to express sympathy and aid for Armenian and Syrian populations. For Wilson, the call to create the League of Nations was in part catalyzed by the moral demand to help Armenians and other defenseless populations across the globe. Later, Wilson, in poor health, would become responsible for drawing a section of the border for an independent Armenia. However, as the United States shifted to reliance on foreign oil, political sympathies toward the Armenian cause became inconvenient, and for decades afterward, Turkey exerted geopolitical power to silence American politicians.

While perhaps unintentionally ambiguous, the wording in the closing sentence of Biden's statement is significant. For more than a century, the Armenian Genocide has been widely contested, denied, and erased, even though there is overwhelming historical documentation and confirmation among historians and academics. Violence against Armenians remains both a concrete and an existential threat today. In 2020, Recep Tayyip Erdoğan, the president of Turkey, made a veiled reference to the ongoing violence and erasure of the Armenian Genocide when he stated, "We will continue to fulfill the mission our grandfathers have carried out for centuries in the Caucasus." Today, Turkey is regularly ranked among the world's top three countries for imprisoning journalists, writers, and other artists. The country's current penal code contains wide-ranging articles that prohibit free speech, including Article 301, which, as cited in a 2021 report by PEN America, criminalizes "publicly de-grad[ing] the Turkish Nation, State of the Turkish Republic, Turkish Grand National Assembly, the Government of the Republic of Turkey and the judicial bodies of the State."

Yet denial of the Armenian Genocide extends well beyond malicious campaigns to bury the past. On November 9, 2020, while Americans remained enraptured in the presidential election, Azerbaijan successfully achieved a long-desired land grab in the independent, ethnically Armenian Republic of Artsakh, known more widely as Nagorno-Karabakh. After six weeks of horrific warfare, during which Armenians were terrified that full-scale ethnic cleansing was imminent, Russia brokered a vague treaty that proved beneficial for every party except Armenians. During the war, thousands of Armenian soldiers and civilians were killed. Over one hundred thousand have been permanently displaced. As Azerbaijan repopulates seized areas of the region, countless Armenian religious sites dating back to early Christianity are at risk of destruction. This was not without warning. In late October of the same year, well before the ceasefire, dozens of genocide scholars had signed a statement drawing attention to the Nagorno-Karabakh situation, which included the following: "Current political statements, economic policies, sentiments of the societies and military actions by the Azerbaijani and Turkish leadership should warn us that genocide of the Armenians in Nagorno-Karabakh, and perhaps even Armenia, is a very real possibility."

Unrelated to this specific statement, the Armenian Genocide literature scholar Dr. Rubina Peroomian notes in her extensive literary research, "How forceful and profound is the impact of Turkish denial, such that the pain does not subside even when myriad genocide scholars, historians, and government officials around the world make sympathetic remarks in recognition of the Armenian Genocide?"

Today, there are an estimated eleven million Armenians living around the world but fewer than three million living within the country of Armenia. However, much of the Armenian diaspora remains extremely vocal and active about their distant homeland. For many, acknowledgment and reparations from Turkey remain central to breaking the cycle of intergenerational trauma.

Storytelling and activism have also always been important aspects of Armenian culture, since long before countless writers and artists were murdered under Ottoman rule. For recent generations of diasporan Armenian writers, telling their stories often requires a complex balance of contextualizing the past and reporting on the present, respecting a culture that has been shattered and glued back together across the globe while feeling lost in its cracks and forgotten remnants. Diasporan Armenian writers, particularly in their fiction and creative nonfiction, thus have found esoteric ways of experimenting with form, style, and narrative structure to tell hybrid stories.

In the back of this collection, you'll find a helpful but far from comprehensive list of Armenian and diasporan Armenian literature that spans genres and offers wider insights to Armenian religion, literature, history, and culture. Of course, the essays included here provide personal perspectives on these themes as well. I hope the included selections fill you with light and outrage, joy and concern, and an equal demand for self-reflection and urgent action.

How Armenian Funeral Halva Helped My Family Find Home in America

LIANA AGHAJANIAN

THERE WAS ONLY ONE THING I understood about death as a child: when it arrived, it brought with it halva.

Halva (which means "sweetmeat" in Arabic) is a confectionary made with assorted ingredients like tahini (sesame paste) or semolina and eaten in various forms across the world, from the Middle East to the Balkans to India. It's even sold commercially in the United States. The recipe I knew, however, involved four key things: sugar, butter, flour, and funerals.

At the funerals I attended as a child, wading through a sea of black outfits with the distinct smell of frankincense in my nose, I'd search through the crowd for my aunts and the glistening, aluminum foil–wrapped treasure they carried on a tray. Multiple days of mourning, house visits, and marathon funeral services administered by the Armenian Apostolic Church—this was the price I had to pay for a tiny piece of halva. It would disappear as quickly as it would materialize, giving me mere seconds of joy in the midst of grief.

I can't remember when I first had funeral halva, a tradition practiced by Armenians as well as other communities including Iranians, Assyrians, Turks, and Greeks. But I know I never forgot what it tasted like: equal parts grainy and sweet, a little nutty. I loved the simplicity of it, how such intensity could be created by stirring together three ingredients that only partially formed other recipes.

I always had trouble taking just one piece.

I was born in Tehran, to an Armenian family whose roots carry the complicated combination of a centuries-old legacy in the country now known as Iran and a history of genocide, exile, and migration. We came to the United States as refugees at the tail end of the Iran–Iraq War, and like many Iranian and Armenian immigrants thrust into a world thousands of miles from the one they knew, we tried to re-create home in Southern California.

I quickly learned that life inside my house—where my name was pronounced the way it was intended to be, where I ate stuffed grape leaves instead of peanut butter and grape jelly sandwiches, and where my parents watched public access programming in Armenian and Farsi instead of the Super Bowl—was different from life elsewhere. Dealing with this contrast as a child often overwhelmed and confused me. Back then, my two identities didn't blend together as easily as they do now; their melding was a slow, simmering process that required patience.

Eventually, working to establish ourselves in the new country, we had stayed long enough to begin burying family, friends, and acquaintances. Funerals formed the backbone of my childhood, the same way weddings did. They were big, expensive, elaborate events full of many people I knew, and many I did not.

I accompanied my parents to Armenian churches scattered across Los Angeles and to cemeteries that held both the immigrants that built L.A. and the Hollywood stars that made the city famous. I went to wakes, where distant relatives spoke quietly under their breath and gulped down endless piping-hot chai from a samovar. I attended drawn-out church services, listening to excruciatingly somber, yet beautiful, Armenian hymns and the booming voice of the priest that bounced off the walls as he read from the Bible. The graveside service was the home stretch. I gripped the grass with my shoes on the hills where we stood and hoped I could hold on until the end. As the casket was lowered into the ground, the frankincense glowed in the brass burner, emitting clouds of smoke that acted as a pathway between mortal prayers and God.

AFTER REQUIEM SERVICES, we would get in our cars once more and drive to a special lunch called the hokeh-jash, which means "soul-meal," a memorial meal for the deceased. Stemming from an age-old tradition in which food was made and distributed to the poor after a death, the hokeh-jash evolved into a service held at home or a nearby restaurant, hosted by bereaved family members.

For my family, that meant heading up to the banquet-style second floor of an Iranian-Armenian restaurant, where we dined on what we always did, whether there was a funeral or not: a table covered from end to end in various dishes and appetizers like koobideh, an Iranian kebab made from beef, saffron-stained rice, and a shallot-yogurt dip called mast o' moosir, among copious amounts of lavash bread, butter, and sumac.

When I couldn't (or didn't want to) attend these funerals, I'd request halva to be brought back home.

"Can you sneak a piece, or maybe two?" I'd ask my parents as they stood in the doorway, heading to the cemetery. Recapturing the taste of halva in the New World became a personal mission of mine.

It must've been significant that my dad began making this funeral food at home for us, where everyone was very much alive. My sister and I would crave it spontaneously, the memory of its taste hitting us when we lingered too long at the dinner table, filling the silent space with reminiscences about when we had last seen our extended family.

We'd wait and watch, witnessing my dad practice his art in a different way. In the making of halva here in America, his skills as an artist came to use, remnants of a life and career he had largely left behind when the war took him from his home and made him a refugee. He'd stir the flour in a saucepan until it turned the color of burnt ivory, then add the butter and sugar. Shaping a glob of burnt flour and butter into a tray was no easy task, and neither was using kitchen utensils to carve uniform designs on top. This process bound us to each other at a time when we were unsure of our place in a new, unfamiliar country.

Funeral halva was that and more.

It was a ritual food, but it also became a marker of my own identity. It made me aware that even in death, the legacy I had to contend with spanned several countries and cultures. It was a tradition practiced for millennia, imported and kept alive in diasporic communities that helped define who we were. It was a little piece of sweetness that always reminded me how complex my history was up until the very end.

They say you don't fully become part of a place until you put your dead in the ground.

My family has created a home in America. Our traditions have become as much a part of this landscape as our deceased kin have. Though I'll always associate halva with funerals, it's become a bigger symbol of all the people and places I could no longer access: the city I never knew as an adult, the languages I never fully learned, the relatives I never got to see over the years. Growing up, I often felt like I didn't have much to ground me in one place or another, but food, especially halva, became a tangible personification of my roots, the same way it has for so many immigrants and their children.

Though much was lost over the years, there was always halva. It helped me explore and connect with a history interrupted by forced migration and political upheaval; it is a sweet intermediary between life and death, a dense fusion made of flour, sugar, and butter.

Hava Nagila

NAIRA KUZMICH

IF GOD WANTS PEOPLE TO SUFFER,
HE SENDS THEM TOO MUCH UNDERSTANDING.

YIDDISH PROVERB

BEFORE I TELL YOU about the strange night I danced to "Hava Nagila" in a bar in Berlin, I have to admit that I think about this night often, and I think about it on two different occasions. I think about it when I find myself at a loss for words, when I am confused about how to feel, what to do or say or think. A new horror on the news, and suddenly I picture myself dancing. A colleague at work proposes a "Diversity Field Guide Manual," and I smell the spilled cocktails, the heavy breath of the man beside me. People keep tweeting "Protest is fun!" and that famous Hassidic melody spins round and round in my head; the sticky bar floor spins under my feet too. But I also think about that night when I am most clearheaded, when I feel I have finally grasped something beyond my reach. A moment of enlightenment, perhaps, a moment of profound pleasure. I hold my niece in my arms, swing her to sleep, and it is she who has her hand on my shoulder that night in Berlin.

I was twenty years old and traveling through Germany with two girl-friends. We had met while we were studying abroad in Ireland, and two weeks in Germany after the fall semester ended sounded like a good way to cap off our European adventure, especially after meeting a considerable number of Germans in Ireland who were funny and hospitable, friends who would host us if we came through their towns.

We began our trip in Berlin. F. was a green-eyed, brown-skinned Indian American, born and bred in Southern California, and B. was Canadian, pale and short, with Macedonian and Caribbean family roots. And me, at five feet ten and 180 pounds, I was the big, black-haired, black-eyed Armenian American immigrant girl who was finally free of her family, her culture, all those obligations and expectations and traditions that made her desperate, had her saving money and begging her parents for years before they finally agreed to let her leave home.

I have to say here, too, that I was mostly happy when I was abroad. Even now, when I look back with a more cynical eye at my youth, embarrassed of my desperation, my rush to embrace the American Dream of an endlessly forgotten past, a constant clean slate, I can say that I was happy. And I'm glad. Glad to have felt for a while what so many feel every day. Glad that my shame now does not take away from my happiness then.

There was, however, one evening, one moment, one dance that I danced during my time abroad when my shame triumphed and triumphs still. For this, I am glad too. Understanding, for me, when it does not come from the sudden surprise of pleasure, comes from anger. When I danced that dance in a bar in Berlin, I felt a momentary happiness, and it is because I felt it for a moment when I should have felt it for none that I will feel ashamed forever. I am, however, grateful for this feeling. It is a small burden to suffer, after all, compared to what so many others shoulder. A small burden and a reminder. Not only of the heavier prices others have paid for their actions, feelings, and words, but also of those who float in this life light as a feather, thinking that they do no harm, cause no damage, leave no dead in their wake. It is these people I fear. Those who do not suffer. Those who do not understand.

THE MIDDLE-AGED GERMAN WOMAN who ran the hostel told us where to go for a night out: the immigrant part of town, Kreuzberg. Young people like the area, she explained. Travelers feel comfortable there. Like they could be locals. But, please, she advised, keep an eye on your wallets and on each other. Comfort and safety, she knew, were not always the same thing.

When we came out of the subway an hour later, the three of us looked at each other uneasily. We were twenty, twenty-one, twenty-two. We were women. Girls, really. It was not only what we saw: the graffiti, the smell of garbage, the homeless strewn on the streets like decorations. It was that small pedestrian fear coupled with something deeper. For we had come here to party. We had come to drink cheap beer and dance hard and make out with handsome strangers.

But we were not like the majority of the North American girls studying abroad in Ireland. That's what we told ourselves. We were not White Girls. Girls with diluted ethnicity. We thought they were a different breed. They did not eat floss halva or homemade pickled cauliflower, did not dance unironically to turbofolk music or curse in multiple languages. When confronted with "the foreign" abroad, there was always an extra layer for us to work through, because we knew that sometimes we were one of them— the *others*—but other times we weren't.

In Berlin, coming out of the subway, we felt American. We felt uneasy. By that, of course, I mean we felt white. White girls come to party in the hood. We walked quietly, not wanting to draw attention to ourselves, not wanting to see ourselves for who we were at that moment. We walked until we found the recommended bar, a packed place bright with bodies. We took off our layers of clothing, our white-girl skins, and felt like ourselves again, whatever that was. All we knew was that we did not stand out in any way here, and it was a relief. Inside the bar, it was clear that everyone forgot what the outside had looked like, the streets they had crossed, the roads they had traveled to get here. We quickly forgot too. Here was a common destination: party. The great equalizer.

We squeezed past German and tourist bodies to get to the bar, got our beers, and by the time we finished them—quickly, that first beer always the fastest to go—we had a group of men talking to us. We let them talk. In the way of that strange magical algebra of bar-floor meetings, there were three men, suddenly, for the three of us. The one who happened upon me was German. German through and through. Tall, blond hair closely cropped, cool blue eyes. Big in the German way: lean muscles, wide shoulders, thick neck. Standing next to him, and looking up, I smiled and settled into the conversation, taking delight in my comparative smallness.

He asked where I was from, and I answered L.A. Like that—"L.A." With a confidence I did not share when I was asked the same question in America. But it was the most truthful answer after living twenty years in my white, but foreign, body, and it was easier to tell the truth in Europe, where no one was trying to prove me a liar. No one in Europe knew that when I said L.A., I really meant Little Armenia, the ethnic enclave of Los Angeles where I spent almost my entire life after leaving Armenia at the age of five. In Europe, I let others believe what they wanted about me. Let them think I was a rich girl, steps away from being discovered, instead of a twenty-year-old who slept on the fold-out couch with her grandmother in the living room of a one-bedroom apartment in Little Armenia, Los Angeles.

And what did my German man think about my city? The German

abruptly handed me his glass, turned around, and raised his shirt up across his shoulder blades. Stunned, I reached out with my fingers to touch the pale pink skin of his back but pulled away at the last moment, confused. He pulled his shirt down and turned to face me again.

"I want to tattoo *To Live and Die in Los Angeles* right there!" He grinned at me expectantly. "Tupac!"

I blinked at him, trying to find an appropriate response. Did this white boy really want to tattoo a Tupac lyric on his body? Because he *was* white. Particular notions of German whiteness—Aryan identity—certainly figure significantly in European history, but the Germanic roots of American white people are also what give most white Americans today the security of their racial identity. I knew that most white Americans thought they were Irish by heritage; I also knew they were wrong. We ethnic people are often forced to educate ourselves on the ethnicity of whiteness in America as part of our arsenal of facts, our weapons against racism and xenophobia. There's a certain American romanticism at work, we know, when white people believe in their Irish roots as opposed to their German ones. By romanticism, of course, I mean that remarkable power of self-deception Americans are known for throughout the world.

I had felt no discomfort among the white Germans I met in Ireland because, I had realized quickly, they were open about their country's past: apologetic without being defensive, a stance that struck me as just right. Complex and difficult to navigate, but right nonetheless. They were not responsible for the deaths of over six million, but they knew who were. Their predecessors. Relatives. They spoke about the Holocaust gravely, with sincere mortification, but without a sense of individual guilt. Sitting in our living rooms in the west of Ireland, talking politics in that silly, naive way that young people love to do, it was fascinating to see how shame translated into the young German consciousness, and how that compared to America's own history of genocide and racism. My German friends were afraid of nationalism and wary of any demonstration of patriotism. *This* line, they said, was too thin to navigate. Listening to them talk, I knew that despite the general liberal climate of Southern California, my white neighbors, classmates, teachers, and strangers on the street all wielded the American flag like a weapon against the past.

So I peered at this German and tried to make sense of his desire to claim Tupac's words and all that they represented as his own, to carve them, in fact, into his own white skin. "Have you been to California?"

"Yes!" He pumped his free hand in the air. "Venice Beach and Rose Bowl!"

And, unexpectedly, I was charmed. "Was USC playing?" I asked coyly. "I go to USC."

His mouth dropped open, and I threw my head back and laughed. I could be his California girl, like one of the real ones he had seen during his vacation. I've strolled the boardwalk at Venice; I've cheered at college football games. I've been in a car on the winding streets of Los Angeles, "California Love" blasting on the radio. In the arms of this German eager to embrace another's culture, I would be safe from suspicion. And what better place than L.A. for two people to take on the role of a lifetime?

"USC," he breathed gleefully, and then he noticed the empty glasses in both of our hands. "One minute. I'm going to get us more beer."

I smiled and watched him go, enjoying the way he so assuredly disappeared into the crowd. As I moved my gaze away, I caught the conspiratorial wink of his friend, a handsome cornrowed man with North African features who was speaking to my friend, B. I blushed and kept my gaze moving. Before it had a chance to settle on anything, a Frenchman moved intimately close and began to speak flirtatiously. I apologized and told him I was "with someone," pointing at a nondescript spot in the crowd huddled by the bar, and kept repeating, pointing, until he walked away. I felt a strange sense of loyalty to the German, though he had no claim on me or my attention. He had, however, been to my city. He had thought me a California girl.

In Europe, particularly among European men, I had felt my Americanness shine through and my foreignness fade away. Outside of a bar in rainy Dublin, I had kissed a Swiss-Italian who kept exclaiming "American girls are so hot" every time we parted for air. I felt silly but proud, reveling in my beauty, its power, but also the power that came with being American. European men had, perhaps, "different" expectations for what constituted an American woman, but whatever suggestion or fantasy they had in their mind's eye, I fit it. And it was a wondrous, dizzying feeling, much better than simply feeling desired. It was a freedom these men afforded me, akin to flying with an American passport—the knowledge that no place could hold you without your permission. While my passport *was* American, I felt American only on paper, bubbling in "White" for my "Race" in college applications, for example. In person, Americans could not get over how different I looked, sounded, even behaved, which was the most hurtful.

My reserve was foreign snobbery or a symptom of my oppression. My passion was too aggressive or too contained. Everything I did, everything I believed in, could be explained away by my foreignness—no, not explained away by. Blamed on. A difference there too.

But here I was in Europe, no one batting a lash when I said American, when I said California, when I said L.A. In Europe, among European men, my Americanness was exoticized but never in the way my Armenianness was, and is still, exoticized in America. That difference is the difference in relation to power. As an American in Europe, I had the clout of financial means and national support. I had a right to be there. For the most part, I was even wanted. Even the jokes at the Americans' expense—our ignorance, arrogance, propensity to wear sneakers—were not a threat. They posed no danger to my, or to any American's, sense of safety *or* comfort. Obama had just won the presidential election, and all of Europe was singing America's praises. But even before, though we'd gone to war with Afghanistan and Iraq, and anti-American feeling was high in Europe, you could say you were American and not *worry* about that affecting your ability to get a taxi, an apartment, a job, a handsome man's phone number.

Being ethnic or being a person of color in America means constantly having to accommodate other people's feelings while tempering your own, means constantly having to gauge whether it's safe to look, talk, think like you want, like you find natural, because for some people that seems like the most unnatural thing in the world. With our "ethnically ambiguous" features, being Armenian, specifically, means being confronted with American resentment toward a large variety of people: Muslims and Jews, Arabs, Slavs, Latinos (especially Mexicans), the French, Greeks, Indians, and Pakistanis. White Americans have confused me for everything and everyone, and when they didn't confuse me, when they knew exactly what an Armenian was, they had very specific feelings about what that meant too. Because to be Armenian in L.A. had its own xenophobic narrative: we were considered welfare-draining, BMW-driving, wife-beating, odor-reeking leeches of American generosity.

When my Armenianness was sometimes of interest to men in America, I always felt uncomfortable, like I was behind a glass wall in a museum, an audience of curious onlookers reading excitedly from their guidebooks about the defining features of the Armenian Woman, pointing at the strength of my thighs, the tangles of my hair, my childbearing hips. I still don't feel safe when a white American man's eyes fall attentively on me, and I know many women of color who feel the same.

But in Europe, *I* was the American. I was the one throwing my powerful net all over these men. Making them anecdotes, curiosities for my friends' pleasure. These men thought they were getting something novel? Let them. I knew I was getting something better.

THE GERMAN REAPPEARED WITH A BEER for me but had to get going, he said, visibly irritated, pointing to the door and shaking his head. He had to take a friend home, too much to drink. I swallowed my disappointment and gave him a hug, thanked him for the beer and conversation, and said that perhaps we'd meet in L.A. someday. "Yes!" he said eagerly, grabbing me by both shoulders. "Make sure you don't leave!"

I don't remember who I was talking to or about what when "Hava Nagila" came on. I heard the beginning chords of the Jewish song and caught B.'s eye. *What the hell is going on?* And then, in a blur, like a carefully planned '90s teen comedy routine, everyone in the bar rushed toward the tiny dance floor, by the deejay. People began putting their arms around each other's shoulders, forming a circle, and there we were, B. and I, right in the thick of it. The music was loud and dizzying, everyone drunk and dancing, moving awkwardly in the dense formation, shoulders and underarms pressed painfully close. Everyone grinning, everyone loudly shouting the only words they knew to the song: "Hava Nagila." I was shouting too.

It's hard to truly describe the rush of that moment, its absurdity, how perfect it all felt. This could not be more surreal, I distinctly remember thinking. Germany! This was Germany!

And then a Turk broached our circle, coming in between me and my Canadian friend, and my body tensed. I knew he was a Turk because I just knew—some people may never understand what it means to have history simmering always in the blood.

But perhaps they can understand this: Germany is home to the largest population of Turks outside of Turkey, and they make up the largest ethnic minority in Germany, approximately three million. Understand that Germany, with its notorious history of genocide, is home to a people whose ancestors tried to wipe mine off this earth. Understand also that when I walked in Germany, I may have been confused for a Turk, but I confused no Turk, no German, no hybrid, for an Armenian. Not once did I see a dark-haired, dark-eyed, big-hipped woman and think, *Maybe.* Every time I saw someone who a bystander would argue looked like me, I immediately identified the ways they were different: the Turkishness in the shape of their eyes, an Asiatic turn, for example; or the color of their skin, either too dark or too pale, not that sandy shade of brown that could only come from centuries living on a land of stone, bearing the brunt of the powerful color in the sky. But I mostly felt their Turkishness in the pit of my stomach, an instinctive jolt, a pressure climbing, spreading throughout my body. It was not hatred I felt, not fear. It was history, the collective memory of my people, and it was real and beating hard and fast inside of me.

Turkey refuses to call the systematic extermination of one and a half million Ottoman Armenians in 1915 genocide; in fact, there is widespread propaganda in place to convince Turks that it was their ancestors who were slaughtered at the hands of the Armenians. There are other "official" Turkish explanations for the large number of Armenian dead. Most Armenians starved and were not killed outright—so, blame poverty! Armenians were Russian sympathizers and had to be neutralized for the well-being of the empire—Turks were defending themselves against treason! Armenians were killed by marauding gangs—what a coincidence! Deaths from "relocation" efforts cannot be considered genocide—it's all just part of empire-building! And my favorite: it was not genocide because the term "genocide" was not coined before 1943. If a tree falls in the woods, does it make a sound?

Still. I know what some readers want me to say now. I know that as the Turk approached our circle, put his arm on my shoulder, pressed his hip into my hip, smiled widely into my face—some readers want me to find beauty in the moment. Poetry. They want me to say that here we were, a Turk and an Armenian, dancing to a Jewish song in a bar in Berlin, shoulder to shoulder, coming together through art, travel, serendipity—that we were reconciling our horrific histories with our dreams of peace, a future for us all. The past forgotten, the past replaced by something more palatable. A song and dance.

But it is so easy for some people to say this. White Americans. Because they have been trying to dismiss history for centuries.

Even before his hand dropped from my shoulder to squeeze my ass, that American Dream crumpled before me. This surreal, seemingly magical scene lost its dazzling glow, its profound poignancy. Why were Germans so carelessly playing this song, I thought angrily, as if it would atone for their sins, bring back to life six million dead? All around me people were drunk, shouting, laughing, reveling in a stupid, naive fantasy or a horrific, racist joke. Oh, how stupid I felt in finding meaning in this bar! How angry I was at myself—I feel my rage even now. Hava Nagila-ing in Berlin. Apparently,

I was just another American traveler, White Girl Extraordinaire, *Eat-Pray-Love*-ing myself into contented oblivion.

I knew then that "Hava Nagila" was a Jewish song of celebration. But I didn't know that it was an expression of praise for the revival of the Hebrew language after its oppression for two millennia, when Jews were forced to speak the language of their conquerors. And I didn't know then that it was written in 1915, the year the Ottoman Turkish government began the slaughter of my people.

But there is no meaning here, either. A coincidence. Like the fact that it was a Turk grabbing my ass as I moved in a circle in Berlin. When his hand didn't move away, I squirmed and pressed myself against the body on my other side. But this new gap between us he quickly closed. Something in my expression, something in my body, something in the air. But suddenly a man came between us. It was the Moroccan who earlier had been talking to my friend B. He put his mouth close to the Turk's ear and said something I couldn't hear. The Turk didn't look at me as he left the circle, disappearing into the same crowd my German had.

The Moroccan put his arm around my shoulder. "Keep dancing," he said with a kind smile and distinct accent. But I could no longer move.

LATER, we were hungry, unsteady on our feet. It was a long subway ride back to our hostel, and we needed to sober up. We wandered around until we found a place open and smelling good. Sumac and cumin and fresh dill. A Mediterranean or Middle Eastern place—the food from those regions, I knew, often overlapped.

It was one of those ethnic fast food places specializing in numbered combos, with large, appetizing photos of full plates beside each oversize number, the name of the actual meal in smaller font, seemingly not as important. I took my time looking at the menu plastered on the wall behind the cashier. And then I saw exactly what I wanted: a beautiful picture of lahmajun, that thin, round dough covered in minced beef (or lamb), tomatoes, parsley, and peppers. Lahmajun is popular in both the Middle East and the Mediterranean, but its origins are clouded in mystery, though the word itself is Arabic. Syria, Lebanon, and many parts of the Levant make their own versions of lahmajun, but it is most famously a dish claimed by two distinct groups of people: the Armenians and the Turks.

In America it is referred to as Armenian Pizza, but in many parts of Europe, in this restaurant in which I stood, tipsy and increasingly emotional, it was labeled "Turkish Pizza." I narrowed my eyes to make sure of what I was seeing. It was my turn to order, and as I stood in front of the clerk, my eyes were still on the picture above him and the words beside that picture. Turkish Pizza.

There are more Turks than Armenians in Europe, and there are more Armenians than Turks in America. That is fact, and it goes a long way in explaining why the names of the dish are accepted and popularized in those regions. But these were facts, too: I was born in Armenia. I lived in a neighborhood called Little Armenia. Every week I ate my Armenian mother's Armenian lahmajun. Standing in that restaurant in Berlin, I was not an American, not by any means.

The clerk said something in German, and I finally looked at him. Dark hair, dark eyes, darker skin than mine, a beard dense and unfashionable in Armenian circles. I glanced up above him again, saw the words, and he spoke once more, loudly, annoyed. Probably to ask what I wanted to order. There were people behind me, I realized, who did not care, had no idea what I was feeling at that moment. There was someone in front of me, too, who may have suspected but probably didn't care either. I cleared my throat, but my voice wouldn't come. I lifted my arm and it shook as it indicated the lahmajun. The clerk said something again. I thrust my finger in the air, pointing. He raised his eyebrows, spoke once more in German. I put my hand to my throat, swallowed, and said the number in English. Almost everyone we had met in Germany spoke some English. He would know numbers. I said the number. And he smiled. He smiled big, said in a thick accent, "Turkish Pizza?" I repeated the number in English. He repeated his question. My heart was racing, and I knew I was seconds away from bursting into tears. I felt the drunken restlessness behind me. I felt his Turkish eyes on my Armenian face. I said the number in English again. He smiled wider, leaned forward: "Turkish Pizza." And this time it was not a question. I felt a feeling akin to humiliation but tinged with anger. I shook my head. "Lahmajun," I said, meeting his eyes. "That is its name. That is what I want." I presented the Euros to him, and he took them.

I don't know if he understood me. I don't know if he took it as a peace offering. This word we both use to refer to the same dish, a word not in any one of our languages.

Because I didn't mean it as a peace offering. I only wanted him to know I would never say "Turkish Pizza," like I knew he would never say "Armenian Genocide."

※　※　※

WHILE MANY STATES individually recognize the Armenian Genocide, the US federal government will not, as Turkey is vital to US military interests in the Middle East.[1] Most of the Western world, however, has acknowledged the Armenian Genocide as historical fact. Last year, there was a surprising addition to the list: Germany.

Germany was an ally of Ottoman Turkey, and official recognition of the Armenian Genocide by the German Parliament also implies Germany's own culpability in the death of over a million people. The German military often stood by as the deportations and executions took place, and they even supplied weapons to the Turks. Armenians were encouraged by this admission and moved deeply by the fact that it was a German politician with Turkish roots who initiated the resolution.

Of course, Turkey's government was not pleased with Germany's decision, nor were many Turkish-German people living within Germany. These days, the tensions between Turkey and Germany have escalated dramatically: the German government tried to curb President Erdogan's campaigning for Turkish-German votes that would sustain his autocratic rule of Turkey, and Turkish officials have made accusations of Nazism against the modern German government.

It is easy, perhaps, to write that the world is changing rapidly these days, that alliances are shifting as the global leadership struggles to figure out how to deal with millions of refugees, people they have displaced with their foreign policies, their scheming, their wars; it's easy, too, to forget the past. I've heard many Americans ask why we should suffer for centuries-old European imperialism, overlooking conveniently the role of modern American corporate and political powers in supporting puppet states, revolutions and counterrevolutions, terrorist groups and antiterrorist groups. And it becomes hard, then, to not cry and point out that history is not just centuries-old; history makes up today's borders, the lines—imaginary and otherwise—around our nations, and the very real boundaries to our sense of compassion.

It's no surprise to me that Germany has accepted so many refugees and America so few. Some countries are quicker to reflect, to feel remorse. Some countries can confront their past, look it dead in the eye, and feel ashamed.

All this I came to understand after Berlin.

MY FRIENDS AND I sat eating around the small table in the Turkish restaurant. B. told F. about dancing to "Hava Nagila," and F. was disappointed to have missed it. She was in a different part of the bar, talking, kissing, feeling light in her skin. I told F. she didn't miss much, and I chewed my lahmajun energetically, hoping the sounds of my jaw would drown out B.'s surprised exclamations. The lahmajun tasted fine. I didn't wonder if the clerk spat on it. I didn't compare it to my mother's. It seemed a very foreign thing, this meaty dough in my hands. My hands felt strange, too, a strange shade. And what were these strange, light expressions on my friends' faces? Why were they laughing? I didn't understand why they weren't discussing the ugly implications of dancing to "Hava Nagila" in a German bar. These girls were marked by ethnicity, by foreignness, in a way I thought I was, in a way that explained my sensitivity.

And so I began to wonder if my experience was shaped more by the Turk grabbing my behind than I wanted to believe, if it was that specific fact that shone a light on the ugliness of the situation. Was I pretending to be better than I was, more thoughtful, more aware, by claiming to be made uncomfortable by "Hava Nagila" before the man made the weight of his hand known on my person? I chewed and chewed before I understood that it was not the harassment but his Turkish presence that alerted me to be wary. It was his Turkish body approaching my Armenian body that made me hesitate, that made it suddenly impossible to accept the dream of reconciliation, the beauty of a dance being danced in a bar in Berlin. It was the past there intruding on the present—but I welcomed that intrusion. I welcome it still. I needed it to understand that history is not the passing of time but time's inability to heal all wounds.

I was twenty years old and tired already of what my ethnicity meant to others, which made it impossible to understand what it meant to me. My parents kept trying to *keep* me Armenian: you're Armenian, they'd say, don't forget, never American. And Americans seemed to agree: you're Armenian, you're foreign, you're this or this, but no, not American; your parents are right about that. You're not white like me. So I had reveled in the fact that, in Europe, I finally was. Free from everyone's expectations, which let me finally be free. This was the power of whiteness. America!

But then I danced a dance in Berlin and I understood that when my parents pressed upon me my Armenianness, it was not the same as white strangers pressing upon me my foreignness. My Armenianness was a gift from my parents. It was not a weapon. It was a book I could turn to again and again and find myself there. A reminder: I was not a gap in the history pages. Not 1915. When my parents said, "You're Armenian, not American," they meant I knew where I came from, and I knew what that meant: I'd be confronted by my past everywhere. It meant I could not dance to another culture's song, in another culture's bar, and feel light in my skin. It meant I smelled the stink in the air, heard the laughter dark and mean. Long.

I thought about explaining this to my friends, thinking they'd get it because of their own histories, but then I realized I couldn't expect that of them. How to say to someone you love that they could never understand your pain because they haven't been in your shoes? They have not danced the same dance as you. Even when the music playing is the same, the body dancing is not. The body moves to a different rhythm.

So I will say it to someone I don't love. I will say it to the stranger reading: there are some things you will never understand, but you must listen.

Note

1. Editor's note: This essay was written in 2015, and the author passed away in 2017. In 2019, both the US House of Representatives and the US Senate passed resolutions acknowledging the Armenian Genocide. In 2021, President Joe Biden also released a full statement of acknowledgment on Armenian Genocide Remembrance Day.

"Where Are You From?
No, Where Are You *Really* From?"

SOPHIA ARMEN

i

The first time a middle-aged white man yelled at me, "Get out and go back to your country!" I froze. It was in the immediate days following 9/11. I was nine years old and at my school. I didn't understand. I could not hold this stranger's well of hate in my small body. I did not understand what he needed from me. I remember having two thoughts. One, while I clenched my small fists, was "no, no, NO!" That "no" was rage. The "no" I felt that day was important: it was one of the first times in my life I felt my power, my rejection of immorality and injustice; it's the everyday feeling I get as I work in community today. That it doesn't have to be this way. That these systems *feel* wrong.

But something else happened that day. I heard my insides scream in anger, but then it came, a deep and unexplainable rush of sadness. It engulfed me, poured over all the contours of my young body. A second thought rushed into my head. Even though I was so young, I remember I wanted to yell back at this man, "I can't."

It does not exist. Not really.

ii

WE ARE THE LOST ONES

UNANCHORED, A CIRCLING SHIP UNALLOWED TO PORT

STILL TAKING ON THE SEA

They say that when the Armenian refugees came to the Central Valley, they were sure it was Eden. Heck, they even named the town, well, Yettem.

Growing up, the Central Valley was where my friends lived, where the air was dry and the land fertile. There were the two Kevins, Kalfayan and Yahnian, who were the Visalia boys. And then, of course, there was the other Kevin, who lived in between the citrus orchards. They were thick skinned on the outside, tough and leathered like jerky or bastegh, but pure honey inside. *These are Armenian men*, I would think. *These are the men with hearts of gold.* We would all see each other at least once a year at Hye Camp in Dunlap, California. And maybe down south at the beach for Armenian Christian Youth Organization (ACYO) gatherings when the Central Valley boys would come down and meet the Los Angeles girls and spend the day on the sand.

For me, Fresno was like Disneyland. Each year my large Armenian family would gather from miles away and take over an inn or hotel that looked straight out of a 1970s movie. The Piccadilly, or some years the Holiday Inn or Rio Bravo in Bakersfield, when we chose to meet halfway to be kinder to the Los Angeles crew.

For my cousins, sister, and I, we had it made. We would run all over the place, splash in the pool until day's end, and chase each other over the grounds. We were mostly girls, but we were Armenian girls, and we got down in the dirt. Holding the land with our noses.

When we had become so pruned from the pool that our fingers looked like the raisins and dried apricots we ate throughout the weekend, our eyes bloodshot from chlorine overload, we would sneak to our favorite spot of the whole trip, a small, white room our overflowing family always rented no matter what year, what motel, or what part of the town we were in—the hospitality room. Arriving at the door, our small cherub fists would pound until some uncle would come out and let us in, telling us to shush with a big grin. Inside was anything but a shush, the sounds of laughter and chatter overwhelming you in a wave that clearly was different than all other parts of the hotel. Opening the doors felt like the scene in Willy Wonka when they entered the chocolate room. *If you want to view paradise, simply look around and view it.*

Here we were. In all our glory. This was our place.

We would try to pass through the sea of legs that felt like hundreds and hundreds and hundreds of aunts, uncles, cousins, and dads. Everywhere you looked, everyone was smiling full-toothed and laughing, talking in small groups, trying to catch each other up on everything that we had missed during the year. Auntie Rima wore her beautiful plum-red lipstick as always, the tint mirrored in her hair, which she brushed back into a ponytail. Uncle Haig made a short joke about my dad, who retaliated by leaning over to hold his belly in laughter with a quick quip about Haig's age.

It was impossible to keep the noise contained in a small box of a room with plain white walls, bland and sad like unbuttered toast. It deeply contrasted with us. We were alive. We were packed so tightly into the room, receiving noise complaints was just the beginning of it.

But that wasn't why we kids were here. For the pinched cheeks, the *Oh!*, or the slobbery kisses. We were here for the holy grail. Trying not to get stopped by each and every relative, climbing on hands and knees at one point was the best tactic. When we finally pushed our way into the middle of the room, there it was. The best mezze ever.

It was the mezze of our dreams.

The most overwhelming mound of scrumptious and mouthwatering food, which the aunts kept replenished all hours of the day by any means necessary for the hordes of family members coming in and out of the room to snack on. Basterma, cheese boreg, yalanchi, Karoun string cheese, lavash, kufta, lahmajun, and kadaif that my mom brought; I could already feel the sugary syrup across my teeth as she scraped and cut them in the metal tray. All at the same time, bigger and better than just any day. Platters of the best dried fruit that I ate until I got a stomachache. And, of course, later, shish kebab, tabouleh, and pilaf. Everyone brought food and everyone helped out. I was in heaven. My grandfather Barr was there with his five siblings, looking tall and strong like an ox. *We* were *there*. *We* were *here*. None of the kids at school could come close to my school breaks.

We are the lost ones
unanchored, a circling ship unallowed to port

a century in, still taking on the sea

we are the lost ones
who crafted an island of
ship wood and barnacles
and made home
without making it
home

iii

In my early twenties, in the hours not filled with organizing, I worked a variety of retail jobs. One was at Cost Plus, which stood between the wide stretches of sizzling black asphalt of used car dealerships on Topanga Canyon Boulevard in Canoga Park, California.

Cost Plus was branded a "world market," or at least that is what corporate, whoever they were, wanted us to say. Every day, I would arrange cheap "imports," or hand-size figurines from India, China, Turkey, and elsewhere, on shaky shelves that reached as tall as the large, gray, three-story warehouse building that housed them. They even rotated a new "travel to" display, meaning a new country, that I was in charge of setting up when I became the point of sales coordinator. Despite putting on scented lotion every day, I always smelled of the shrink-wrap and plastic from the boxes because of the sheer volume of items that went through that place. I was happy the day I got the announcement that I would be moving from the stock team to the register, because it meant no longer having to be at work at 4:00 a.m.

The cash register is always an adventure at any job. At Cost Plus, besides the number of loyalty sign-ups you had to hit, it's the place you have the most interactions with customers. My full hospitality host came out, and she has a distinct voice.

As I scanned items, the red line beeping on each small trinket, a blond woman approached, next in the queue. She complimented my earrings, small black triangles. She stared.

"Where are you from?"

"Here. I live a ten-minute drive . . . without traffic, of course."

"No, where are you *really* from?"

Ah yes, the phrase had become an everyday occurrence in my life, but at work with each new customer, each new one in line, well, I was stuck. Stuck physically at the register, and stuck with this question like a CD caught on a scratch. It worsened when I began working in "luxury retail," a world of codes and knowing when to shut up. The question *Where are you really from?* of course exposes its orator and its empire. It is racial project in action—nation-state-making, identity-making, and human-making too. You are not from *here*. By extending me as outside the nation, it tells little about me and more about who or what the nation is, how power defines itself by what it is defining itself against. On our TV screens and at Trump rallies, the "our" says little about who really is the targeted group at the time; it is more a revelation of the mechanisms and optics of power. And its intended goals. *Power reveals itself*.

"Oh, I love your blouse, where are you from?" There were days I was cast as another "exotic" thing on the shelves. For the customers, largely white suburban women, I was a land to travel to, a story to explore. An enchanted part of the environment I was ringing up. I could not shake the feeling that if I looked different, I would not be blended into the shelves of objects behind me, nor an object of study.

I had, of course, grown up with people calling me exotic, mysterious, with—that ridiculous phrase—"dark features." As a girl and then as a woman, these were always deeply gendered, and then they were sexualized. It felt like I was supposed to be accessed by everyone. Like I did not have control over the boundaries of my own body. Everyone had an opinion and wanted to make it known. A question, an inquiry, a quest. In my classrooms playing with the other kids, then on dating profiles and with coworkers. At work I finally understood what Arlie Hochschild meant by "emotional labor." But what she didn't seem to get to was what the hell you do when people are literally asking you for a magical carpet ride.

Where are you from?

First—Hi, I am Sophia.

And second—Do you have an hour?

iv

My name is Sophia Rakel Armen. There is much in a name. Who was there and who was lost. I carry them in my body. I carry them every time I say my name out loud or write it down.

My name is Sophia Rakel Armen. My last name, Armen, is the story of Armenians from Istanbul, or Bolis, as we say. My father's side of my family was from Istanbul, a place of intellectual exchange, art, and culture. My great-grandfather, whose first name was Armen (a popular Armenian first name for boys), was very young when Talaat Pasha gave the orders for the mass extermination of the Armenians.

The Turkish soldiers came to his home, and he watched his entire family slaughtered. Now orphaned and shaking with fear, he was found by American missionaries, the same ones who were forcibly trying to convert Indigenous people in the Americas, who were in Turkey at the time trying to convert Eastern Christians en masse to American Protestantism. When they found him, they asked for his name and all he could say was "Armen, Armen, Armen" as he relived the images of terror. These Americans changed his name to an Anglo name, Albert, and made his first name his new last name. From that moment on, our family name changed forever. He became Albert Armen. Because of these decisions by others, the

Turkish government's bloody massacre of my family and Western colonial presence, my family tree stops abruptly; its branches are cut.

When he eventually made it to the United States, my great-grandfather had no idea who his family was or who was left of them. He struggled with reliving the scenes of his family's massacre. In an act of resistance, he changed his name to an Armenian name, Avedis. In his moment of refusal, navigating both the trauma of genocide and the assimilationist forces of the United States, he became known as Avedis Armen.

My middle name, Rakel, is from my mother's family, the Der Mugrdechians. My mother's grandmother had several children at the time of the genocide. My family was active in political parties and in the Armenian resistance against the incoming Turkish troops looking to massacre the residents of the city of Van, in Southeastern Turkey. Van is a specifically important reference in this debate today; it is the resistance in Van that the current Turkish government uses to say that the Armenians deserve their fate because they were "terrorists" and "traitors." But my family were village people, the marginalized and forgotten, and they were as much part of the society as everyone else.

The city of Van is racialized today by the Turkish government as a "terrorist haven" because it is a center of the Kurdish struggle. The Turkish government today uses the rhetoric of "national security," like the United States does, to bomb the lands my family was displaced from. The ideology of racial supremacy in Turkey may look different today, but its core tenets are the same and they originate from the same logics of the Armenian Genocide.

My family from Van was deported on a death march through Der Zor, Syria, where they were sending Armenians knowing they would die in the desert of starvation and disease; or be shot en masse. Rakel, my great-grandmother, had her children with her in the line of Armenians being forced from their homes. They marched these Armenians through the desert to execute the orders of ethnic cleansing, to massacre them or force them to die of starvation.

Along the way, Turkish troops would randomly target Armenians for execution, take all their belongings, and select women in the line to rape. Rakel's daughter, my aunt Lucy, was crying the whole time because she, a small child, was disturbed by the commotion. The other Armenians in the line got angry at Rakel because Lucy was drawing attention to them. If anything attracted the attention of Turkish soldiers, they would be killed. Rakel, as Lucy told it to us, was forced to leave Lucy behind a rock so the caravan could move on undetected. But after two nights, her heart beckoned to her, and she went back for her daughter even though she could have been killed. I am named for her, for her bravery and her laugh.

Both sides of my family are from some of the largest centers of massacres of Armenians. We know our stories, our customs, our food, and our culture. The Armenian language of my family is peppered with village dialect Turkish no longer spoken. And we keep these realities alive in diaspora, in our bodies and in our prayers. A century later.

When my family came to Fresno to one of the first Armenian communities in the United States, largely made up of these displaced families, they came to a place with a climate charged with white supremacy and racial discrimination. There were covenants that Armenians could not own property; some Armenians were chased out of using the same public facilities, like bathrooms or pools, as white Americans, and as refugees they were taunted with racial slurs. They faced a fatal concoction of anti-immigrant/anti-refugee racism and Orientalism; many of the tropes used today against all Middle Eastern refugees have origins from this time. Many of the oldest Armenian-American organizations in the United States started because the first Armenians to come here needed them for protection and community, to help each other work through discrimination, violence, assimilation, and displacement. But we tell ourselves this is not true and speak of our accomplishments. *Did you know an Armenian invented the MRI?*

Today, my face in the United States is a constant marker for racist America to tell me I don't belong "here." My name is a constant reminder that I have nowhere "there." That unexplainable feeling that washed over me in the schoolyard that day when I was nine is something I navigate every day.

V

When we dance
as preteens
me and my best friend
children
hold big arms spread
hands up over head
take the male side during Tamzara
Pull out a napkin and lead the shoorchbar chain
Break the inner circle of old men in the Halay

Take off our heels and throw them off the dance floor
Dance until our toes are blistered and pulsing
Clap on one knee for our fellow sisters
As the elders stare
and our parents
Chase after us telling us to look at the underside of our feet
My mom yells, with a smile, "where are your shoeeeeeeesssss Sophia!"
At weddings
And Sunday school
And camp
And every single celebration
Of us Armenians being alive
And here we are
Two rough and tumble girls
Claiming
Our ground
Our land too

online memes circulate calling me a radical feminist, captioned with "idiot," "shameful," and, my favorite, "Western sheep." yes, and *I learned it at your wedding*

vi

On this land, in meetings and late-night strategy sessions and town halls, I meet and learn from elders of the Black radical tradition, Indigenous organizers, and other communities built from immigrants and refugees. We build comradeship, and we build commitments. And we do not post them on IG.

The contradictions of organizing on this land are infuriating, maddening even. The three pillars of white supremacy still mean those impacted by Orientalism/imperialism fleeing genocide and empire come to a land of genocide and empire, too, and enable it.

In school, Otis Madison teaches us, "In the US, the guns are pointed inward and outward." On my first day of college, my would-be elder-mentor-hero Cedric Robinson writes on the board, "Race is myth. Racism is reality" in white chalk while wearing a large-brimmed yellow straw hat. Grace Chang says "fuck" during her lectures and cusses out the boy in class who says white privilege does not exist. It is a feminist rebellion, and I am hooked. Ralph Armbruster-Sandoval not only teaches us about the history of hunger strikes but shows up to our student occupation of the chancellor's office, twice. I meet Razmig Sarkissian, who would become a lifelong comrade, in a room in Wisconsin, and we teach a hall of organizers to dance while he tells me of a thriving political home—that Western Armenia lives.

At school I read and then collage a DisOrientation guide.[1] After driving in a caravan to the University of California Board of Regents, at the meeting I learn from the minutes that the University of California operates the United States government's nuclear weapons labs at Los Alamos and Livermore, and a shipment of military firearms have been delivered to Afghanistan ahead of schedule. The university president, accurately called the UCOP, remarks, "Good" at the announcement of the news.

I reconsider whether it matters that I am a feminist studies major, really, when my schooling means people around the world wake up to guns and bombs.

In school, a friend gives me a copy of *We Charge Genocide* (1951). In the introduction, the case is made, "We maintain, therefore, that the oppressed Negro citizens of the United States, segregated, discriminated against and long the target of violence, suffer from genocide as the result of the consistent, conscious, unified policies of every branch of government."

> We came from genocide to a land with its own.
> Everything we do is a contradiction,
> and a choice.

vii

As a girl, when I was struggling, the place I would always picture, the place I imagine even now when I am feeling low or the critics' choir has a particularly zealous day, is my church. Well, not really my whole church, but the top of it. My favorite part.

There is a row of stained-glass pictures of the apostles at the tip of the dome. In the picture is Peter, flanked by Thaddeus and Bartholomew, the apostles who came to Armenia from Jesus's Palestine, and, yes, I am pretty sure they were promptly martyred as they were a threat to the pagan status quo at the time, but there they look so glowing in the glass, so alive. I think I am always drawn to our churches because of their octagon-like shape and because the top is almost always the most beautiful. In mine, when the light hits it, the top of the dome is an overwhelming blue. This is always where I have become myself, in the ferocity of the blue.

Church seems like a secret society for us in the overwhelming Americanness of Van Nuys, California, one where you have to be a member. Or at least this idea of a secret club, where lineage, genealogy is part; it is how it is practiced. When you arrive at church, the first question asked of you is never "Who are you?"; it is "Who is your family?" I would say this is the eternal Armenian greeting. We understand we come from a collective.

When I try to explain this to people here, that you can't really convert in or out, they don't understand it. They ask, "Well how do you gain members?" I say, "We don't." We're just born into it, and that's why in diaspora we die.

When I was young, church seemed like a chore. Sixteen years of extra school on Sundays where the men would tell us this was just the way things were. This is where I would hone my debating skills over time, through these confrontations with my male teachers. This is where I would have my first kiss when the elders weren't watching; this was how I became me. For others in the United States, Christianity can seem like death and oppression, or the absolute opposite, salvation. But I have realized jarringly since I was very young that when they talk about Christianity in this country, they are never really talking about me. This was weird growing up. There was an implicit, actually often explicit, white, Western assumption to which I wasn't allowed to belong, even when I wanted to at some points in my life.

I think now, of course, about this structurally and historically. Fucking ruminating on Samuel Huntington's clash of civilizations thesis will give you the blues. And, yes, we can all throw baba Edward Said back at him, but sometimes it just seems like these missionizers win.

Missionaries.

Like, for example, in the less than two years I have been at the University of California, San Diego, people have tried to convert me dozens of times. We are in a border town, nestled between a military base and Trump's proposed wall, and the level of conservative zeal can get violent. As we protested the dropping of the MOAB on eastern Afghanistan outside the Federal Building downtown, men stopped us to say, "I served two tours there," and "If you don't like it, get the hell out."

On campus, I have to walk the same path every day to get to class. It's almost always the same type—tall, built white man with a Bible in his hands. Their heads are shaved, military or former military, tabling in front of the library that looks like a spaceship, on the main throughway at UCSD called Library Walk.

I always thought they were trying to convert all the kids; really that's what these people do, right? I was just another passerby. Until one man with gray-blue eyes the color of a puddle, whom I had encountered many times before, said it.

"Well I am sure this goes against your family, but we can all find strength in the lord Jesus Christ."

"My family?" I ask.

He stutters and says, "Uhhhh . . . well . . ." He looks noticeably uncomfortable. "Yeah uhhh . . . uhhh I thought you were . . . well . . . you know."

I finish his sentence for him because my guilt sets in watching him struggle so much.

"Muslim," I say.

He repeats it back to me.

I chew him out for being an Islamophobe. But in my head I think, *They think they own everything.*

On the phone later, my friend tells me of his similar experiences; he tells me that once he snapped. He yelled, "My people were Christians while yours were eating stones . . . you Viking."

I can't help but laugh, though I know this is not the answer either.

How overwhelming we are, that vibrant blue.

viii

Hrant Dink, the organizer and journalist, was too busy organizing. He never got to write all his stuff down.

When the Hrant Dink Foundation published his work after his assassination, they noted in the preface that his works are not complete. He did not finish.

In the late-night hours because of the time difference, Arno Kalayci and I message back and forth on Facebook. We have been daily virtual pen pals for nearly two years. We have never met in person, but I feel like I know him. He shows me pictures of the water and land of Istanbul, and I show him the chaparral on the mountains off Kanan Road by my cousins' house. He tells me of Nor Zartonk's latest campaign, and I tell him how the campaign for ethnic studies in California is unraveling.[2] I complain about the gatekeeping elders and internal fights in our organizations, that it feels like the government is winning, the perils of nationalism, the frustrations in the community, the strategies that worked, and how most didn't.

He tells me about the gatekeeping elders and internal fights in their organizations, that it feels like the government is winning, the perils of nationalism, the frustrations in the community, the strategies that worked, and how most didn't.

We laugh because though our *where* is different, sometimes it's not.

ix

And here we are, sharp and lodged. Because the Armenian diaspora from the genocide lives across the world like shattered glass, it's a community you cannot reassemble into what it was. So we have to make it into something else, something more beautiful—a mosaic of sorts, with its pieces. But this is difficult. Because when the oppressor pretends that everything is fine, there's no ability to move forward or to develop a future Armenian identity that can encapsulate all of us. Because if we have to stay rooted in what has not been recognized, we will be unable to dream Armenian identity beyond the past, beyond loss.

When you take someone's identity // you take the air out their lungs.

x

When I submit an essay on the genocide to a prominent leftist, anti-imperialist publication, they ask me to take out all of the political analysis and leave in the portion about the suffering of my family. They want a story, a prepackaged tableau with none of the teeth. We will take the victimhood, but none of the analysis. We want the trope, but no action steps.

I refuse. And pull the piece.

xi

Self-love does not exist without community love. And it definitely does not cost $9.99 nor is it packaged by Dove. Each morning, I wake up and choose to love this hair, this nose, these arms, this belly, these eyes. I have been young and have not. And I have been young and peered out between masses of matte black hair, and I have said yes to the day.

On the internet, the men in our community, when you step out of place—which can mean anything from threatening their power explicitly or threatening their power just by existing—let you know something specific: you are ugly. Your nose, your skin, your arm hair, from playground preteens to Mari Manoogian.[3] It doesn't matter how many scholarly essays I write about the history of Armenian woman fedayis. They let us know. In patriarchy this is a promise, a threat, and a reminder: you are small.

I show up every day as I am. I roll out of bed (no shame to any other routine), and I say I am here. Deal with it.

xii

Armenia is a *nation*, an indigenous one. One that has existed long before Western notions of nation-states in the region. One with a historical relationship to land. The borders have changed, have crossed us many times, but largely within similar triangulations of soil, we continue to exist. We predate European theories of nationalism. We are eternal. The spiral. The wheel.

And so is our struggle. In the United States, our struggle is erased both in the discourse of power and in its counterhegemonic forces. I have grown up deeply entrenched in spaces of "Arab and Muslim" organizing and scholarship. I have built relationships to weather many storms from many places, often under immense pressure and when it is deeply unpopular. And still in these spaces, the erasure is apparent: "Arab and Muslim" as the phrase to refer to the racialization of all people under Orientalism, anti-refugee racism, and anti-Muslim racism has a glaring omission. The Armenians and Assyrians are nowhere to be found. Erasure in action. This isn't coincidence.

Turanism, the ideology that motivated the genocide and helped shape the modern Middle East, is not just a piece of government legislation or a nationalist slogan; it is a racial ideology. I would argue that pan-Turkism, or Turanism, *is a structure of power used to justify and execute the erasure of non-Turks, constructed via racial figure as foreign and not Indigenous, as means to "purify" the land.*

When we build anti-colonial, anti-imperialist, anti-racist struggle, we do so on many scales at many times. We do so from many *locations*. The where of Armenians.

xiii

I am interested in our *where*. Not for anyone else's sake. But for our own.

They all want to *place us*. How do we tell them it is *place* that is so charged? I am interested instead in where *we* place us. Where do we put ourselves, where do we build community, where do we show up?

The where in the United States for people from our region is everything. It is your racialization. It is how you fall into the national project. It is how resources are distributed or not. You are a two-second Google search after a Twitter beef. You are borders. You are a headline on the news. The United States makes Southwest Asian and North African (SWANA) people carry our homeland on our backs, whether we want to or don't. Whether we wear it with pride or it is used for our targeting.

Over *there* the where is tangible—either stolen, under attack, thriving, or destroyed based on the perspective or, perhaps, even privilege. Meanwhile we keep floating out in space debating our identity; there is a global web of Armenian bickering you cannot leave. But somehow, we build constellations, like stars holding hands, anchoring each other around the world.

Sometimes I get so angry at English I want to scream. There are not enough words here to carry these memories; there aren't enough words to name our future, our Spring. Karoun, Karoun, Karoun-eh.

If "Zartonk" means "awakening," it means you have to wake up the people. It means at various times throughout history, then, that we have been asleep.

Notes

1. The DisOrientation guide is a popular punk and DIY organizing tool for university campuses. Rather than giving the sanitized and often neoliberal history of a campus, the DisOrientation guide gives students the true history of organizing on campus and exposes university ties to systems such as the prison-industrial complex, the military-industrial complex, union busting, and the privatization of public education.
2. Editor's note: The Nor Zartonk (New Awakening) movement began in 2004 as a discussion forum for Armenian youth. In the early years, they held panels with the journalist Hrant Dink before his assassination in 2007. In 2015, Nor Zartonk held a successful 175-day protest and occupation of Kamp Armen, an Armenian orphanage in Istanbul, to prevent its destruction.
3. Mari Manoogian is an Armenian American politician who represents the Fortieth District in the Michigan House of Representatives. Online, when Manoogian spoke on an issue of national politics, young Armenian men critical of her began circulating pictures of her arm hair.

An Inter/Racial Love History

KOHAR AVAKIAN

GROWING UP, I genuinely believed that when you married someone, you became that person's race. My sisters did too. In our eyes, everyone in our family was the same. We shared the same interests, habits, and characteristics. We celebrated and took part in the same cultures. We spoke the same language and we understood the same things. After all, we even had the same last name. We were one Armenian, Black, and Nipmuc family because that was just what we were. There was nothing else to it.

You see, Mommy could cook all of Nene's recipes like they were her own, effortless like rolling sarma from the backyard at the kitchen table while holding a conversation across the hall. She always seemed to resort to Armenian to scold me—small hands reaching for Kinder eggs at Bahnan's Bakery—Mi tepnar! Don't touch. Mommy was the one who insisted that she and Baba give us Armenian names. I know Nene appreciated that. Talin, Gariné, Nairi, and Kohar. Good Armenian names. *Now everyone will know what they are.* She was—and still is—on the board of our church, drove us to and from Kid's Club, all the way down Highland Street and back. Kid's Club. That's what we called Armenian school. It all started in Hokour and Nene's third-floor apartment, a triple-decker on Hudson Street. Nene would make us sit for hours at the dining room table . . . ayp, pen, keem, ta, yetch, za . . . just like she did for Dikran Amo, Moses Amo, Hokour, and Baba before us, in the old country. Candy bowls filled with sweets were our incentive, accompanied by *The Price Is Right* playing in the background—Nene's favorite show. I wonder what she liked most about it. I remember staring in amazement at those bright gleaming cars, showcased by skinny white models with pretty white teeth, and those money-hungry contestants, jumping up and down for the opportunity to get a hold of that one thing we all came here for: "a better life."[1]

As for Baba, he always allowed me and my sisters to be as we were, embracing every part of us so that we never felt like we had to choose. With his cool and charismatic demeanor, he could talk to anyone—I mean, *anyone*—and he fit right in with my mom's family too. He even learned how to do our hair, usually in pigtail braids with colorful hairballs tied to the ends. Mommy did it better, of course, but it was the effort and care that mattered. In Worcester, Baba was the glue that fused our families together, a father figure for his daughters, nieces, and nephews alike. We always had cousins at our home, from all sides, usually in the backyard with Dede's grapevines cradling us in, pinkies strung together Michigan-hopping toward the future that was almost stolen from his past. I never knew Dede, but I felt like I did. He died in 1993, two years before I was born, yet his imprint remains. One of his plants is still blooming in our home today. He and Nene were in an arranged marriage—"the odd couple," as Baba says—but somehow it worked.[2] Posing for a picture on their wedding day in Bourj Hammoud, Nene stood tall, chin up, on a wooden stool, attempting to look proportional to Dede's height. I heard so many stories about Dede to the point that he seemed larger than life, literally. Then I realized that maybe Nene—barely reaching five feet herself—was just really short.

But don't be mistaken. Nene was small but mighty, and very pious too. She could command attention from an entire room without making a sound. That's where Baba gets it from. Naturally, she was always the one to bless our meals. When she spoke, everyone stopped to listen to what she had to say. It was the type of reverence reserved for really important people. You just knew that she had seen some things. And she had. Nene's family came from Marash and Kayseri in Western Armenia, from a time and space now kept alive only in memory, where I might visit only on Google Maps, or in my dreams. Movses Yeranian and Takouhie Boudakian were her parents, my great-grandparents. Known as Movses Hoja, Movses Dede was a shoemaker who occasionally filled in for the minister of the Protestant Church in town while he was away. Before Nene was born, he was married to a woman from the Shnorokyan family and had two sons named Manasseh and Yeprem. When word got out about the killings of young men, his wife told him to run away. And so he went, with two of his friends. They traveled by night and hid by day, trekking hundreds of miles through the Syrian desert. He never saw his wife or sons again. Years later, Nene tried but was never able to find them either.

Movses Dede safely made it to Syria, but not without injury. A Turkish gendarme hit him on the head with a thick wooden board covered in sharp nails, giving him seizures for the rest of his life, an indelible physical reminder of his deportation. Nene used to tell Hokour about how Movses Dede often fell in the middle of the street and foamed at the mouth while she was walking with him as a child. He didn't deserve those permanent scars for being who he was, and neither did she. In Syria, he met and married my great-grandmother Takouhie from Kayseri, who gave birth to Nene—Semagül Yeranian—in 1923, the same year that the new Turkish republic was founded upon their people's bones, their stolen homes, and the ghosts of the kin they unwillingly left behind. Sometimes I think about Takouhie Nene. I wonder how she made it through the desert on foot all the way from Kayseri to Syria, how determined she must have been to survive. I wonder which pieces of herself she had to leave behind, at home. Pregnant once more, she died during her next childbirth, when Nene was three years old. The baby died too. Takouhie Nene's memory remains preserved today in the form of my sister Gariné's middle name. Movses Dede and Nene had no choice but to pick up the broken pieces once more. They eventually made their way to Beirut "because that was where Marashtsis went," laying their roots in a new fertile home.[3] Movses Dede soon remarried—"a woman named Ossanna"—and soon, Nene's sister Mary, or Mokour, was born.[4] A few years later, Movses Dede died when Nene was fourteen and Mokour was still a child, leaving Nene without any parents. *Did they ever get time to grieve? To process what they had lost? Did we?*

Born in Yozgat in 1920, Dede was an orphan too. His parents were named Guluzar and Haji. Of them, we do not know much more, other than that they died when he was very young. As a result, he was raised by aunts and other relatives playing parent. Just like Nene. That was the way it went. We always take care of our own. In Yozgat, he used to ride horses through the watermelon fields, a memory he must have held close to his heart because he passed it down to his children, who then bestowed it to me. Sometimes I think about those watermelon fields in Yozgat, replaying those inherited memories over and over in my head, of a time and space that must have tasted sweeter than watermelon itself, because it was *undeniably* home. Perhaps he clung to those childhood memories because they represented a life before the rupture that split his world apart. Like the millions of other Armenians, Assyrians, and Greeks displaced with him, Dede escaped Turkey to Syria, a center of refuge for orphaned children, where he spent a few years of his adolescence. Finally he reached Beirut, where he met, married, and started a family with Nene in Bourj Hammoud, the de facto Armenian capital of the city.

Out of the fragments of their lives, Nene and Dede worked hard to nurture a sense of wholeness for their family in Lebanon. They had four children in total, just like Baba and Mommy would after them. Dikran, Moses, Seza, and Zareh. Born in 1959, my dad, Zareh, is the youngest, like me. Nene named Moses Amo after her late father, as did Mokour for her own son. We call him Uncle Moussa. Mokour married an Assyrian man named Benyamin Bahnan, or Kehrayr. Before they moved to Bourj Hammoud, they lived in Kamishlii, Syria. They had seven children in total, all sons. Alfred, Henri, Antranig, Moses, Jano, Gabrielle, and Raffi. I'm not sure how Mokour did it, but she did it well. In the '60s, she and her family moved to Beirut to be closer to Nene and for a better life. The Bahnans soon opened a bakery a block away from their home, serving an abundant supply of fresh manaeesh and lahmajun every day. With seven sons, Kehrayr never had a shortage of helpers. The Bakery thrived. "Living in Lebanon was like living in Armenia."[5] In Bourj Hammoud, the Avakians and the Bahnans were able to speak Armenian, go to Armenian schools and churches, and be with each other freely, a luxury they did not take lightly because it had almost been taken away from them in Turkey. They also spoke Turkish and Arabic, and some English too. In the vibrant Armenian quarter, the Bahnans ran the bakery, Nene worked as a nurse at the Karagheusian Clinic, and Dede worked as a shoe cobbler and ran a convenience store. Together, Nene, Dede, Mokour, and Kehrayr planted seeds and created a village that still stands strong. And for a while, life was really good.

Until one day, Nene could sense that things were beginning to change. She warned her family that she could feel that a war was on its way. Divine intervention, a mother's intuition, or maybe it was just in her blood, but her foresight saved her family. Nene's old headmaster and dear friend, Reverend Hassessian, and his wife, who had worked with Nene at the clinic, had migrated to Worcester, Massachusetts, a few years earlier, and he served as the minister of the Armenian Church of the Martyrs, the eventual headquarters of Kid's Club and our church. Following their advice, Nene applied for visas for her family in 1967, listing her job and education as their asset. They got rejected over and over again. "I mean, we thought we were never going to get it."[6] Seven years went by. Then some-one suggested that they list Dede's job on the application instead, something they had never thought of because he didn't have a formal education. They tried. Immediately, their application was accepted. Apparently, the United States was in need of cobblers that year.

In 1974, Nene, Dede, Hokour, and Baba got ready to say their good-byes and leave Lebanon for good. Well, not for good. Hokour and Dikran Amo went back for the first time in forty-five years in 2019. I hope to go back with Baba and my family one day. Baba was only fifteen when he left Beirut. Though he was sad to leave his home, he had dreamed about America—the land of big bright billboards, pretty models with nice white teeth, and luxury cars. Growing up, *The Sound of Music* was his favorite movie. I wonder what he liked most about it. He had always wanted to go to the states, and now it was actually happening. Since Dikran Amo had married Takoush Tantig and Moses Amo Auntie Maggie, they had to apply and go separately. The Bahnans stayed behind too. For the sake of their survival, my family sacrificed the one thing they had finally found in Lebanon: the right to be together. Nene and Dede led the way, collecting their things once more, all that they could carry from a place they had shaped into a sound home. They would go first, and the rest would follow, how it had always been. Before they left, Baba made one promise to Nene: he would marry an Armenian woman and always keep the culture alive in her name.

Boston Logan Airport, 1974

"WELL WHERE ARE YOU FOLKS GOING?"

"WE'RE GOING TO WOR-CES-TER."

"NO, YOU'RE GOING TO WUH-STER."

"NO, NO WE'RE NOT GOING TO WUH-STER . . . WE'RE GOING TO WOR-CES-TER. W-O-R-C-E-S-T-E-R. IT'S WOR-CES-TER."

"NO, THAT'S HOW IT'S SPELLED. THIS IS HOW IT'S PRONOUNCED."

"SO, THAT WAS MY FIRST LESSON IN THE U.S. . . . THEN WE GO OUTSIDE, AND WE WAIT, AND WAIT, AND WAIT FOR OUR FRIENDS WHO WERE GOING TO COME PICK US UP FOR AT LEAST A GOOD HOUR. SO WE HAD OUR SUITCASES, IN A NEW COUNTRY, WE'RE JUST STANDING, AND WE NOTICE A TAXI CAB AND YOU KNOW, I WALK OVER AND I TALK TO HIM, AND I SAID, 'WILL YOU TAKE US TO WORCESTER?' YOU KNOW, 'WE'LL PAY YOU FOR IT' AND SUCH, AND HE HAPPENED TO BE FROM LEBANON. AND HE LOOKS AT ME AND SAYS, 'SIR, THIS IS NOT HOW IT IS

IN THE OLD COUNTRY. YOU DO NOT WANT TO TAKE A TAXICAB ALL THE
WAY TO WORCESTER. IT'S GOING TO BE ONE HUNDRED AND SOMEWHAT
DOLLARS. YOU MIGHT AS WELL SIT HERE AND WAIT FOR YOUR FRIENDS
TO SHOW UP.' SO THAT WAS GOOD ADVICE HE GAVE US, BUT WHAT ARE
THE ODDS THAT WE WOULD MEET AN ARMENIAN ON THE AIRPLANE, AT
HEATHROW AIRPORT, AND AN ARMENIAN TAXI DRIVER?"

ZAREH AVAKIAN, 2015

"We didn't know Watertown from Worcester." But those were the two
options because that was where the Armenians were.[7] When Nene, Dede,
Hokour, and Baba landed at Logan Airport in Boston, they were met
by Reverend Hassessian from the Armenian Church of the Martyrs in
Worcester and their friend Sahag, the brother of the patriarch of the Apostolic church in Watertown. Because Reverend Hassessian was "of higher
standing," out of respect, Sahag yielded.[8] And so it was decided that they
would go to Worcester and live with the Hassessians until they got on their
feet. At first, it was difficult. The people were not as nice as they were in the
movies. In Lebanon, they had learned some English, but now, their entire
world was in a different font. But just like Movses Dede and Takouhie
Nene before them, Nene and Dede "sacrificed the future of their lives and
their comfort to come here for their kids. It's as simple as that, like almost
all immigrants have done."[9] I smile to myself thinking about how Baba felt
like he had to explain that to me, as if that wasn't exactly what he did for
us by leaving his home behind and coming to this foreign country.

After some time, Baba and his family began to adjust. They found
an apartment near Elm Park, up the street from the Church of the Martyrs. In 1977, Mokour's oldest sons, Uncle Alfred and Uncle Henri, joined
them. Just like Baba's family, they both got jobs and worked with the
goal of bringing the rest of the family over. Worcester was no stranger to
Armenians; it was there that Armenians first permanently settled in the
United States. Our church, the Armenian Church of the Martyrs, is the
oldest Protestant Armenian church in the United States. Founded in 1888
in the home of Hovhannes and Sara Yazijian, who notably amended their
last name to "Writer" and officially consecrated in 1901, the Church of the
Martyrs was named in honor of the victims of the Hamidian Massacres
(1894–1896) and became a center of Armenian life in Worcester, along with
the Church of Our Savior and, in due course, Holy Trinity Church.[10]

During the late nineteenth and early twentieth centuries, New
England Protestant missionaries who worked in the Ottoman Empire

fused the first connections between the old country and the United States—largely between Kharpert and Worcester—when they sponsored Armenian converts to find work in America.[11] Movses Dede also must have converted around this time because that was when the American Board of Commissioners for Foreign Missions (ABCFM) came to convert Apostolic Armenians. Many of these same missionaries were also responsible for the "Christianization" of numerous Indigenous tribes in North America and other "heathen" peoples across the globe.[12] Upon arrival in America, Armenians often found jobs in Worcester's factories, many of which were owned by the same Protestants who brought them to America in the first place. Others worked as domestic servants in English households.[13] "The Protestant work ethic" was a common phrase repeated in my household growing up. Work hard and you will be successful. It wasn't until I grew up that I understood where we inherited that language from. When it became clear that the first wave of Armenian refugees would no longer be able to return home as a result of the Armenian Genocide, they transplanted their roots and transformed Worcester, soon known as "Little Kharpert," into a new Armenia.

As the first Armenians landed on American shores, they encountered an entirely new social order: a racial hierarchy ruled by whiteness. Michael Omi and Howard Winant define racial formation as "the socio-historical process by which racial categories are created, inhabited, transformed, and destroyed . . . in which human bodies and social structures are represented and organized."[14] In the United States, conceptions of race were historically constructed through intersecting mechanisms of religion, law, and "science," all rooted in ideologies of white supremacy. Following the Naturalization Act of 1790, one had to fit into the category of "free white persons" in order to become a naturalized US citizen.[15] Writing on the 1790 act in *Whiteness of a Different Color* (1998), Matthew Frye Jacobson remarks, "So natural was the relationship of whiteness to citizenship that, in a debate which followed, the racial dimension of the act remained unquestioned."[16] To put it bluntly, citizenship was a conditional process; assimilation into the white mainstream was the prerequisite. Exclusion was written into the Constitution.

Consequently, Armenians and other immigrants from Asia, such as the Chinese, Japanese, Syrians, Indians, and Koreans—whose position within the black-white racial binary remained uncertain—applied for citizenship on the basis of their ability to demonstrate their "whiteness." According to John Tehranian, legal whiteness rulings came down to how well "a petitioner could point to his own adoption of white values" and "to the assimilation of his ethnic group into the core Western European, Christian tradition as evidence of his whiteness."[17] As a result of the court decisions *In re Halladjian* (1909) and *U.S. v. Cartozian* (1925), Armenians were deemed white by law in the United States, a condition that enabled them not simply to survive but, in many instances, to prosper and thrive.[18] Christian since 301 CE and affiliated with Protestant missionaries since the mid-nineteenth century, Armenian refugees, now vulnerable and stateless, successfully defended their claims to collective citizenship.

Nevertheless, legal whiteness did not protect Armenians from every-day violence, discrimination, or long-lasting identity battles. The law never truly encompassed the immigrants' experiences on the ground. "There was the Black bubbler and the white bubbler. . . . The Armenians had to use the Black bubbler."[19] The reason why they had to apply to naturalize in the first place was because their whiteness was contested. "I'm definitely not white 'cause I grew up in an Irish Catholic neighborhood. Blue eyes, blonde hair. They did not consider me one of them."[20] When they initially arrived in the United States, Armenians were called slurs and beaten in the streets, as narrated by the first generation of those who lived in Worcester.[21] "I could never forget some of those early workers were given difficulties from other immigrants . . . and they couldn't necessarily walk the streets of Worcester at night, so I often think of that."[22] In Fresno, California, they were subjected to restrictive covenants, which made it illegal for them to settle in certain areas as a result of their Armenianness.[23] Genocide survivors arrived during the Americanization movement, which coincided with World War I, an era of fervent patriotism, nativism, and xenophobia. "We were good Armenians by being good Americans."[24] National Americanization efforts were developed as a means to assimilate heterogeneous immigrant groups and shape them into one common "American" identity. "My father was the same way; he never spoke Armenian. You know, he was totally Armenian, but for some reason, he only replied in English. I think it was so he could fit in. He didn't want people to think he wasn't American."[25] During this time, many immigrants changed their last names to sound more American and were forbidden from speaking their languages in school. "Because that's how you proved you were an American."[26] These sentiments were internalized and passed down through generations. "They sent a note home telling my parents they're not allowed to speak any language at home other than English from now on."[27] Armenians who had just barely survived with their culture under the oppressive Ottoman regime were now being forced to conform to a new standard. Though the Americanization movement did not explicitly mention race, it was inherently racist; the standard was whiteness, as written into the Constitution.

During the last half of the twentieth century, Little Kharpert received a number of new Armenian immigrants from the Middle East, including the rest of my family. The same generation that had survived the Armenian Genocide was uprooted once more. Nene's intuition was right. They had left just in time. Less than a year later, in April 1975, the Lebanese Civil War broke out. Life had been really good for a while, but now uncertainty loomed over the horizon. Dikran Amo, Moses Amo, and the Bahnans were still living in Bourj Hammoud when the war began. Uncle Gabby told me about how in Beirut the railroad split the Christians and the Muslims from one another. According to him, in the United States we have a race problem, but there they had a religion problem. Uncle Moussa (Mokour's Moses) and Uncle Anto joined the other Armenians and took up arms in protection of their community. Uncle Jano, Uncle Gabby, and Uncle Raffi were too young at the time, but that didn't stop them from keeping busy at the agump. Just thirteen and fifteen at the time, Uncle Gabby and Uncle Jano served coffee and clean rifles to the soldiers in the neighborhood, including their brothers. Uncle Raffi, the youngest of them all, always tagged along too.

As time went on, it became clear that they had no choice but to leave Lebanon. One time, the Bahnans were stuck in the cellar of their apartment building with the rest of their neighbors for eight days straight with nothing to eat but some bread and water. Bombs, snipers, and wreckage, of both buildings and people, became commonplace. During the eight days of heavy fighting, Mokour got scared that the immigration papers they needed to get to America would be destroyed. She sent Uncle Gabby to deliver a backpack containing the documents to their old neighbor, who lived next to the bakery, for safekeeping. With Uncle Raffi on his back, he went, quietly sneaking past the snipers and crouching behind cars. It took him over an hour to get to the other side of the neighborhood. When he got there, he saw that the bakery had not been spared from the destruction. It had burned down; the metal front had exploded off. "Everything was gone."[28] And yet they never wanted to leave Beirut. No matter how bad things got, they were happy to be there because it was home. *Did they ever get time to grieve? To process what they had lost? Did we?*

In 1979, the Bahnans' visa application was accepted because of Keh-rayr's job as a baker. Following Dikran Amo and Moses Amo, who had left for America a few years earlier, they went to Worcester to be with Nene's family. Uncle Anto stayed behind and fought for five more years because he was too old to go with them. The rest of the Bahnans landed in JFK on September 11, 1979:

> We came into Kennedy airport. We needed help, someone to guide us somewhere, because we had no idea where to go and there's a language barrier. So, no one knows how to speak English.
>
> And we met this older—I'm going to say in his seventies—older Black guy, white hair, darker skin. I'd never seen anything like it in my life . . . I couldn't help myself, but to look at his skin. I was fascinated . . . I'd never seen a person like that before. Anyways, he was the nicest person on the face of this earth. Even though there was a language barrier, with sign language and everything, we snuck by. All he wanted to do was help us, honestly . . . I thought, *Wow, what a country. If this guy is like that, then they all must be like that. Everybody that lives in this country must be like that.*[29]

In Worcester, they were in for a rude awakening. "What the hell am I doing here?"[30] On his second day in the country, Uncle Gabby got into a fight at Burncoat Junior High as he tried to tell a kid who was cutting other people to get to the back of the line. They fought. "Then, we became best friends for the rest of the year."[31] The school wanted to kick him out, but Hokour, who was twenty-five at the time, came by and successfully reasoned with the principal. A few months later, trouble found him and his brothers on the bus:

> We did have some problems on the bus one time. Some people asked us where we were from and we said Armenian and they thought we said Iranian. Back then, remember the hostages in Iran? . . . during Khomeini's day. So this country had problems with Iran and the hostages and all that, so there was a miscommunication between Iranian to Armenian. So push came to shove on the bus in downtown Worcester. One of them pulled a knife on us. We were pushing and shoving and punching, whatever, so the bus driver had to kick the guy with the knife out, and he got arrested by the cop and we left.[32]

After the newness of everything wore off, they began to feel home-sick, longing to go back to the streets of Bourj Hammoud once more, but they made do with what they had, like our family always had. In their ESL classes, they met other Beirutis, like the Aprahamians from church, and at the YMCA they played soccer with other kids from all around the world. Symbolic of their regeneration in a new place, the Bahnans reopened the bakery at the corner of Pleasant and Russell. Out of the ashes, they forged a new future, rebuilding all that had been shattered even stronger than before to feed a new generation. Our bellies were always full as kids, and our hearts too. It wasn't until I learned about the destruction of the old bakery that I realized how much we had taken it all for granted growing up. But I'm sure our parents never did. Every day, Dede would walk from his apartment to the bakery to have coffee and a cigarette with Kehrayr. Then, he would take the old, unsellable bread to feed to the birds at Elm Park. Wherever they went, my family fostered new life. Weekends consisted of cookouts, church picnics on Lake Quinsigamond, and walks in Elm Park on Sunday afternoons. The Armenians in town, now second and third generation, were happy to receive the new immigrants. And even though the new immigrants thought the old ones spoke Armenian with "a funny accent," they were happy to be there too. "We really accentuated each other. We got along very well. They taught us things, you know, the ways of America."[33] The best moment of all was when the whole family was finally together once again.

After some time, the Avakians and Bahnans embraced the vibrancy of life in Worcester during the 1980s and '90s. Personalities too bright to capture in black and white, Dikran Amo worked as a jeweler and Moses Amo was quite skilled with leather work, taking his craft all the way to Newport, Rhode Island; Burlington, Vermont; New York; and California. Hokour followed Nene's footsteps and pursued nursing. In Lebanon, she attended the American University of Beirut. And of course, she would also become my very own Armenian schoolteacher and math tutor, and the culture bearer of her family. As for Baba, he started playing soccer for the first time at age fifteen, went All-American at age seventeen, and got recruited to play for UVM; he was my own personal soccer coach and World Cup watching buddy. Then he went into the car business, where he has flourished since. Ironically, I didn't get my license until years after my sixteenth birthday. As for Uncle Alfred, he worked as a car mechanic by day and won disco competitions by night. Uncle Henri mastered the art of painting and hairdressing and eventually took over the family bakery. He was also occasionally the singer for the annual barahantes and at family weddings. He performed at Worcester's annual Armenian benefit dance last year. Once he finally got to America in 1984, Uncle Anto owned gas

stations, remodeled homes, and perfected his gymnastics on the weekends. As a kid, Uncle Jano had already known how to hot-wire a car, so
naturally, he worked as a car mechanic, just like Uncle Alfred and Uncle
Moussa. Uncle Gabby graduated from Worcester State with a degree in
general business because he promised his mom he would. Uncle Raffi, the
baby of them all, graduated high school and helped out at the bakery. And
for a long while, life was really good.

Quinsigamond

In 1984, Baba met Mommy in Worcester, ten years after he first arrived
there as a teenager with Dede, Nene, and Hokour. Mommy—Crystal Mae
Ellis Wheaton—was born in Boston in 1961. Her parents' names are Ruth
Fannings and Ronald E. Wheaton. Her mother, Gram Gram, is African
American, and her father was Native—Nipmuc, to be exact. Her grandparents were named Muriel Wheaton, Harold C. Wheaton, Carrie Bell
Fannings Gilbert, and Andrew Lee Fannings. While Mommy's Nipmuc
side of the family comes from Massachusetts, her mother's side comes
from Georgia. My great-grandmother Carrie, whom we called Ma, lived
in Georgia up until the 1910s, when she trekked up north at the age of
sixteen, all the way to Boston. Her grandparents were enslaved. As for
Muriel Wheaton, or Grandma, she was the oldest living Nipmuc of central
Massachusetts when she died in 2014. My sisters and I were lucky enough
to meet her own mother before her, our great-great grandmother, Marion
B. Belden Braxton West Stanton, who lived until the age of 102. We come
from a lineage of strong and powerful matriarchs on all sides.

For thousands of years before Worcester's colonization, the Nipmuc people carved out mishoons and traversed their ancestral waters of
Lake Quinsigamond. Known as the "freshwater people" of the Algonquin
region, our ancestors thrived off the four-mile body of water as they fished,
farmed, and hunted along its fertile shores and adjacent hills. Some of our
ancestors' mishoons still remain at the bottom of Lake Quinsigamond
today, where they were intentionally submerged with rocks for safekeeping during the winter. That's survival. The seventeenth century proved
devastating for the Nipmuc people and the rest of the Indigenous people
of the Northeast, as European colonizers brought over deadly diseases,
incited warfare, and forced the Natives to convert and relocate, under the
guise of Christian philanthropy. Reverend John Eliot and Daniel Gookin

are credited with establishing villages, called "Praying towns," between 1646 and 1675 for the "Christianization" of Natives in New England.[34] While the Puritans' efforts may seem beneficial, the underlying purpose of the missions was to assimilate, erase, and exercise control over the people and the land.[35]

In America, the same religion that would get my Armenian relatives killed in Turkey was used to justify the genocide of my Nipmuc ancestors. As the colonizers gradually encroached on Nipmuc territory and other Native lands of New England, the Nipmuc people collectively resisted the English during King Philip's War (1675–1676). In the name of "vindictive justice" and "on the ground of necessity," the English used intimidation tactics, ranging from relocation to public extermination, to remove us from our land. In addition to suffering "judicial slaughters," many Nipmucs from Worcester were forcibly interned on Deer Island in Boston Harbor, where they were left to starve to death in the cold.[36] A number of Nipmuc children were taken away from their homes and enslaved in the households of English families in Worcester against their will.[37] Although the physical violence was threatening in itself, the ideologies that emerged from these encounters served to displace and erase Native people—and many others—long after the seventeenth century. For the sake of their survival, Nipmucs strategically blended into the backdrop of Worcester and frequently intermarried with Black Northerners. However, as a result of these interracial unions, white Americans characterized Natives as "disappearing," a myth notably promulgated by census takers who viewed their mixture as a sign of their extinction.[38] Even though my ancestors had survived and thrived so that I could be here today, I have read about my own people's extinction too many times to count.

In June 1862, the *Worcester Spy* reported that a former slave from New Bern, North Carolina, arrived in Worcester with his family in the midst of the Civil War. The newspaper referred to the family as "contrabands" on account of the conditions that brought them to the small New England city.[39] Their arrival marked the beginning of the "small but steady" migration of Southern Black Americans to Worcester County during the 1860s.[40] During the same era of religious fervor that touched Armenians abroad, New England Protestant missionaries also traveled south in the midst of the Civil War, where they, along with Northern white soldiers, formed personal connections with fugitive slaves who sought refuge in Union camps. As a result of these relationships, a number of free people of color accompanied Union missionaries and soldiers home, north to Worcester. Between 1862 and 1870, the Black community in Worcester nearly doubled as a result of this migration; about 370 Southern Blacks, predominantly from North Carolina and Virginia, took the journey up north to Worcester.[41]

Exposing the racial hierarchy on which the country was founded, the factories that helped the early Armenian immigrants get on their feet were not accessible to everyone. In 1893, Franklin Rice, the founder of what would become the Worcester Historical Museum, noted that the overall treatment of Worcester's Black community had worsened over the years as a result of the waning existence of white sympathizers. He concluded, "Negroes are not treated with the consideration they were before the war, when Worcester was thought a paradise for the fugitive from oppression."[42] Some factories refused to hire Black Americans, which drastically stunted the collective growth of the Black community in Worcester. They remained in the same occupations, often domestic service jobs, that they acquired after the war. The possibility of social and economic mobility was close to impossible for them, as demonstrated by the complete exclusion of Black women: "The city's corset-making industry, boot and shoe factories and textile mills, which employed thousands of white women, many of them French Canadian and Irish, did not employ a single Black woman."[43]

I didn't learn about any of this history in school growing up. My high school, named after Mount Wachusett, the Nipmuc word for "mountain place," made no mention of us. It was as if we did not exist. Instead, I heard stories that celebrated America's "great" founding fathers—how they won wars, amassed riches, and accumulated land. But the textbooks never mentioned how they committed genocide, owned other human beings (my ancestors), and violated our women and children. They neglected to recognize the nation's true founding fathers and mothers: the Black and Native peoples who were massacred, looted from, and violently uprooted from their ancestral land—a debt that has yet to be repaid. In my heart, I knew this omission was wrong. In addition to erasing the racial violence, history books failed to capture the unbelievable strength, sovereignty, and resilience of America's original Black and Native stewards. My ancestors had survived and thrived despite all attempts at their decimation so that I could be here today. They deserved to live and have their stories of survival celebrated and told, just like my Armenian predecessors. For them, I write.

Did my Armenian ancestors know that my Black ancestors, who were stripped from their Indigenous African homeland to be considered mere property, also sought employment opportunities in Worcester only to be turned away from the same factories that gave Armenians a future? Did they know that on the same land where they found refuge, others had not been given the chance? Did they know that the blood of genocide had already long been imprinted in Worcester's soil and steeped in the waters along its lakes' shores? Did they know that Lake Quinsigamond—derived from the Nipmuc words "qunnosu" (pickerel) and "amaug" (fishing place)—bore the name of the very people their Protestant allies' forefathers sought to "civilize," displace, and erase? That nearly three hundred years earlier, along the same waters where they picnicked, thousands of Nipmuc individuals, too, had been massacred, torn away from their Indigenous land, and—despite their persistence—deliberately written out of history, just like they did to us in Turkey?

MOMMY AND BABA GOT MARRIED IN 1987. "Never knew I would fall in love." When Nene initially raised her doubts because Baba had broken his promise, it was the Bahnans who reminded her that marrying someone outside of his community wouldn't make him or his family any less Armenian. Instead, it was an opportunity to introduce someone new to the culture and gain another member of the family. After all, the Bahnans were half Armenian and half Assyrian, and that hadn't changed a damn thing. "Like you, we're all mixed up."[44] Even if his family hadn't approved, Baba was ready to leave on behalf of Mommy because he loved her so much, just like Mokour loved Kehrayr. They shared the same interests, habits, and characteristics. They spoke the same language and they understood the same things. They both knew what it was like to be the legacy of a failed genocide. They understood how it felt to live in a country that refused to recognize their people's humanity, trauma, and claims to their homelands. They shared an unspoken understanding that our ancestors didn't walk thousands of miles for us to put down each other for who we are. There was nothing else to it.

"Race": noun. The *Merriam-Webster* definition reads as follows: "a family, tribe, people, or nation belonging to the same stock" or "a class or kind of people unified by shared interests, habits, or characteristics." If race is supposed to be about our shared interests, habits, and characteristics, then why do we spend so much time talking about our differences? Why do we let humanmade boundaries and narrow racial categories dictate how we see one another? When I was six, my parents revealed to me that my understanding of marriage wasn't exactly the way race works. I remember feeling shocked, hurt, and deceived. I could not comprehend how the world could be any other way than how I already saw it. Looking back, I realize that my outlook never really changed. Even though I eventually went on to study race and immigration in college and in graduate school, I learned everything that I know during my childhood. It was my family who taught me the meaning of global indigeneity and showed me the importance of intersectionality through action and love. They have given me a wealth of knowledge in the form of oral histories, making it possible for me to share this story. Kuttabottomish taubotne, shad shnorhagalem, thank you to my family for teaching me more than I could ever learn in a classroom. We hold a love for one another that's as deep as Lake Quinsigamond and as vast as Yozgat's watermelon fields, for in each other we can always find home when all else fails.

Notes

1. Zareh Avakian, interview by Kohar Avakian, February 8, 2015, Paxton, Massachusetts.
2. Zareh Avakian, interview, 2015.
3. Zareh Avakian, interview, 2015.
4. Seza Avakian, interview by Kohar Avakian and Rita Bahnan, August, 20, 2016, Paxton, Massachusetts.
5. Seza Avakian, interview, 2016.
6. Zareh Avakian, interview, 2015.
7. Zareh Avakian, interview, 2015.
8. Zareh Avakian, interview, 2015.
9. Zareh Avakian, interview, 2015.
10. Hagop Martin Deranian, *Worcester Is America: The Story of Worcester's Armenians: The Early Years* (Worcester, MA: Bennate Publishing, 1998), 15, 127–131.
11. Deranian, *Worcester Is America*, 3.
12. Enoch Mack, William Cutter, Enoch Mudge, Solomon Peck, and Joseph Tracy, *History of American Missions to the Heathen, from Their Commencement to the Present Time* (Worcester, MA: Spooner and Howland, 1840), 11.
13. Deranian, *Worcester Is America*, 13.
14. Michael Omi and Howard Winant, *Racial Formation in the United States from the 1960s to the 1990s*, 2nd ed. (New York: Routledge, 1994), 55–56, 66.
15. Matthew Frye Jacobson, *Whiteness of a Different Color: European Immigrants and the Alchemy of Race* (Cambridge, MA: Harvard University Press, 1998), 22.
16. Jacobson, *Whiteness of a Different Color*, 22.
17. John Tehranian, *Whitewashed: America's Invisible Middle Eastern Minority* (New York: New York University Press, 2009), 40.
18. Ian Haney-López, *White by Law: The Legal Construction of Race* (New York: New York University Press, 1996), 130–131.

19. Gina Piligian Zalauskus, interview by Kohar Avakian, July 29, 2016, Paxton, Massachusetts.

20. Zalauskus, interview, 2016.

21. Deranian, *Worcester Is America*, 47.

22. Hagop Martin Deranian, interview by Kohar Avakian, August 11, 2016, Worcester, Massachusetts.

23. Diana Aguilera, "Diversity in Fresno: How Racial Covenants Once Ruled Prestigious Neighborhoods," KVPR: NPR for Central California, December 8, 2015, https://www.kvpr.org/post/diversity-fresno-how-racial-covenants-once-ruled -prestigious-neighborhoods.

24. Deranian, interview, 2016.

25. Zalauskus, interview, 2016.

26. Michael Soojian, interview by Kohar Avakian, August 11, 2016, Worcester, Massachusetts.

27. Zalauskus, interview, 2016.

28. Gabrielle Bahnan, interview by Kohar Avakian, August 19, 2016, Paxton, Massachusetts.

29. Bahnan, interview, 2016.

30. Bahnan, interview, 2016.

31. Bahnan, interview, 2016.

32. Bahnan, interview, 2016.

33. Zareh Avakian, interview, 2015.

34. Dennis Connole, *The Indians of the Nipmuck Country in Southern New England, 1630–1750: An Historical Geography* (Jefferson, NC: McFarland, 2001), 7–9.

35. William Lincoln, *History of Worcester, Massachusetts, from Its Earliest Settlement to September, 1836; with Various Notices Relating to the History of Worcester County* (Worcester, MA: Charles Hersey, 1862), 16.

36. Lincoln, *History of Worcester*, 31.

37. Henry F. Waters, *The New England Historical and Genealogical Register* (Boston: The Society, 1854), 273.

38. Thomas Doughton, "Unseen Neighbors: Native Americans of Central Massachusetts," in *After King Philip's War: Presence and Persistence in Indian New England*, ed. Colin G. Calloway (Hanover, NH: University Press of New England, 1997), 218.

39. Janette Thomas Greenwood, *First Fruits of Freedom: The Migration of Former Slaves and Their Search for Equality in Worcester, Massachusetts, 1862–1900* (Chapel Hill: University of North Carolina Press, 2009), 1.

40. Reed Ueda and Conrad Edick Wright, *Faces of Community: Immigrant Massachusetts, 1860–2000* (Boston: Massachusetts Historical Society, 2003), 23.

41. Ueda and Wright, *Faces of Community*, 24–25.

42. Quoted in Ueda and Wright, *Faces of Community*, 45.

43. Ueda and Wright, *Faces of Community*, 46.

44. Bahnan, interview, 2016.

Language Lessons

NANCY KRICORIAN

OUR HOUSE IN WATERTOWN was built on a double lot, with the front door on Walnut Street and the back door on Lincoln. We lived oriented toward Lincoln Street, where in our large backyard, my father tended a vegetable garden and my grandmother managed the annual beds and the perennials—lilacs, forsythia, viburnum, two types of hydrangeas, and three kinds of roses. There were two pear trees, a peach tree, and a grapevine that climbed up the house and grew over one side of the second-story porch.

This porch was where my grandmother stored her large pickle crock under an enamel-topped table. In spring, summer, and autumn, she sat on a vinyl-covered couch watching over the yard and the neighbors. In addition to the wood-framed clothesline in the backyard, my grandmother also strung a rope above her porch railing, where she hung dishtowels and clothes out to dry. She stored the wooden clothespins in a bag she had fashioned from a dress that I had worn as a toddler. She had sewn closed the hem of the dress and suspended it from the line on a wire hanger.

Many of the families on Lincoln Street were Armenian—Masoyan, Moushigian, Kazanjian, Kasparian, Kricorian, Mekjian, and Gayzagian—and my grandmother referred to the ones who weren't not by name but by nationality: the Greek, the Irish, the Italian, and the Portuguese. Many of the surrounding houses were built as single-family dwellings, but ours was a three-story, two-family house. My father and his three siblings had grown up in the top two floors. When I was growing up, my grandmother and my father's youngest brother lived there. My parents, my sister, and I inhabited the ground floor.

We were officially two separate households with two independent apartments, and in the basement there were even two washing machines, one for my grandmother and one for my mother. But we were one family. My sister and I were often upstairs with my grandmother, watching old Shirley Temple movies in her living room or sitting on her back porch eating watermelon or pelting butternuts at a brazen squirrel that was feasting in the pear tree. There was another second-story porch on the front of the house, and sometimes I took a nap or read a book on a daybed there because it was quiet and shaded by an enormous spruce tree that grew in the front yard.

My grandmother would pound with a broom handle on the floor of her apartment by the utility closet, calling for my father, "Eddie!" He would open the closet in our apartment and shout, "What is it, Ma?" She'd reply, "I'm sending the bucket." Either my sister or I would be dispatched to our back porch as a plastic bucket tied to a length of clothesline rope descended. Inside, we might find a pot of fresh-made yogurt, a basket of fresh choereg sweet rolls, or a plastic bag filled with manta, tiny meat dumplings shaped like boats.

Our family attended the United Armenian Brethren Church on Arlington Street in Watertown. It had been founded and built in 1938 by Armenians from Cilicia, most of them genocide survivors, and was led by the Reverend Vartan Bilezikian until his retirement in the early 1950s. My grandfather Levon (Leo) Kricorian, who had been one of the founders of Watertown's Saint James Armenian Apostolic Church in the early 1930s, had converted to Protestantism and was also among the founders of the Brethren Church.

During my grandfather's day, our family pew was the second one from the front on the right-hand side, but after his death and with the arrival of my squirmy sister, we moved to the left-hand side, second from the back. In this second location, the Amiralians sat behind us, the Haroutunians were in front of us, and the Bilezekians were across the aisle.

By the time I was seven, the church had been renamed the Watertown Evangelical Church and Reverend Proctor Davis, a Southern Baptist who resembled the evangelist Billy Graham, held sway from the pulpit. When we sang from the hymnal, the Armenian widows in the front row with their black hats and white buns chorused in a minor key.

IN ELEMENTARY SCHOOL, many of my close friends were Armenian. I watched with envy on Monday and Wednesday afternoons at the end of the school day as they marched off together for Armenian language lessons at the cultural center attached to the Saint James Church. My grandmother had offered to pay my Armenian school tuition, but my mother, who was French-Canadian, made clear without words that she preferred I decline the offer. This was another silent skirmish by proxy in the power struggle between my mother and my grandmother.

My mother never learned Armenian, despite living in the same house with her Armenian mother-in-law. My grandmother and father often spoke the language together, or rather my grandmother spoke to him in Armenian and he replied in English. The fact that my mother knew hardly one word of Armenian when the language flowed around her in our house, in the neighborhood, and at church was remarkable. Recently I asked her why she had never learned it, and she said, "They didn't accept me because I wasn't Armenian, and I didn't want to know what they were saying about me."

My father's first language was Armenian, but when he went to kindergarten, he spoke more Turkish than English because his paternal grandmother, who spoke only Turkish, lived with his family. My mother's first language was French, but she was shamed out of speaking it when she went to elementary school, and she lost almost all of it after she was sent to an orphanage at age eight.

I knew a little Armenian, or rather I knew several dozen phrases in Armenian and various words. My grandmother taught me how to count to ten in Armenian, but beyond that I learned through hearing certain phrases over and again. I understood my grandmother's commands—give me a spoon of sugar, shut the door, open the light, take this, come here, sit there, stay there, walk, run, hurry up, go slowly—without knowing the language. I understood what she was saying when she called my uncle a squash head. It was clear that the word "amot" meant "shame," and when she said "amot kezi" I knew that I was or had done something shameful. This generally involved my "vardik" (underwear) or my "vorik" (bottom), and often specifically referred to my ballet and tap-dancing outfits. She also said, often, in English, "Cover your shame."

Her English was heavily accented and full of grammatical errors and mispronunciations, and I cringed at the thought that anyone outside our family would hear her mistakes, particularly her misuse of the personal pronouns "he" and "she." One time she said to me, "Your mother, he is not a lazy woman." It never occurred to me that I should wonder why these gendered pronouns gave her so much trouble. She also called window wipers "vipers," and instead of "throw" she said "trow," as in "trow dees een dee ash barrel."

I loved my Armenian grandmother, but I wanted to be as American as possible and to speak perfect English. When I was about ten years old, I started wishing that I were a WASP with a simple, muscular last name that didn't broadcast my family's immigrant origins. This was probably as much at the heart of my not going to Armenian school as my mother's disapproval. I kept my distance from the recently arrived Armenian kids from Beirut with their accents and their mismatched clothes. Some of the other kids—particularly the Irish and Italians, whose whiteness was relatively recently established—picked on the Armenians, calling them insulting names such as FOB, which I thought was an acronym involving a swear word but eventually learned meant "fresh off the boat." One day in the parking lot after school, I saw a tough girl named Dana surrounded by a scrum of kids as she slapped around a dowdily dressed immigrant girl with the unfortunate name of Pearlene.

In fifth grade, our teacher asked us each to bring in a homemade food that represented our ethnic backgrounds. My grandmother, who was an excellent cook, baked a batch of gurabia, Armenian butter cookies dusted with confectioner's sugar. She carefully packed them in a tin lined with waxed paper. As I walked to school carrying the cookie tin, I felt a growing sense of dread. I was sure my Armenian classmates would find the cookies to be ordinary and the non-Armenian kids would think they were bland and disgusting, so unlike the Oreos and Chips Ahoy they brought in their lunchboxes. I left the gurabia in my locker. I knew that I couldn't bring them home with me. A few days later I dumped them in a trash can.

I remember being shocked when an Irish boy named Howie, who lived in the projects, called me an "Armo camel driver" and an "Armo rugbeater." Howie had somehow seen beyond my impeccable English and the clothes I had carefully chosen at the Jordan Marsh department store. He had magically surmised that my grandmother spoke fractured English and that my father came home from his meat cutter job with dried blood on his cuffs and bits of hamburger and sawdust in the seams of his shoes.

In junior high, I signed up for French class. My grandmother told me that after the deportations she had learned French in the orphanage. "Comment allez-vous?" she said to me. This was also my mother's first language, although the only vestiges of it that I witnessed were on our monthly visits to the tarpaper shack in New Hampshire where her bedridden father growled in a language I couldn't understand and my maternal cousins referred to my mother as "Ma tount."

But my mother's French and the French at school were two very different things. At the time, French was the language that all the serious students studied, and it was considered very classy. Classier still was our French class's field trip to Du Barry Restaurant on Newberry Street in Boston, where incidentally I was horrified to discover that people ate snails, frog legs, and rabbits.

At Watertown High School, Mrs. Yacoubian offered Armenian classes, but no one I knew in the college track signed up for them. I developed a rapport with my French teacher, Monsieur Craig, who wore a beard and a beret, and made allusions to some mysterious suffering he had endured during World War II. He loaned me books by Jean Paul Sartre, and I sometimes stayed after class to discuss French existentialism with him. He said to me, "You and I are intellectuals," dismissing the football cheerleaders as anti-intellectual riffraff.

I WANTED TO ESCAPE Watertown High School and those cheerleaders, who carried red and white pom-poms to homeroom on the days we were forced to the auditorium for football pep rallies. I was tired of the old Armenian ladies at church who looked out of the sides of their eyes at the scandalous length of my skirt. I hoped to find other people who had read *The Brothers Karamazov*.

When I left for a college three hours from home, I kitted myself out in wide-wale corduroys, button-down shirts, and Fair Isle sweaters, naively believing this was an effective disguise. Maybe it was growing up, maybe it was my wealthy American boyfriend telling me I wasn't fooling anyone, or maybe it was living for a term with a *pied noir* family in Toulouse during a foreign study program, but by my second year in college I felt more Armenian than ever.

I interviewed my grandmother for an oral history project that was assigned in a class about mothers and daughters in literature. Sitting on the second-story back porch, shaded by the grapevine, she told me the story of what had happened to her family when they were driven from Mersin during the deportations and massacres. It was the first time she had told anyone in the family the details of her parents' deaths and how she had managed to survive. The history of this familial and communal trauma had suffused the air that I breathed growing up in Watertown's Armenian community while never having been articulated. Now my grandmother's voice telling the story was in my head. It was both a burden and a legacy.

My grandmother died at the end of my first year of a graduate writing program in New York City. That summer, I went to talk with her oldest friend, Alice Kharibian, who had been with my grandmother at the concentration camp in the Syrian desert outside Ras al-Ain when they were girls. Alice said, "Your grandmother was so wishy-washy. I was jarbig [clever, resourceful] for all of us. She and her brother would have been dead in the desert without me." Now I had Alice's voice sounding in my head along with my grandmother's.

BACK AT THE UNIVERSITY the following autumn, I enrolled in my first Armenian language class. I realized then that my grandmother's confusion about "he" and "she" was due to the fact that in Armenian the third-person singular pronoun is gender neutral. I was again surrounded by Armenians and the Armenian language, this time by choice. I began writing about my grandmother, and I wrote poems in her voice and in the voices of other women from our church. I remember reading out loud in Sharon Olds's workshop a prose poem I drafted a few months after my grandmother died. Titled "The Angel," it started, "My grandmother is in heaven. This heaven has no Turks, no women in skimpy bathing suits, no squirrels in the pear trees."

Later, I switched genres to fiction and began drafting the interlocking stories that would become my first novel, *Zabelle*, which was a fictionalized account of my grandmother's life as a genocide survivor and immigrant bride. When the novel was published, many Armenians came to my book tour events around the country. Zabelle Chahasbanian was a stand-in for many people's beloved mother or grandmother, so the book was popular in the community.

During the question-and-answer sessions after these readings, I was repeatedly asked about my credentials: "Are you ALL Armenian? Do you speak Armenian? Is your husband Armenian? Do you know how to make choereg?" It was the first time that I was made to feel that I wasn't Armenian enough. At one event, a man in the audience stood up to denounce me, saying, "You're not Armenian. You're an American writer exploiting your grandmother's story to make money." I replied, "If you calculated the number of hours that I spent writing this book and divided it into the advance I received, I made less than minimum wage. If I wanted to make money, I'd write porn." The absurdity of what he said was apparent, but it stung because I was ashamed about having failed my grandmother. I was not a good Armenian girl, I hadn't produced Armenian children, and I was in fact some kind of mongrel. If I had spoken fluent Armenian, I might have been forgiven the rest.

Over the years, I continued studying the Armenian language at the Armenian Diocese, at the Prelacy, and then with three excellent private tutors, one after the other. I learned the alphabet, I was able to read at a first-grade level, and I could write simple paragraphs in the present tense. But I still couldn't carry on a more than basic conversation. I should have studied harder. I should have gone to one of those language immersion programs in Venice or Jerusalem or Beirut. But I was living my American life, raising my American children, writing my Armenian-themed American novels, and working first as an adjunct writing instructor, then as a literary scout for European publishers, and later as an organizer for a women's peace group.

Here I am, decades later, still studying Armenian. It's a language rooted in my childhood, forever echoing with the sound of my grandmother's voice. I have loved discovering the ways the expressions and words I learned from her are part of the vast and intricate network of Western Armenian, a language that has the sturdiness and delicacy of a needle lace tablecloth but that is categorized by UNESCO as "definitely endangered."

For the past four years, I've been taking private lessons over Skype with Sosy, a teacher who fled Aleppo for Yerevan because of the Syrian Civil War. I have finally learned the simple past and the imperfect tenses. I have been writing microstories in Armenian, which Sosy proofreads and corrects. Recently she said to me, "Now you have the grammar, you understand the workings of the language; you just need more vocabulary. You need to listen, and to talk, talk, talk."

I keep walking this long road back to my grandmother. Talking to myself as I walk, I eventually end up climbing the steps to the back porch of her house in heaven, where together she and I will roll stuffed grape leaves at the enamel-topped table as we talk and talk in her native tongue.

A Good, Solid Name

OLIVIA KATRANDJIAN

"THERE'S A LOT in life you can't protect your kids against," a friend from Nebraska advised me when I told him I wanted to have a baby. "The one thing you *can* do is put them into the world with a good, solid name."

I knew what he meant: a recognizable name the general American public can pronounce. But even then, before my daughter was conceived, I knew I wouldn't follow his advice.

Olivia Gayane Katrandjian

Olivia is a good, solid name. In the United States, Katrandjian is so far from good and solid that I'm astounded when non-Armenians pronounce it correctly on the first try. More often, people pause five letters in and look at me for guidance. "Katra—" "Katrandjian. No, not Katranjistan. Katrandjian." Don't get me started on my middle name. Children mispronounced Gayane so badly that on my high school diploma I replaced it with Grace.

John Christopher Wildt

My husband is a thoughtful, funny, well-read, and open-minded man who loves the outdoors and respects women. Born in Connecticut, he has Irish, French, German, and English roots, not Armenian, but he quickly learned to heat up lahmajun when he didn't feel like cooking and stay in his seat after a movie to scan the credits for names ending in "ian." When we decided to marry, I knew he would be an equal partner in housework and parenthood, and a good role model for our children. But the patriarchy dies hard.

I didn't expect him to take up Katrandjian, but I did offer an Armenianization of his name we could both adopt: Wildtian. He refused to budge from the five letters of his good, solid, Germanic name. He was surprised I didn't jump at the opportunity to leave Katrandjian behind. Most Armenian names were still so foreign to him that he remembered one of my friend's by referring to him in private as Chocolate Babken. Why wouldn't I want to join him in a world where making a dinner reservation over the phone takes under a minute?

But to become a Wildt would be to strip myself of my identity. Forget the bylines I'd acquired as a journalist; I wasn't so delusional as to think I had built my name into a recognizable brand I couldn't afford to lose. Only a few years before, I'd been the tiny, blurred body pretending to work at a computer behind Diane Sawyer on *World News Tonight*, placed there so it seemed that she reported from a buzzing newsroom. My task was to look professional answering the phone, as if the Washington bureau was calling, though in reality my nearly blind grandmother was on the other end, binoculars hanging from her neck, shouting as if her voice had to reach across the Hudson River: "Are you wearing turquoise? I think we saw you for a second before the break!"

I could start again as Olivia Wildt, or change my name and keep Katrandjian as my byline. But I didn't want to. I could not fathom going through life without an Armenian name. Though Katrandjian is unpronounceable to most, I had come to see it as my golden ticket—an instant connection to Armenians all over the world. I could cold call or email any one of the tribe, no matter how famous. And in my twenties, as I built a career in journalism, an industry in which connections are crucial, I did. I had coffee with an opinion writer for the *Los Angeles Times*. A veteran *Washington Post* journalist forwarded one of my pitches to the appropriate editor. An ABC News reporter introduced me to her contacts around the globe.

I even connected to people whose names only sounded Armenian. For my first summer internship, through a program run by the Armenian General Benevolent Union (AGBU), AGBU sent my resume to Laura Trevelyan at the BBC's United Nations bureau, not realizing that Trevelyan comes from a long line of British journalists with absolutely no Armenian heritage. I took it upon myself to show her the Armenian khachkar on display in the building, and after an instructive and inspiring summer, Trevelyan gifted me her book, *A Very British Family*.

As my publication credits grew, young Armenians started emailing me for advice. Grateful to have been supported by others, I was always eager to help in any way I could. I firmly believed then, as I do now, that we must lift each other up if we want to thrive. To that end, I founded the International Armenian Literary Alliance (IALA) to mentor emerging writers, support established authors, and celebrate Armenian literature. Through this platform, we have built a global Armenian literary community, championed historically marginalized voices, and fostered intercultural exchange.

I would not give up membership to this tribe for anything. My name is my diasporan passport, and I couldn't imagine raising children who did not have that visual pronouncement of their Armenian identity. So my husband and I struck a deal: our children would have his last name and an Armenian first name. My daughter can eat bright-green scrambled eggs with her paternal grandparents on Saint Patrick's Day, but you'd better believe before that she's munching on yalanchi (and she did, beginning at ten months, alongside her iron-fortified cereal).

Lusinè Zabelle Wildt

It took a while to get pregnant. After invasive tests, medication, and award-winning mood swings, I finally had a choereg in the oven, a kufte in the pot. When my husband and I found out the baby was a girl, we chose the name Lusinè, after my cousin who had left her family in Yerevan as a teenager, taught herself English, and built a life and career in the United States with little help. We wanted our daughter to be so strong and independent. And we loved that Lusinè means "moon": after we had tried so hard to conceive, she would bring light to our lives. We added an accent over the "e" in the hope it would make the pronunciation clearer, at least where we live, in Luxembourg, where accents are common. We chose Lusinè's middle name, Zabelle, after Zabel Yesayan, the Armenian writer and feminist who fought for human rights and social justice and was the only woman on the list of Armenian intellectuals to be arrested on April 24, 1915.

I struggled with this decision. Older generations who fled to the United States with long, complicated names often felt pressured to assimilate. My maternal grandfather, born Hampartzoom Hampartzoomian, changed his name to Lee Hamptian after returning to New York from World War II. He never mentioned being the subject of overt racism, only that he simply "couldn't take it anymore." My grandmother was born Grace Tufenkjian, which literally translates to "son of a gun." "Sometimes I shortened it to Tufenk, to make it easier for people," she said. "In college, a professor took one look at my name and said Smith instead."

I was choosing to give my daughter what brought my grandparents so much difficulty. Studies show that your name shapes the way you're treated. In the United States, people with English-sounding names have better job prospects, make more money, and are even more likely to be helped in a life-or-death situation. In a 2001 study, the psychologist Albert Mehrabian found that individuals with unusual given names are perceived to be less moral, less popular and fun, and less successful.

But to me, the benefits outweighed the potential setbacks. Lusinè looked like her father even before she was born, in the 3D ultrasound images. While I have dark hair and eyes, and eyebrows that rival Frida's when unplucked, Lusinè is fair skinned with light brown hair that curls into blonde, and blue eyes that at times appear green. When she was four months old, the three of us traveled from Luxembourg to New York via Frankfurt. A German customs agent stopped us: Lusinè had no Luxembourgish identification but instead an American passport that had never been stamped, and not only did she and I not share a last name but she looked nothing like me. "I was in labor for three days," I said in the most measured tone I could muster, trying not to lose it on the eşek who had the power to block our passage. After an admonishing look from a female agent, he let us through. When we finally reached Newark Airport, I pushed Lusinè's stroller into an elevator while my husband got our bags. An elderly couple asked me where her parents were, as if I were the nanny.

It is strange to look at a child you carried inside you for nine months, one who calls for you at all hours of the day and night, who clings to your legs and buries her face in your hair, and not see yourself in her features. But no matter how little Lusinè's appearance resembles mine, she is branded with an inextricable part of me: an undoubtedly Armenian name that links her to her people.

I will not give my children recognizable names so others don't have to stretch beyond their comfort zones. I know that on most occasions when Lusinè introduces herself, she'll be asked to repeat her name. And if it gets to be too much of a hassle, if she hates her name and resents me for giving it to her, she can change it.

But I hope she comes to see Lusinè Zabelle Wildt as good and solid. I hope I have given her a sense of the difficulties minorities face and respect for others no matter what they look like, where they come from, what religion they practice, or whom they love. I hope I have paid homage to those who came before her and were stripped of their identity by murder, conversion, or assimilation. I hope I have given her instant membership to a community of people who want to help each other thrive. I hope, when she introduces herself and people say, "What?" it will be an opportunity to explain her name and identity.

"It's Armenian," I imagine her saying. "I am Armenian."

My Armenia

On Imagining and Seeing

CHRIS MCCORMICK

IN THE CAPITAL CITY of a former Soviet republic, under the chandelier-scattered light of a hotel chain's lobby, I stun the bellhop by speaking his language. "You're Armenian?" he asks, and he looks so much like my cousin's teenage son back in Los Angeles—the same ancient and boyishly disproportionate eyes and nose—that I want to squish him in a hug. "I'm half," I explain, the first of many such explanations I'll offer, to the first of many such strangers with my family's face. By the time we arrive at my room on the twelfth floor, the bellhop and I have agreed to an arrangement: during my stay in Yerevan over the next two weeks, he won't speak a word to me in English. "Lav," I say, meaning "good," one of only about a hundred words I can speak with any confidence. I promise to tip once I exchange my dollars for Armenian dram, but Davit—"Like David," he says, starting our language lessons at the toddler level—refuses. Even the idea of a transaction occurring between us seems to offend him, as if he were not an employee of the hotel but a helpful stranger offering a hand, or a long-lost friend recognized across a vast and crowded pavilion, or someone even dearer to me than that.

I was in Armenia to research a novel I had already written, to see a place I'd imagined all my life. My book, *The Gimmicks*, is set in a fictionalized version of my mother's Soviet Armenian hometown, where a family wrestles with the legacy of the genocide after one of their own is recruited by extremists intent on bringing the Turkish government, however violently, to justice. Only after I finished the book and sold it to a publishing house, in that suspended moment between signing the contract and finalizing the manuscript, when every possibility of love and anguish was as tangible as the forthcoming book itself, did I arrange to make the trip. When the plane began its final descent, somewhere between Paris and Yerevan, I felt suddenly ill. What if every detail I'd imagined was a false one, if every scene I'd depicted was wrong? Who did I think I was, anyway, inventing a place that didn't need invention? As the plane descended, I spiraled. I would have to scrap the book, it was obvious, and start from scratch.

I calmed myself by thinking of my mother—I was being a baby, after all. In 1975, when she immigrated to the United States from then-Soviet Armenia at the age of nineteen, she had flown from the same airport I now approached. What had she imagined, standing at the gate with a suitcase in her grip? Certainly not a white husband from the American Midwest, a pair of half-Armenian children, and one of them growing up to write books in a language she didn't yet speak to imagine his own version of her country, to arrive in the place she'd left behind—the very same spot—without her.

I'd been imagining Armenia for a long time, though I knew much of my early imagining had been muddled and wrong. I was four or five when I first heard my family members tell stories of the 1915 Armenian Genocide, and the gruesome facts of that event grew intertwined, in my mind, with the details of my mother's otherworldly childhood. I pictured the violence taking place on the quiet streets of her hometown; I pictured her at my age hiding from Turkish soldiers, though the genocide had occurred forty years before her birth. Time and place grew confused in my imagination, maybe because the crimes, I was told, had never been punished. I found it difficult to grasp that the Armenia my mother called home was only a sliver of the Armenia it had once been, or that my mother was the granddaughter of genocide victims, growing up in a country hundreds of miles away from the deportations and the murders. In my imagination, my mother's childhood converged with history in a swirling mess of achronological images called Armenia: massacres and forced marches; the rubble aftermath of the earthquake that killed my uncle's sister; my grandfather's illegal tailor shop; Soviet machinery and ancient shepherds; the shadowed plains beneath Mount Ararat; my mother and her childhood friend, who still sent kiss-stained letters back and forth across the world; my mother in the knee-deep snow; my mother, my age, climbing the apple trees that sprouted, somehow, from the silver smokestacks of a textile factory in the radiant dawn light.

After winning the Nobel Prize for Literature in 2017, Kazuo Ishiguro delivered a lecture that included a profound rumination on the link between fiction and memory. His parents had taken him from Japan to England when he was five, and when he began to write, he had yet to return. "My Japan was unique," he said,

> and at the same time terribly fragile, something not open to verification from outside that drove me on to work. . . . What I was doing was getting down on paper that world's special colors, mores, etiquette, its dignity, its shortcomings, everything I'd ever thought about the place, before they faded forever from my mind. It was my wish to rebuild my Japan in fiction, to make it safe, so that I could thereafter point to a book and say, "Yes, there's my Japan—inside there."[1]

Was this why I'd waited so long to travel to Armenia? Was this why I'd set my novel there in the first place? Only after getting down on paper the special colors of the world I'd been imagining—for the five years spent writing the novel, yes, but also for all the years of my life—was I ready to see the other Armenia, the real one. I hoped so, anyway. My claim to the country was flimsy, after all, my remove from it even greater than Ishiguro's from Japan. It was possible—likely, even—that my increasingly hazy imaginings would never seem as true to others as they felt to me. It was possible the real Armenia would bear no resemblance to my own and in supplanting the place of my imagination would prove its falseness, unbearably, once and for all.

The first few days in Yerevan, I felt a certain dissonance, a disorienting kind of recognition. So much in the city—from the beautiful stonework on the grounds of the central square, which reminded me of the rugs I grew up playing on, to the familiar feasts of lavash and salted cheese and fresh tomatoes at cafes on Abovyan Street—revived my own memories of home, that place far from Armenia that I had no need to imagine, knowing it intimately. I began to speak with increasing confidence in Armenian. I felt I had come a long way in order to travel not very far at all.

One day early in my trip, over small cups of strong coffee at an outdoor cafe, I met with my mother's cousin, Hatchik. Family lore has it that he tried and failed to convince my mother not to leave Armenia more than four decades ago. Now he'd heard I was in the country, and he wanted to meet me. Hatchik is in his seventies, and on the day I met him a heatwave roiled across the continent. He would invite me to his apartment, he said, if not for the lack of air conditioning. Besides, when his wife died she left a mess. I tried to offer my condolences, but my aunt, who'd traveled with me to help translate, was laughing. Hatchik's wife had died forty years ago.

Hatchik asked about my other half, and I thought he meant Mairead, my fiancée, who had come to Armenia but was off that day on her own adventure. But Hatchik meant blood—where did my father come from? "Irish," I said. "Whiskey," Hatchik said, and that was the end of his curiosity about the man my mother loves.

Hatchik was there to talk, and since I can't speak Armenian nearly as well as I can understand it, I was glad for his stories. One of them went like this: Before his wife died, she and Hatchik would go to parties and come home with completely different kinds of information. She would ask him if he saw the crystal dish the hosts had purchased for the sweets, or the new stemware their drinks had been served in. But Hatchik had noticed none of that. "I came home talking about the short way two old friends had spoken to each other, belying a hidden tension," he said, "or the way a wife had placed a hand gently on her husband's arm when he reached for another glass of cognac."

"You sound like a writer," I said, and my aunt translated. Then we were talking about Saroyan—"Bravo," Hatchik said, when I expressed my love for *My Name Is Aram*—and the injustice of Pushkin's worldwide fame compared to Toumanyan's relative unknown stature. "But who cares about fame?" Hatchik said. "A writer is interested only in his origins. That's why you're here, isn't it? A writer wants to know, at every level, where it is he comes from."

His words were on my mind a few days later when I visited the Temple of Garni, a first-century pagan temple restored in 1975 by a process called anastylosis, a method of architectural restoration that uses as many of the original stones as possible. Where the Garni restorers had to use new materials, they chose blank stones that stood out next to the ancient ones, the difference between the materials stark. They wanted visitors to be able to discern between the original and the added. In this way, I could see exactly what had been salvaged and what had been supplied.

When Hatchik said "origins," he meant genealogy and geography; he meant blood. But as I compared the spongy touch of the ancient basalt to the smooth faces of the blank stones, I considered the combination of memory and imagination I was really there to investigate. A kind of inventive anastylosis, memory and imagination, only I wasn't sure which was the original and which the support.

The question followed me. A week into our trip, we left Yerevan for my mother's hometown. The road to Kirovakan was a neatly combed part, one hundred kilometers long, in the russet valleys of summertime Armenia. Thin poplars lined the road on either side like pickets, and the distant hills remained fixed, the way objects in the distance stay true. The signs along the road had been updated: the Kirovakan of my mother's time, and of my novel's, has been replaced with Vanadzor. As we drew nearer, and as the elevation increased, the golden plains softened into lush and craggy vistas. A far-off, stone-walled village loomed in the hills, and Mairead—the only other person in the car who'd read my nascent book—nudged me to look. The village reminded her of one I'd written.

Was it pleasure I felt, or relief? Some aspect of my imagination had broken through to reality, and I felt a strange sense that I was returning to a place I had never been.

My aunt's brother-in-law, Goryun, the brother of my uncle in Los Angeles, a painter I had grown up admiring, was behind the wheel. It was Goryun's apartment we'd be staying at, and when I tried to thank him for the inconvenient trip—he'd driven the two hours to our hotel in Yerevan only to turn around and bring us the two hours back—he waved my thanks away like a petty insult. He spoke no English, but his meaning was clear. Goryun was bald except for a dark, meticulously trimmed mustache, and the bridge of his nose was strong and angular. I thought the word "chiseled" just as my aunt explained what Goryun did for a living: masonry. "Those tiles in the central square in Yerevan," my aunt said, "he did those."

Halfway between Yerevan and my mother's hometown, Goryun pulled the car over at a market called Gntuniq Bakery. For an hour in each direction, there was nothing but valley grasses and mountainous landscape, dotted every now and then by a village in the distance. We had seen people selling watermelons and corn along the side of the road, but Gntuniq Bakery was no small roadside affair. With its bright awnings and glistening rows of parked cars, it reminded me of the kind of park-and-browse enterprise I'd grown up visiting in desert towns between Los Angeles and Las Vegas.

Inside was the bakery itself: a mile-long display of pastries, breads, boregs, sweets, and traditional sandwiches. Beside and beyond the counter were shelves and shelves of market goods—beverages and spices and candies and the like. But the main attraction was up front, as soon as you walked in. If I hadn't known what a tonir was before seeing the clay ovens—if I hadn't written a character using one into my novel—I might've worried for the lives of the bakers. Two smooth, gray mounds rose from the floor to the height of the baker's navel, each with an opening at its peak just wide enough for that same baker to topple inside, which is exactly what several men were doing when we entered the store.

After rolling and loading dough onto a cushion held in one hand, each baker approached the tonir and swung headfirst into it, holding onto the lip of the oven with his free hand and balancing his upside-down body by splaying his legs in the air. What he was doing inside the oven—slapping flat dough onto the piping hot inner walls—was invisible from where I stood. All I could see was a pair of legs emerging from a smoking hole, as if from a crater in the ground. Forget Ishiguro and Saroyan, I thought of Dante. But the bakers—the performers, I want to say, because I wasn't the only one aiming my camera at them while they worked—didn't seem damned. They dove and posed their legs in wild shapes, like skateboarders at the edge of the half-pipe. They winked at the audience as they sauntered between the table where they rolled the dough and the tonir, and back again.

As we drove into Vanadzor, the gray sky threatened a storm over the green hills; throughout my bleached childhood in the Mojave Desert, my mother often told me she grew up in a place so green and gray she was teased for smelling like the rain. I'd had one of my own characters teased with the same strange insult, and I'd given another a job at the now-abandoned factories that loomed above us. I pictured the man I'd invented walking the potholed road below my feet.

But where was the statue of Kirov in the city square, so central to my characters' childhoods? Obliterated since independence, maybe? (I asked, but it had never existed). Where was the apartment complex—the tallest building in the city—on whose rooftop my characters confessed their secrets? No roof stood out from the others as a likely spot. And why had I taken my characters to the Black Sea on the Georgian coast instead of nearby Lake Sevan, that turquoise cleft in the Ararat Plain?

The map said Vanadzor, but Goryun and the locals still called it Kirovakan. As far as I could tell, this refusal on the population's part to update its lexicon had little to do with a rigor-mortis grip on Soviet loyalties, but rather with the city's uncanny sense of being frozen in time. The cause of that sensation occurred on December 7, 1988, when a convergence between the Eurasian and Arabian tectonic plates brought Kirovakan to the ground and sent my cousins—Goryun's nieces—to America. More than thirty years later, I could still see the damage to the city: empty lots where build-

ings had once come down, roads split like old leather upholstery. A population cut nearly in half, from 150,000 in 1979 to 82,000 in 2016.

Compared to sunny, bustling Yerevan, Kirovakan was overcast and
strikingly still, silent and easily mistaken for bleak, but beautifully surrounded by the hiddenite green of forested hills. When we arrived at the
apartment building where Goryun lived with his wife, Gyuli, we found
a nondescript, Soviet-era complex, and I followed Goryun up an echoing stairwell carved out of the building itself, concrete and poorly lit, the
steps fissured and fairly creased. But when we arrived at the apartment—
pristine hardwood floors covered in ornately colorful and handmade rugs,
Ionian columns abutting a bay window, an oil painting of flowers bursting
from a vase that I recognized as the work of Goryun's brother, my uncle
in Los Angeles—the whole of Kirovakan seemed to shift and brighten.

We took a walk through the city, stopping first at the storefront where
my grandfather had owned and operated a private tailor shop. I cupped
my hands and looked through the glass panes. The place was empty, but
my aunt drew vivid pictures in my mind: the sewing machines lined along
the center of the floor, the pin-cushioned dummies, and my grandfather's
office in the back, where he would meet with Soviet officials, charming
them—bribing, I inferred but couldn't confirm—in order to keep the business running. My mother had told me about her father's business, about
how she and her sister would hide the equipment when an official came
around snooping. But in my muddled imagining, I'd pictured the secrecy
happening at their own home, not in some storefront on the main thor-
oughfare of the city. The reality turned my grandfather, whom I'd known
only vaguely for the last years of his life, when he suffered from Alzhei-
mer's, into someone more brazen and influential than I'd imagined.

For twenty blocks or so, we traced the long walk my mother would take as
a girl to her music school. The buildings themselves were less interesting to
me than the story my aunt told of my mother's strut: with her instrument—
a heavy lap-harp called a qanun—wedged under her arm, she let her chin
lead the way, putting on an un-girlish air of unapproachability and business. In my novel, I'd described a girl walking through Kirovakan with her
instrument—a backgammon board, as it were—wedged just so under her
arm, and I smiled at the coincidence of my mother appearing, however
accidentally and obscurely, in my own imagination.

Finally, I was beginning to escape the cereal-box game of comparison
I'd been playing. Far more interesting than what I'd got "right" and what I'd

got "wrong" were the surprising harmonies I was starting to hear between the two worlds, these two Armenias in my mind. At my mother's grade school, a small building with a lobby downstairs and classrooms above, I imagined my characters dragging their soaking boots out of the rain and up the steps, nearly running into my mother as a girl at the top of the stairwell. My aunt called me over to her. She had discovered a series of class photos from the 1960s hanging on the wall and pointed out the children and teachers she remembered, looking for my mother's face.

Watching my aunt take photographs of the photographs, it occurred to me that I was not (and had never been) the only one comparing imagination to reality, memory to the present. We all do this, in one way or another, all the time. By writing a novel, I had made the process external, but it was a common task: to negotiate the imagined with the experienced, the remembered with the re-encountered, the original with the added-on. Constant but syncopated, the rhythm of this undertaking was impossible to plot out or predict, and how we danced to it was how we lived.

Back in Yerevan, I said goodbye to the bellboys, the cleaning crews, the bartenders, and the front desk clerks who had rallied around Davit's mission to help me learn the language. They asked about my stay, and I wanted to tell them what I'd seen: an uncle I'd never met throwing his arm around me like a son . . . a shot of mulberry vodka at a picnic table outside an eleventh-century monastery . . . the staircase on the other side of a blue gate where my grandfather used to sit with a dog and smoke . . . my aunt dancing with her sister-in-law, thirty years after the earthquake that made them housemates . . . a local woman on the streets of Kirovakan, curious about my looks and my limited language, following me for blocks and blocks . . . my book, imperfect but more than mine . . . my mother, who was not there, and everywhere.

But I'd said enough. On paper, I'd gone to fact-check my fiction, to verify the details in a story I was telling. In the end, though, just the opposite was true. I hadn't gone to test the accuracy of my storytelling, but to measure how well I had listened.

Note

1. Kazuo Ishiguro, "Nobel Lecture: Kazuo Ishiguro, Nobel Prize in Literature, 2017," Nobel Prize, streamed live on December 7, 2017, YouTube video, https://www.youtube.com/watch?v=ZW_5Y6ekUEw.

Inside the Walls

Reflections on Revolutionary Armenians

NANCY AGABIAN

I

When I asked my friend Diana what she thought about the revolution, she said it was dying.

"Really?" I asked, a bit stunned. Diana had lived her entire life in Armenia and was in New York City now for her studies. It was mid-April 2018, and I had been watching street protests unfold on my computer screen in the wee hours of the morning. "Everyone says it's different this time," I offered, "because the young people are leading it."

"No," Diana said, solemnly, assuredly, "there are so many police, more than protesters."

I respected Diana's opinion. I had first met her in Armenia about a dozen years before. I knew her to have a mind of her own and a strong moral core. Many times, I had observed her listening carefully to conversations, her long face inscrutable, before expressing a contrary yet paradigm-shifting opinion. It was true that too many movements in Armenia had been stifled and squashed. I supposed Diana was right, though I hoped she was wrong.

For those few weeks in April and May, change seemed more possible than ever before when Armenians from all walks of life protested in unprecedented numbers, estimated to be as large as 100,000, shutting streets down all over Yerevan, the capital, as they wreaked havoc against the status quo.[1] They self-organized and showed up en masse, open to collaborate. Women and children and old people were involved. The disabled banged on pots and pans, inspired by a protest in Spain.[2] The new middle class of tech sector workers contributed their skills to distribute information online.[3] Musicians and artists brought ingenuity to the streets with impromptu concerts and creative signs.[4] People everywhere brought their boomboxes and danced traditional dances in a circle.[5] Low-level pawns of the old regime, the ones everyone knew had corrupted elections at polling stations, weren't turned away from the protests. Even queer people, who had long been oppressed and demonized, were now included. Absolutely everyone was united in forcing out the corrupt regime and its tentacles, the oligarchs, who had exacted so much harm since Armenia fought for its independence from the Soviet Union in 1991. The people had had enough. They were angry, but they also cared about each other. They were angry, and they put their bodies on the line. They used their imagination, creativity, and love for each other in a mass tidal wave of disruption. Not one person died as a result.

The revolution began when just one hundred people supported the opposition member of Parliament Nikol Pashinyan, a scruffy guy in a backpack and baseball cap, in his protest against President Serzh Sargsyan. Over two weeks, they walked more than seventy-five miles to Yerevan, dubbing their protest My Step.[6] Their goal: to force Sargsyan to step down. He had just reached his term limit after ten years in office, but he'd finagled his way into a new prime minister position with essentially the same powers. Once in Yerevan, Pashinyan installed himself in Opera Square and gave a speech, impressing no one. But then his group made the rounds to the universities, and students joined him. Over time, as he kept insisting on the power of the people, Nikol, as he came to be known, won Armenians' hearts; a former journalist, he used Facebook Live to speak directly to everyone, a marked contrast to Sargsyan's formal appearances and removed countenance. Nikol also knew the abuses of the regime well: he had been falsely accused years before when Sargsyan was elected president and mass demonstrations against his corrupt election on March 1, 2008, had been quelled by state forces that killed ten people. He landed in prison for three years on charges of encouraging violence.

As I watched the events of the revolution from my bedroom in New York, glued to my computer till 4:00 a.m. because of the eight-hour time difference, I found myself in awe of not just the growing rebellion but the tactical response by protesters at every threat of state-enacted violence. Protesting students handed flowers to the police, who responded by hanging up concertina wire around Parliament to deter them; Nikol damaged his hand trying to tear it down, video of which brought out even more students, who shut down the metro by lying between the doors of the cars. Riot police showed up after that, in their helmets and shields. But when young women appeared on the streets, the police didn't know how to push their shields at them. Eventually the police yelled at the women and threw them around like they did at home. Soon, women showed up with their children. I watched video of one little girl asking a cop why he wouldn't join the protesters; he patted her on the head. Soon after, the police wore balaclavas to appear fearsome. By now the protests had spread to the far reaches of the capital, where poor people lived. Here, black-clad goons jumped out of vans and beat protesters while the police yawned and watched. Still, everyday people—middle-aged aunts and uncles—joined in the protests. I watched a video of a bus driver refusing to cart protesters to the police station, allowing them to stream out the back door to escape. People used their cars to block traffic. I smiled as I watched a truck driver handing out ice cream to everyone stopped on the road. As crowds continued to grow, police weren't amused. They lodged tear gas and stun grenades at the crowds. But people documented these acts on social media, which brought out even more folks.[7] It seemed nothing could stop the will of the people to join together.

If the revolution was dying, it was putting up quite a fight.

I'M NOT SURE WHY I was initially surprised at Diana's response. I had lived in Armenia from 2006 to 2007 and had visited a handful of other times, often encountering widespread despair among feminists, queer people, activists, and intellectuals. Corruption was rampant at every level of society. People often told me that it would take two generations for there to be any change, suggesting that justice could be found only with those born with a pure sense of right and wrong, and indicating that no one thought the current living, breathing populace was capable of reform. Though civil society was growing after the breakup of the Soviet Union, and there had been a number of successful protest movements—against the privatization of a public park, mining in the mountains, pension taxes, fraudulent elections, bus fare hikes, electricity prices—liberation was still a far-fetched dream.

From my vantage point, as a granddaughter of immigrants and refugees who had fled oppression and genocide, born and raised in the United States, a sheltered, idealistic artist, Armenia seemed to be a brutal place, violence as widespread as corruption. Trauma from the genocide rippled through society yet remained buried beneath Soviet and contemporary oligarchic oppression, frequently dismissed as an obsession of the diaspora. Domestic violence was rampant but denied. The army was known to haze soldiers to death, then blame it on suicide. It was easy to jump from the idea of protesting the government to fear of unrest, which would render Armenia vulnerable to attack by Azerbaijan. Though activism and empowerment were growing, fear was deeply entrenched in minds and bodies.

"The only way to make any change is for all the oligarchs to be rounded up, shot, and killed," my frustrated friend Amal had told me in the summer of 2015. We were sitting in a cafe drinking beer among friends and discussing Electric Yerevan, the largest protest yet. For days people showed up, around twenty thousand strong, on Baghramyan Avenue in front of Parliament to protest a hike in electricity prices mandated by a Russian-owned utility company. When it was all over, the proposed price hikes had been reversed, but not all of the protesters' demands were met by the government.[8]

Amal is a feminist artist and scholar as well as Diana's partner; her point of view is one of the main lenses I use to view and understand Armenia. She is strong willed and holds a dignified composure, so I was taken aback when she suddenly insisted that all the oligarchs be exterminated. "It's the only way to rid the country of corruption!" she posited.

"No!" I said in reaction. "That would only create more violence."

"You don't understand, Nancy. These men are like vermin. They won't go away. They won't go away unless they're destroyed!"

People in the group looked around, for what I'm not sure, but I assumed that such words could get Amal in trouble if the wrong person heard them. Diana sighed and said, "This is why I don't like her to drink."

Though alcohol-induced, Amal's argument for violence was portentous. The following summer, an activist group named after the medieval epic poem *Sasna Tsrer*, or *The Daredevils of Sassoun*, daringly captured a police station and held nine cops hostage. They demanded the release of the opposition leader Jirair Sefilian as well as Serzh's resignation, which drew wide-scale protests. Unfortunately, the protests resulted in wide-scale violence, injuring many people, taking the life of an officer, and landing the members of Sasna Tsrer behind bars with little way out.[9]

By the spring of 2018, a cycle of violence, empowerment, and fear had pushed people to and fro, back and forth. On April 16, Amal emailed:

> I'm writing from a besieged house! The cops have chained us all in, like good dogs trained to defend their master—tomorrow the Parliament is supposed to vote for Serzh as Prime Minister. Nikol Pashinyan and hundreds of citizens have taken to the streets, the transport has been shut down and many people have refused to go to work or school.

Not a week later, and only a few days after Diana told me the movement was dying, Serzh Sargsyan met with Nikol Pashinyan at the Marriott in Republic Square and left after three minutes. I watched the circus on my computer screen in astonishment, then went back to bed as Nikol emerged from the hotel and entered the enormous throng of crowds. When I woke up, I learned that Nikol had been arrested.[10]

But the people were not deterred. That night, those who couldn't come to the streets—the housewives, children, elderly, and disabled—leaned out their windows and banged on their pots and pans, most clanging for just fifteen minutes but in some neighborhoods playing their makeshift drums for an hour. The next morning, dozens of troops were seen marching down the street, not in formation but in their own gait.[11] They had actually joined the protesters! This was the moment everyone had been waiting for, the turning point.

After Amal had read that Nikol had been released from detention, she heard crowds marching down the street and stepped out with her baby.

> I kept walking down toward the opera with zora. we didn't go too far, because then the cars started to come and they were honking loudly, zora got scared and cried. so we went back home!! only to find out that while we were out there—serzh had resigned!!!!!!!!!!! and then the honking and the cheering started! people honked and cheered all day long—till one or two in the morning!

The people now had to force the government to accept Nikol as their leader. As the Parliament pushed back, refusing to vote for him as interim prime minister on May 1, the protests became uber-creative as they shut the city down and blocked the road to the airport. Protesters barbecued, played backgammon, did yoga, and staged theater in the streets. Young children set up roadblocks with toy cars,[12] and grandmothers screamed outside the homes of corrupt MPs. More than any other activity, the protesters danced, everywhere, all the time, in the rain, on top of cars. People of all ages and genders danced side by side, with linked hands or arms in a circle, rotating slowly and joyously as one until May 2, when the ruling Republican party announced they would vote for Nikol.

The revolution may have lagged or faltered, but it clearly didn't die. It was coined the Revolution of Love and Solidarity for the many ways that Armenians united as one.

In contrast, the most outspoken protest in the United States during the spring of 2018 was the comedian Michelle Wolf's takedown of Sarah Huckabee Sanders's smoky eyeliner— "composed of lies"—during the Correspondents' Dinner. After the presidential election of 2016, Americans watched their liberties erode every day as they witnessed the violence waged by the US government on Muslims, immigrants, refugees, women, Black people, and queers. Though there had been a long history of agitation and mass protest in the United States during the civil rights era and the antiwar movement of the 1960s, those Americans who had become varying degrees of white were a docile population who had never had to fight for anything in their lives. In the spring of 2018, we were all dumbstruck and depressed. And enraged. Such a dynamic was manifest through armchair activism on social media and muffled by the participatory escape of streaming TV. Naturally, there was little mainstream television news coverage about the revolution, just as Gil Scott-Heron had predicted. To people in the United States, the revolution in Armenia might as well have not even existed. And yet Americans desperately needed inspiring, imaginative models of widespread protest.

I thought of how jaded Amal had been about the prospect of change just three years before. Now she was elated:

> It feels like a nation died, was reborn and matured right in front of my eyes! we woke up a different people this morning. dignified, self-aware, conscious, happy, but solemn at the same time . . . a whole new society arose, older, wise, with tact and respect for each other . . . there is an inner camaraderie, an inner love for one another—and it glows. people smile at each other as they pass.

As I watched the revolution unfold through my computer screen, I felt connected to Armenia, more so than I had in a long time. The solidarity was infectious, I suppose, but perhaps my attachment was a result of the duality I was experiencing. Armenia is a place that remains hidden from the rest of my world as a single woman, an adjunct professor in New York City, a writer among a diverse community of people of color in Queens, and an assimilated second-generation American. Something about feeling proud of the revolution felt familiar to me: caring for a long-besieged community now realizing their power, taking steps that no one else does to learn about them, waking up in the middle of the night to spend time with them while everyone else sleeps, watching how love transformed them, realizing how love has always been crucial to their identity but had been perverted by powerful entities, expressing a unique creativity that helped to advance their cause. The rest of the world seemed determined to keep this people hidden, perhaps because as humans we are inexplicably drawn to violence and hesitant to love.

My experience of the revolution felt similar to being queer.

II

Armenia is not my homeland in the traditional sense of the word. As far as I know, I have no relatives in Hayastan because all my ancestors scattered to the West after the genocide. The language spoken there is foreign to me, a dialect with a syncopated rhythm compared to the melody of Western Armenian that my relatives spoke. The Eastern Anatolian cuisine of my ancestors as manifest in the United States—roasted chicken and pilaf, giragud like fasulya and batlijan—are not common in Armenia (the one I knew anyway, before Syrian Armenians arrived fleeing war). But in many ways, Armenia has chosen me, and I have chosen it to love like family. And like any family, our love is complicated. We place demands on each other that we can't always fulfill.

A few years after I published a book of poetry about my queer coming of age, some Armenians found it. I never imagined anyone in Armenia reading my poems. I didn't ever imagine that there were queer people in Armenia. Come to think of it, I never really imagined anyone in Armenia, period, except for the stereotypes that came to me through my family: that Armenians were lazy and would trade their eyeteeth for a ticket to America. When I was invited to Armenia as a performance artist in 2005, a portal opened up to me. I was finally among people who looked like me, who shared my culture and history, and lo and behold, they were queer! At that time, silence mostly surrounded LGBTQ people in Armenia; homosexuality had been criminalized by the Soviets and legally tolerated after the collapse but never socially accepted nor given equality status. Gay men in particular were vulnerable to blackmail and coercion. It wouldn't be until 2007 that the first LGBTQ grassroots support and advocacy groups would be formed.

The silence felt like an arm of residual oppression from Soviet times, to keep one's thoughts and private life to oneself for fear of being betrayed to the party. I tried to understand this dynamic through the fractures of my own Armenian family, who never quite accepted my queerness.

In any case, I found there was enough resonance and curiosity for me to return. In 2006, I lived in Armenia as a Fulbright fellow to write about the changing political landscape. A destructive, emotionally abusive relationship with a younger Armenian man damaged me, but it didn't sour me. I kept returning every few years to learn more. I taught writing workshops with women that helped heal me. I developed friendships with artists and queer people, writing books and creating art projects in the United States and Armenia with Amal and Diana and others. I watched in horror in 2012 when DIY, a queer-friendly bar, was firebombed and my friends were under attack and forced to flee into exile. I penned petitions to the government and raised funds for LGBTQ organizations whenever homophobia surfaced in violence, most often as a method to distract from governmental corruption by scapegoating a minority.

Now, during the revolution, there appeared to be an opening. Although not explicitly embraced, queer people were included in the protests in a way that they hadn't experienced in Armenian society before. But a few queer Armenians in the diaspora were questioning on social media whether the revolution was truly revolutionary. Would Nikol support LGBTQ rights? The timing of the question seemed dismissive of the success of the Armenian people to finally achieve widespread change. Homophobia was beside the point, and the expectation that it would disappear overnight was unrealistic to say the least. But now that the regime that was responsible for scapegoating LGBTQ Armenians was out of the picture, it seemed there was some hope.

I had been planning to visit Amal and Diana to meet their new baby, Zora, in the summer of 2018. I also wanted to spread the inspiring message of the revolution to Americans through my writing, and I needed to find interview subjects. Though I, too, hoped change would come for everyone, I chose to interview queer Armenians mostly because they were the Armenians I knew.

ON A PLEASANT AFTERNOON IN JULY, Amal introduced me to the next generation of feminist activists at FemLibrary, located in an old house on a quiet residential side street in the center of Yerevan. As we walked down the street, I noticed overhanging grapevines and heard scary dogs barking viciously behind smooth, eight-foot metal gates. The door to the house opened to a small galley kitchen with counters on both sides, where I met Anna and Arpi, the founders of FemLibrary. Anna had curly, shoulder-length blonde hair, her pointed nose friendly and welcoming. Arpi had a haircut I sported as a teenager, one side short and shaved to the head, one side long, part of it blue. She was petite but compact and tough.

They guided me to a large, wood-paneled dining room with a dusty chandelier and a handful of simple bookcases standing to the right, filled with mostly English-language books on feminism. A hallway behind us led to a bathroom, and a staircase in front of us ascended to the bedrooms. They showed me where an artist-in-residence could stay in the future, and I immediately imagined myself working there.

But wait, there was a garage, where they were hoping to start a cafe. They had already taken down the old motor magazines and girly pinups that had been left behind. Anna and Arpi were concerned about the cafe: they were renting and were fearful that their neighbors would complain. I suggested that maybe there was a way to invite them in, but Anna didn't seem to think this would work.

Anna has a master's degree in gender studies, which she earned abroad, in Great Britain. Arpi is a performance artist. Her recent work brought street art into the exhibition space; it was about feminism and anti-militarism and was shown in Armenia's second cities: Gyumri, Abovian, and Vanadzor.

After coffee and sweets on a small patio under a grape arbor, Anna gave me some background. She told me about some of the women the FemLibrary served, including "queer corps," a play on the words "queer" and "kooyr," the latter meaning "sister" in Armenian. So, essentially, "queer sister." It was a group of thirty women attending film screenings and self-defense workshops. For six months, they rented various locations to hold these events. Now they were happy they would be able to use FemLibrary's safe space.

Both Anna and Arpi had found that most queer spaces they encountered were male dominated and less political. The same was true for the revolution. Arpi mentioned how Telecon, a gather app, connected people to lots of events during the revolution, but most of them weren't by and for feminists.

Anna clarified: "There were feminist elements at the local level, but not at the macro level. Overall, the revolution was patriarchal."

I asked why they got involved. Anna explained that queer people had been used by the Republican-run government for years, scapegoated to divert the public's attention. "We don't want the republic to continue ruling over our bodies and minds."

Additionally, police had recently raided the home of an activist, and Anna had been caught spray-painting anti-military graffiti, so she was on the police's radar. Conditions were getting more dangerous, and they felt if they didn't protest, if change didn't happen, they would soon face a further degradation of their rights.

Fearing for their future safety while also confronted with the reality of the sexism of the current movement, they tailored their protests to express themselves. They were against patriarchal society as a whole. When the women closed streets, they chanted, "Serzh is not our father," and "Kick out the father of the republic."

Bystanders joined them in their chants but also exhibited sexist attitudes. Arpi was at a location where a lot of girls and women were jumping in front of cars to close the street. A middle-aged female bystander watched the proceedings. When a young guy jumped in front of cars, she called out to him, "I'm proud of you," after previously saying nothing to the countless women who had just done the same.

They also had to fight for space to be heard. "There was a guy with a megaphone near the medical university, and I asked to read a text," Anna said. "He refused to let me have the megaphone until he could see my text. So I didn't use the megaphone. I have a loud voice and I projected instead, and people listened. Suddenly this man was no longer an actor in this situation.

"'Who are you?' he asked, and I told him I'd been an activist for ten years. 'How come I don't know about you, then?' It was as if I couldn't exist without his knowledge or control," Anna noted.

The women shut down streets, then moved quickly to a new location when police arrived, unless they got arrested. Once when Anna was detained, she organized other people being held by police and informed those arrested of their rights. "I knew the law, so the police were threatened by me," she said. She told other protesters to neither testify nor give up their passport info. As she was doing so, a police officer reacted: "Look at how you're sitting!" Her offense? She was seated cross-legged on the floor. "I'm tired of you," he said. And that's how she was let free.

"I rejoined my sisters," she said, enthused. "And I felt how strong our sisterhood was." She told me how seven people were staying on the floor in her apartment in the center. "It was a communal space for us," she continued. "We started a Facebook Messenger group called aghchignotz, which means 'girls' space,' for girls and women who wanted to share information on closing the streets." Seventy people joined and invited their friends. At first it was a space to organize and communicate. Then it became a political platform for conversation. "Chat and conversation were important, too. We realized that it was a place where you could send a message and at least one person would support you."

Anna and Arpi talked about ownership of the protests. It was clear that everyone could find a way into it. They let me know that feminists started Anti-Taron, a movement to oust the corrupt mayor of Yerevan, who resigned in July.[13] Their own aghchignotz group was active in closing the SAS supermarket chain and organizing their workers, using the slogan "power to the people" at their protests.

I hadn't realized that women—and queer women—had taken such leadership roles. For every sexist encounter they subverted to their advantage, it seemed there were also moments when they were embraced. Arpi told a story about protesting at the municipality. Security wouldn't let her by, but a girl inside the police barricade was pulling her in. The police said to the stranger, "Pulling your friend is illegal." The woman replied, "She's not my friend; she's my sister!" It could have been a ruse, but it also had a double and welcoming meaning: people on the streets in Yerevan use these family terms toward each other, calling the woman selling them coffee "auntie," for example. Arpi and the stranger were sisters, united in the struggle.

Arpi was hopeful for the prospects of LGBTQ acceptance. She mentioned that the Yerevan City Council member Zaruhi Batoyan, who had organized the pots and pans protest, made a speech in Republic Square during the revolution in which she called for ending discrimination against anyone on any basis, including sexual orientation.[14]

Anna replied, "We still need to fight a lot against nationalism and for sexuality." She warned that Nikol and the new government were not progressive enough. "It won't be worse. It also won't be extreme violence supported by the state," she noted, contrasting to the fear of the former regime. She didn't have a positive outlook; she was simply acknowledging survival.

Still, I left their space feeling hopeful that a new generation was becoming more active and visible: it signaled that all the work of Amal, Diana, and others was not futile. In small ways, I had contributed to these efforts over the years, and I felt a sense of hope.

Not long after our conversation, Anna and Arpi had to flee the Fem-Library—the grapevines, the galley kitchen, the wood-paneled dining room, the bookcases, the chandelier, the staircase, the artist-in-residence bedrooms, the garage cafe—because their landlord had ousted them, citing their political convictions as the reason. They started over in a new space, only to be evicted again, recently, for the same reason. They've been fundraising to buy their own building.

AFTER OUR CONVERSATION AT FEMLIBRARY, Anna and Arpi directed me to Pink Armenia's offices, just up the hill from their space. Pink is a human rights defender NGO that supports LGBTQ people in Armenia and was founded around 2007. The office was in a large house behind a school, and I followed the GPS on my phone, but I still had trouble finding it. When I had visited three years prior, Pink was located on the second floor of an office building right off Abovian Street, smack in the center. Now it was in a house behind a smooth white wall, a security buzzer with a camera mounted at the gate.

Mamikon, one of the founders of Pink and now its executive director, informed me they had moved here for greater security since they often received death threats. He seemed markedly different from the last time I visited: tired and worn out, his auburn brown eyes ringed with dark circles. While most folks seem energized by the impossible, it had clearly taken a toll on him.

After Mamikon gave me a tour of their offices and a warren of small rooms designated for legal and psychological counseling, we sat down in a large, bright central space that operated as a communal office. Here's where they hung out during the protests, Mamikon told me. While a handful of office workers typed on laptops nearby, he recounted how Pink got involved with the revolution after an initial feeling that the My Step protest would soon die out like all the others.

Even as the protests grew, they were cautious. "We didn't imagine there'd be changes so quickly. We thought it would be a long fight. We didn't know if it would be the results we wanted; we thought it would be like Electric Yerevan. When there was a huge number of people, we realized 'this is the moment.'" Mamikon identified April 23 as the turning point: when Serzh stepped down, and "one hundred times" more people showed up. "We also saw lots of LGBTQ people on the streets and felt we had an obligation to be with our community. It was inspiring to see LGBTQ next to others."

Mamikon recounted to me examples of protesters supporting each other, like typical Armenian guys dancing with trans people. At a food station where a trans woman was helping out, someone called her "Aghber jan" (Brother dear). She said, "No, I'm a woman."

"Okay then, kooyr jan [sister dear]," the brother responded.

Someone else asked, "Are you a boy or a girl?"

A woman, another stranger, intervened: "Just call her a citizen of the Republic of Armenia."

It seemed the revolution brought out a tolerance that hadn't been allowed to emerge before, at least among citizens on the streets.

It wasn't all rosy, though. One of their staff got beaten up. He was with a crowd of people when the police targeted him, pulling him away for arrest. A man next to him asked, "Why don't you take me?"

"Because you're a normal guy," the cop answered. The police beat the staff member in their patrol car, and there were no witnesses. But this gay man had black and blue marks as proof.

It was the only report of police abuse on one individual that I had heard. I remembered watching from afar, in my bedroom in New York City, when violence erupted; it was the day Nikol tried to get into Parliament and tore his hand on barbed wire. From then on, it was a Velvet Revolution, as Nikol claimed. But no one was discussing this violence toward Pink's staff member: it got washed under the current of great change.

And now there was already a new wave of homophobia. On social media, there were elements trying to undermine Nikol and the new government with homophobic fake news. Mamikon showed me one video with an outraged caption that the new minister of justice was legalizing homosexuality (but it was already legal). Another video depicted the press secretary of the health ministry saying why she was against homophobia, but her words were spliced, falsely taken out of context to imply she was pro-gay.

I hoped that people wouldn't be duped by efforts like these as they had in the past. It didn't seem the fledgling government was concerned; it wasn't making statements or speaking out about the homophobic attacks on social media. Mamikon thought the government wouldn't say or do anything regarding LGBTQ rights until after the snap elections on December 9, when Nikol would resign and be elected again. Nikol wouldn't touch such a controversial issue and jeopardize his election.

"I don't think it's a real revolution," Mamikon said. "There has been a changing power of authorities but not of minds." Here was the echo from what queer Armenians in the diaspora had alleged on social media.

I'd been in Yerevan for several days now, looking for visible signs of revolution. People seemed lighter and happier. No one was glued to a cell phone, even on public transportation. Gender presentation felt more diverse. Gone were the ubiquitous high heels; I saw many young women wearing jeans and sneakers, and they looked empowered.

But the city was gentrified. An underground passageway at the Metro by Yeridasartagan used to be filled with lively used booksellers and flea market stands: notebooks, linens, underwear, flower shops, batteries. It was now pristine, white and shiny, a fancy mall. When I continued down Abovyan, instead of fifty-dram lahmajun and peroshki stands, I encountered expensive French cafes.

There were so many cars on the streets, many more than before. Amal told me that the banks were offering loans to people, and they used them to buy cars and fix up their homes only to land in debilitating debt.

At Lake Sevan with Amal, Diana, and Zora, the water looked like a radioactive pea soup. We couldn't go swimming; the algae levels were too high. Nearby mines of European mineral companies, their chemicals dumped into the ground, were to blame.

So, when an art critic told me that Armenia didn't have a revolution because of the neoliberal path it was on, her statement didn't seem as dismissive as previous criticism I'd heard. Or maybe I just didn't want to hear it before.

I asked Mamikon how he thought the revolution happened, and he sighed. "I don't know." He mentioned the four-day war the year before as a breaking point. The government had long claimed that protest would render Armenia vulnerable to its hostile neighbors, Azerbaijan and Turkey. But if the government cared so much about Armenia's safety, why did it not invest in it? Why did Armenia's soldiers not have adequate supplies? (Just recently, a former general was arrested for corruption when a camera crew toured his grounds, revealing many luxury cars and untold boxes of supplies that were never delivered to troops, including donations by Armenian schoolchildren and communities in the diaspora).[15] Finally there was a common goal uniting everyone: they were fed up when Serzh maneuvered himself to stay in power.

Perhaps remembering this unity, Mamikon saw things more positively. He told me that the fight for justice ignited by the revolution would continue, and it would eventually reach LGBTQ Armenians. Taking in his tired eyes, I couldn't tell if he was saying it more for himself, for me, or for all of us.

⁑ ⁑ ⁑

I LEFT ARMENIA ON AUGUST 3, 2018. Sometime during my long flight back to the United States, the LGBTQ activist Hayk Hakobyan invited eight friends to a remote village called Shurnukh, a six-and-a-half-hour drive from Yerevan, for a weekend away from the city. Not all of them were queer, and not all of them were activists.

That night, a couple of men shouted for Hakobyan to come out of the house and he refused. They had harassed him and a friend a few months before, in April. The men jumped over the fence and onto the balcony. His friends called the police and his family who were nearby; the family told the group to leave the village. The group packed their suitcases and were walking out of town when a group of fifteen people showed up and started yelling homophobic slurs, beating them, and throwing rocks at them, even as they ran away.

In an NBC News report, Hakobyan said of his attackers, "They were saying, 'We need to catch Hayk. We need to kill him.'" More villagers joined the melee by the main road until there were thirty people driving the group out of town. At this point, the police finally showed up, but they did not bring enough cars to transport the victims. The group had to flag down a tourist bus to give them a ride, and two went directly to the hospital.[16]

In a village of two hundred people, thirty attackers are significant. The former mayor, about whom Hakobyan's father had previously made a formal complaint for corruption, was also among the crowd.[17] After the fact, some villagers claimed that Hakobyan and his friends had been loud and rowdy during previous visits. Even if this were true, how does this justify hate speech and violence? The police minimally investigated the incident, and no charges were brought on the attackers. They still haven't been brought.

"We want justice. We want these people in jail," Hakobyan said. "I don't have a home anymore."[18]

WHEN I ARRIVED HOME, I was greeted by a note under my door that my apartment building had bedbugs. I'd already battled them in my own apartment twice before. The city that once granted me freedom to find myself and grow now seemed to be interfering in my ability to live well.

I decided to leave New York. The next year was a scramble of saying goodbye to the city and dealing with my parents' illnesses, traveling from my apartment in Queens to Boston every two weeks. By the summer of 2019, I had moved into my parents' home, the house where I had grown up.

The news from Shurnukh dismayed me, but I buried my feelings. I couldn't understand how a people that had turned away from corruption as one body, that had rejected a regime that had lied to them again and again, that had been persuaded by the government's attempts to distract them from its own crimes, was now accepting lies about LGBTQ people that they were the single worst threat to Armenia. In the two years since the attack, there have been other homophobic events and culture war skirmishes that forced Nikol to comment on LGBTQ rights. But I didn't get as emotionally or as politically involved as I had in the past, when I drafted petitions and statements and raised funds. It wasn't just that I couldn't act; I couldn't even follow the events. I cared about what was happening to LGBTQ Armenians. I was glad that I was now seeing straight Armenians in the diaspora express their outrage and organize statements condemning the increased level of violence and backlash; I rationalized that I had done my part and other people now needed to step up. But in reality, my experience of the Revolution of Love and Solidarity had fractured me.

III

Before the attacks in Shurnukh, before the fracture, there was Zora. She was so quick to smile, and it was a pleasure to be with her, a bundle of love. Everything in Amal and Diana's apartment revolved around her. The arched windows and old double-paned glass let in a lovely light that glinted from Zora's eyes, and her coos traveled over the transom into the door of the guest room where I woke every morning. The floor plan was a central hallway with rooms opening onto rooms with swinging doors, and all paths seemed to lead to Zora—taking a nap, nursing, bathing—no matter where she was. In that revolving space it seemed time didn't exist.

From Diana and Amal's back window, where we sat for breakfast, we could see the windows of Sylva Gaboudigian's apartment, which had been turned into a museum after her death in 2009. I didn't know of Gaboudigian or her work, not even her famous poem in which she tells her son that he can forget her but not his mother tongue. But one of my favorite things to do in life is visit house museums. In these spaces, time seems to exist on multiple planes, the past compressed to the present; I feel close to history, understanding it more tacitly than reading a two-dimensional text. The space is intimate and clinical at once.

One afternoon after breakfast, Amal carried Zora in her arms across the parking lot and up the street and into the famous poet's building. She and Diana had all the accessories of slings and strollers, but Zora rebelled against them and Amal wanted to keep her safe in her arms.

The four of us crowded into the tiny elevator, went up a few flights, and knocked on Sylva's door. We encountered two women who gave us a tour. Sylva's apartment was huge; the Soviets built it specially for her in 1975. Her bedroom was tiny, tucked behind a narrow passageway. On her desk nearby sat a massive dictionary that had been eaten by thirty-seven mice. I wanted to ask how they knew the precise number of rodents, but I bit my tongue since it was the only item she possessed from her father, who died when her mother was pregnant. Additionally, I was touched by her tiny bed, surrounded by heavy tapestries. Sylva couldn't sleep at night during the war from 1991 to 1994; the tapestries kept out the light so that she could sleep during the day.

Surprisingly, as a member of the Communist Party, Sylva was also a fervent nationalist. She even met with the Armenian Secret Army for the Liberation of Armenia (ASALA) after they blew up Turkish diplomats. I learned this when the tour guides showed us an ugly clock that ASALA had gifted her. She risked her life by meeting with them. You'd think they would have sprung for a better present, but I suppose terrorists don't have much of a discretionary budget. Say what you will about Gaboudigian's politics and her patriotic poetry; to be respected by both nationalist terrorists and Soviet strongmen is quite a feat, especially for a woman. (Nikol similarly trod a line between powers by making the protests solely about domestic issues in Armenia, which avoided offending Russia or the West.) On her sunporch, the one we could see from Amal and Diana's apartment, there were cases of photos and other mementos that proved Sylva was loved around the world.

The tour guides had known her personally. I widened my eyes when Amal translated this fact for me. We were standing in the kitchen, which had been repurposed as an art room for children, their paintings and drawings, inspired by Sylva's poetry, covering the walls.

As we approached the door and said our thank-yous, one of the guides hugged me. Usually Armenians kiss both cheeks, but even showing this kind of affection seemed odd for the situation. Perhaps she wanted to bring me closer to Gaboudigian's orbit. Maybe it was because I was looking at everything with great interest.

When I lived in Armenia, I had trouble making sense of the harsh ways people could treat each other on the street verses the generosity they showed in their homes. Perhaps the tour guide was simply showing that famous Armenian hospitality. Perhaps her love had been compounded by the revolution.

Because of economic conditions in Armenia, young people typically live with their parents until they marry. Because queer people can't marry in Armenia, they live with their families indefinitely, and their home life can be a site of abuse. After Shurnukh, it seemed to me, queer Armenians couldn't be safe on the streets anymore. They had nowhere to be safe now, not in their homes and not on the streets, either. This is why spaces like FemLibrary and Pink Armenia are so crucial. Sadly, these organizations cannot maintain a safe space either, forced to move from place to place.

I have no idea whether Sylva was supportive to queer people, but I imagine she knew some in her time, operating in the world of poetry. In any case, in the timeless space of her house museum, a place both public and private at once—or neither public nor private—Diana, Amal, Zora, and I were embraced.

AS AN AMERICAN WRITER with one foot in academia and the other in activism, I am familiar with other representations of the street and of home in a political context.

In 1989, the legal scholar Kimberlé Crenshaw coined the term "intersectionality" to explain why Black women should be leaders both within the feminist movement and within the fight against racism. In "Demarginalizing the Intersection of Race and Sex: A Black Feminist Critique of Antidiscrimination Doctrine, Feminist Theory and Antiracist Politics," Crenshaw describes the compounding effects of racism and sexism for Black women, using the metaphor of an accident at an intersection, which can occur from cars traveling in any direction. At the intersection of race and gender, where Black women live, injustice can occur to them in any number of ways:

> Black women sometimes experience discrimination in ways similar to white women's experiences; sometimes they share very similar experiences with Black men. Yet often they experience double-discrimination—the combined effects of practices which discriminate on the basis of race, and on the basis of sex. And sometimes, they experience discrimination as Black women—not the sum of race and sex discrimination, but as Black women.[19]

Later, she constructs another metaphor to illustrate the negative effect of a singular, top-down understanding of discrimination. A basement is filled with people who are stacked from floor to ceiling, standing on each other's shoulders. The people who experience only a singular oppression, like racism, sexism, homophobia, classism, ableism, ageism, and the like are situated at the top, near the ceiling. Those who are disadvantaged in multiple ways are on the floor. Above the ceiling are those who don't experience any oppression; they create a hatch in the floor in order to let others access their privilege. But only folks just below the floor are able to crawl through. In this scenario, constructed to illustrate legal limitations of fighting discrimination, Black women can only rise through the hatch if they make their oppression fit into a single cause and align themselves with a group with a singular oppression.[20] Such an approach allows justice movements to remain hierarchical spaces and creates blind spots in understanding how multiple forms of discrimination disadvantage everyone. Ideally, the way to fight all oppression is for everyone, at every level, to uplift those with the most oppression.[21]

In Armenia there are no specifically anti-LGBTQ discrimination laws, though there are human rights laws in general. Article 29 of the constitution, adopted in December 2015, states, "Discrimination based on sex, race, color, ethnic or social origin, genetic characteristics, language, religion, worldview, political or other views, belonging to an ethnic minority, status of property ownership, origin, disability, age or other private or social factors, is prohibited." You'd think that "other private or social factors" would cover the queer-bashing that took place in Shurnukh. But Article 29 has failed to provide protection for any LGBTQ individuals from the violence they have faced on the streets or in their homes.

Without legal protections, LGBTQ Armenians experience more oppression than other Armenian citizens. They have long sustained violence. Through this position, they've learned strength. Queer Armenians have learned how to fight for themselves. They have long known that they need allies in order to survive. The revolution succeeded partially because those on the bottom of the basement contributed their well-honed skills out in the street. And yet they haven't been liberated. The hierarchy of gender and sexuality is still in place, even if the revolution tore down the ceiling and threw oligarchs to the basement.

But Armenian oppression as an entity is difficult to theorize given the global spaces we occupy. If Armenia is a basement filled with oppression, then what kind of space is the diaspora? And where is it in relation to that basement? Maybe it's more accurate to imagine Armenians all over the world living in the same house or compound. On our different continents, with varying economic privilege, social capital, and political power, we are alienated from each other, living in different structures and rooms, on separate levels, able to hear each other only through muffled sounds through the floors and walls. When we gain clarity, we have opened a door or window to see each other.

Do queer diaspora Armenians and queer Armenians share the same room, somewhere in the attic, the basement, or the proverbial closet? I don't think we are even allowed access to our own room. Yet we also carry varying privileges depending on which letter of LGBTQ we identify with and where in the world we live. Perhaps we are stuck inside the walls throughout the house: our familial and cultural contributions hold together Armenia, but we are relegated to the margins, stifled and silenced.

I DIDN'T ALWAYS view the intersection of my Armenian queerness so negatively. My path to my identity began when I came out as bisexual in my early twenties. As I distanced myself from my family and Armenian community, I periodically informed my parents of my sexuality, who either condemned me or promptly forgot whenever I had a male partner. My family's acceptance was elusive, so in my thirties I sought out other queer Armenians, in the United States and in Armenia. In my forties, I found myself in prominent roles in various LGBTQ Armenian groups. In the fall of 2012, several months after the firebombing attack on DIY, I was invited to give a talk to the senior seminar of the Armenian Youth Federation (AYF) at Camp Hayastan in Franklin, Massachusetts. The site is located a few miles from my parents' home, so I invited them along. To a room of fifty or more young people, I explained the genesis of the Armenian LGBTQ rights movement, starting with figures like Charents and Parjanov, Arlene Avakian and George Stambolian, explaining the fabric of homophobia, moving on to the founding of groups in the United States and Europe in the late 1990s, detailing the founding of groups in Armenia around 2007 and our connections across borders. I theorized that we needed each other, that participating in Pride marches in the West proved the existence of Armenian queerness, just as the cultural events by groups in Armenia brought us together and advanced us forward. We couldn't fight for liberation as queer Armenians without each other.

Something about this experience blew the ceiling off the structure of my parents' shame and denial. Watching young Armenians listen, learn, and begin to break through their prejudices helped them to see me in a different way—as someone fighting successfully for herself and for others. They were proud of me. Afterward, my father bragged about me at the St. James Church bazaar in Watertown to whoever would listen. It was a watershed moment for me as both an activist and a daughter.

I found out years later, from a friend who had mentioned the lecture in passing to Mamikon, that the people who invited me to give that talk were reprimanded by the leadership of their organization. I suppose I shouldn't have been surprised. From previous dealings with the Tashnags, I knew they were dominated by straight men, who to all outside appearances may uphold socialist values but only so much as it maintains their power structure. But this is a problem in any diaspora organization, which exists in its own sexist frameworks, compounded by the failure or inability of our communities to unpack their shame and mourn the gendered crimes of the genocide. The perpetrators raped the women and shot the men. The women were brought into harems and homes; the men were prevented from protecting their family, effectively emasculated by their murders. Anyone with a gender identity outside the binary is hardly ever discussed. But if a man could pass as a woman, he might have survived. Is it possible that when an Armenian man lashes out in anger at queer folx online or in Armenia, it's because he is attacking his own emasculation by oligarchs? By neoliberal economic hierarchies? By the genocide?

What would it look like if he grieved instead?

The people I had associated with at AYF silently cut ties with me, and I was never invited back to the senior seminar. Perhaps my words that day in 2012 made a difference to the young people in that room, but what had seemed like such a positive experience now felt like a sham. In art and intellectual circles in the Armenian community, I am mostly accepted. But to the rest of the Armenian community, eating their chicken and pilaf dinner at the St. James bazaar, my father bragging about me giving a talk on LGBTQ Armenian equality, I am simply a waste of time, a stray comment never reinforced again. Homophobic Armenians rejected not just me but my proud father as well, in service of a "respectable" appearance in line with the dominant white heteropatriarchy of the United States.

I never told my father that I had been shunned by AYF, and yet my silence in the intervening years seems to have made an impact on him. On LGBTQ Pride day, I ask my elderly parents, who both have dementia, if they are proud of me for being queer.

"Well, you're not too queer," my father replies. Does he mean that being queer doesn't make me strange or unusual? Or is he complimenting how I pass for straight as a femme woman? It seems to be more the latter since he doesn't actually say that he's proud.

My mother answers yes, asking if I am proud of *them*. "Yes," I tell her. "Even when it seemed you didn't accept me. But you're not LGBTQ."

And then she says something I've never heard her say before: "You didn't get to choose us."

Had the dementia loosened a thought she had kept to herself? She never chose for me to be queer, and yet she was proud of me. It seemed she was now trying to get inside of my shoes: I hadn't chosen straight parents either.

It's not lost on me that I have been piecing together this essay in spare moments in my parents' basement, where I've set up an office next to the one my father occupied for decades to make a living as our main provider. Now I'm caring for my parents while my queerness hides in the walls, tolerated by my father who was once proud. I write our secrets in the basement, hoping these details will finally get through to some straight Armenian somewhere. Maybe you're reading me in your bedroom or living room or study. We didn't choose each other, and yet here we are.

Writing is a space both intimate and public, like the house museum. Time compresses and stretches in these public/private institutions. Rooms get repurposed. Metaphors get mixed. The hatred for queer Armenians is love that got turned upside down and inside out. It's not so much the result of a power structure, a top-down paradigm. Because we're all queer in some way. Western notions of gender—what a man should look like and say and do, and what a woman should look like and say and do—have been imposed atop our own shame. To the Western gaze, a woman with a prominent nose looks masculine, and a man with large eyes and long lashes appears feminine. I once heard a joke in Armenia: it's the land of hairy women and pregnant men. In reality, there is no role reversal. We are neither feminine nor masculine; our gender is our own, like that of a baby or an old person. This is how a revolution can be dying at the same time that it is growing. The fight isn't a steady trajectory. It's revolving, like any cycle.

NIKOL PASHINYAN WAS SILENT after the Shurnukh attack. He broke his silence on LGBTQ issues only in late October 2018, when his opponents continued their attempts to wage a culture war against him, attempting to pass anti-LGBTQ marriage laws and an anti-gay "propaganda" law. This coincided with protests against a Christian LGBTQ conference that was about to be held in Yerevan in November.[22]

Pashinyan addressed Parliament with a story about meeting an Armenian waiter in Paris who served him coffee in his hotel room. The waiter revealed that he was gay and that he had escaped Armenia's homophobia.[23] Given that a common homophobic refrain about LGBTQ Armenians is "There's no such thing as a gay Armenian," it was an important moment of acknowledgment. No other Armenian leader had expressed anything about queer people. It almost seemed he was about to sympathize with the young man. But then he continued.

"In Armenia and around the world there are people who have a non-traditional sexual orientation," he said. "What we do about these people, how do we treat them? In the Soviet Union it was clear, if someone would be identified [as LGBTQ] there was a law to send them to prison. Before, they would be hanged or shot. So what do we do today? The LGBTQ issue is always a headache for a government."[24]

It certainly wasn't a statement of support, but I thought it vaguely suggested that violence was not the way.

And yet the violence continued. Tensions increased until a week before the Christian LGBTQ conference. The director was attacked in his car, and several staff were followed and harassed because attackers wanted to find the site of the conference. Even some tourists were attacked, suspected of being gay conference participants. The event was eventually canceled due to death threats and the lack of a promise that police would protect attendees.[25]

But snap elections for Parliament and prime minister were still pending. No one expected Nikol to say much on LGBTQ rights until then. The shadow campaign against him continued with fake news and even a fake LGBTQ Pride parade and organization, featuring posters of Nikol alongside a rainbow flag. Such transparently false attempts ultimately didn't work, and he was elected prime minister on December 9.[26]

ON APRIL 5, 2019, something extraordinary happened in the Armenian Parliament. Lilit Martirosyan, of Right Side NGO, addressed the members:

> I am delivering this speech to you as a transgender woman, but I ask
> you to see me as a collective figure. I stand for tortured, raped, burnt,
> stabbed, killed, banished, discriminated, poor and unemployed transgen-
> der people of Armenia. I call upon you to carry out reforms and policies to
> achieve gender equality, and to ensure human rights for everyone.[27]

Lilit was quickly escorted out of the building. She was speaking at a forum on human rights but had not been invited to. Afterward, Lilit explained the dire need for her act of bravery: trans people are continually attacked and beaten in Armenia with no criminal repercussions for the attackers. A trans woman's apartment had been set on fire, and someone else had been attacked with a knife.[28]

A couple of weeks later, Western media outlets such as the *Guardian* and *USA Today* picked up the story when MPs made violent, homophobic remarks, crowds gathered at Parliament to protest, and death threats were waged at Lilit.[29] When Nikol was questioned about Lilit, he sidestepped the issue, blaming the Republican Party, who had been accusing him of supporting LGBTQ rights, for granting Lilit a passport.

A few months later, another controversy erupted when $42,000 was granted to complete a film about Mel Dalusyan, an award-winning weight-lifter and trans man who eventually fled Armenia to escape the widespread transphobia against him. Because the Armenian government funded the film, the same homophobic forces in Armenia took offense.[30]

This time, Nikol stepped up:

> When she was a champion we were cheering and taking photos next to her and when she had a problem we write her off? I didn't know before-hand that the film was financed [by the state] but I'm very glad that it was, it would be immoral not to help this film be made. . . . This person is under my personal protection. This person fled from Armenia but that was not enough to save himself.[31]

It was a step, and, as the revolution demonstrated, one step can make a difference. Some argued that Nikol was only defending Mel for being "exceptional" and that one statement wasn't enough to protect all LGBTQ Armenians. But it seems counterproductive to pin all hopes for quelling homophobia on Nikol. It is dependent on the people, just as the revolution was. When we look at the statistics, they are grim. Armenia consistently ranks near the bottom of the list of countries in terms of LGBTQ rights and safety.[32] When surveyed about queer people, 97 percent of Armenians say homosexuality should not be accepted by society.[33]

Those who attacked the activists in Shurnukh have still not been prop-erly investigated. In response, in 2020, Pink Armenia named August 3 the National Day to Fight for LGBTQ+ Rights.[34]

WHEN AMAL AND DIANA are out in public with their baby, Zora, they are rarely seen as two moms. One is seen as a mother, and the other is seen as a sister or a straight friend. It is a somewhat innocuous situation in a place like a grocery store, but a dangerous one in a place like a hospital, when one of them is giving birth.

After the attack on the nine LGBTQ activists in Shurnukh, Diana returned to New York to complete her studies, and we spent an afternoon on Brighton Beach. She told me a story of overhearing two men discussing the Shurnukh attacks in a Yerevan hardware store.

"These gay people are taking over," they were saying. "They come from outside and ruin our country!"

Diana couldn't help but interject. She pretended she was one of them, a straight person. "No, they're not so bad."

"What?" the men asked.

"Have you met a gay person?"

"No, never!"

"Really? They're not so strange or dangerous. They're just like you and me."

"And they just looked at me with such hatred," Diana said to me.

The sun was high in the sky, it was a beautiful late August day, we had just gone in for a dip, and the water was perfect. We had spoken to Amal and Zora on Diana's phone while the little one was taking a bath, splashing playfully. We were all bathing beauties, we joked.

While Diana told me this story, she wasn't scared or distressed, and she had likely told it before. She chuckled. "So I bought my things and left. I knew by the looks on their faces that I could get hurt."

Considering Martin Luther King Jr.'s long arc of justice, I wonder how far this hatred will take us out of orbit from the sun. We are more than one hundred years from the genocide, and that crime still hasn't been atoned for. Perhaps it doesn't matter; perhaps justice rides alongside our lives, encircling us in small ways that will eventually help everyone to rise.

The cause of LGBTQ rights in Armenia isn't some niche interest. It's a fight that's happening everywhere and for all time: it's a fight for open minds, freedom of thought, and the embrace of imagination. Without envisioning another person's existence, especially those with whom we live side by side, we cannot truly love. Without imagination, we can't burst out from our walls to discover what's in the great big sea.

Before we grabbed our things to leave the beach, Diana mentioned in passing that it was the first time she had swum in the ocean. Armenia is landlocked, but I was astonished nonetheless. I've been swimming in oceans my whole life, but Diana swam out much farther than I would go. I watched her move parallel to the shoreline, her arms arcing steadily, confidently, intersecting the waves.

Notes

1. Neil MacFarquhar, "Denied Power, Armenian Opposition Leader Urges Nation-wide Strikes," *New York Times*, May 1, 2018, www.nytimes.com/2018/05/01/world/europe/armenia-prime-minister.html.
2. Ron Synovitz, "Armenian Women Raise a Clamor for Sarkisian's 'Last Call,'" *Radio Free Europe / Radio Liberty*, April 24, 2018, www.rferl.org/a/armenia-women-raise-clamor-for-sarkisians-last-call-/29187558.html.
3. Neil MacFarquhar, "Behind Armenia's Revolt, Young Shock Troops from the Tech Sector," *New York Times*, May 19, 2018, www.nytimes.com/2018/05/19/world/europe/armenia-revolt-tech-sector.html.
4. Azatutyun Radiogayan, "Ուսանողները Կռմիտաս են Կատարում Հանրապետության Հրապարակում," Facebook Watch, Ազատություն Ռադիոկայան, May 2 2018, www.facebook.com/watch/?v=1924466760932025; Ruben Malayan, "Visual Art and the Revolution," *EVN Report*, May 6, 2018, www.evnreport.com/arts-and-culture/visual-art-and-the-revolution.
5. Amie Ferris-Rotman, "Did Armenia Just Dance Its Way to Revolution?" *Washington Post*, May 3, 2018, www.washingtonpost.com/news/worldviews/wp/2018/05/03/did-armenia-just-dance-its-way-to-revolution/.
6. Anahit Hayrapetyan et al., "My Step," 4plus, April 14, 2018, www.4plus.org/my-step/. As of April 10, 2022, this web page does not exist, but photos from it appear in 4plus's video "Revolution" on its website: https://www.4plus.org/revolution/.
7. I don't have sources for the referenced photos and videos in this paragraph, as they were viewed in the fleeting space of social media before I decided to write this essay. My sources at the time were friends on Facebook and Twitter, and online Armenian news sources such as *EVN Report*, *CivilNet*, *Azatutyun* (Radio Free Europe's Armenian Service), *hetq*, and *a1plus*.
8. Nona Shahnazarian, "'Here Is Not Maidan, Here Is Marshal Baghramian': The 'Electric Yerevan' Protest Movement and Its Consequences," Ponars Euarasia, Policy Memos, January 14, 2016, https://www.ponarseurasia.org/here-is-not-maidan-here-is-marshal-baghramian-the-electric-yerevan-protest-movement-and-its-consequences/.
9. "Armenia: Excessive Police Force at Protest," Human Rights Watch, August 1, 2016, www.hrw.org/news/2016/08/01/armenia-excessive-police-force-protest.
10. "Armenia Detains 3 Opposition Leaders Amid Protests," *New York Times*, April 22, 2018, www.nytimes.com/2018/04/22/world/europe/armenia-opposition-leader-protests.html.
11. Amos Chapple, "Soldiers Join Armenia Protests," *Radio Free Europe / Radio Liberty*, April 23, 2018, https://www.rferl.org/a/armenia-yerevan-politics-protests/29186784.html.
12. Gianluca Mezzofiore, "Protesters Blocked Roads in Armenia's Capital. This Little

Boy Used His Toy Cars," CNN, May 2, 2018, https://www.cnn.com/2018/05/02
/europe/kid-blocking-street-toy-cars-yerevan-armenia/index.html.

13. Joshua Kucera, "Armenia's Protesters Take Fight to Yerevan Mayor's Office,"
Eurasianet, May 16, 2018, eurasianet.org/armenias-protesters-take-fight-to-yerevan
-mayors-office.

14. Kyle Khandikian, "Rainbow Hysteria: How LGBTQ Issues Became a Mainstream
Topic of Conversation," *EVN Report*, February 26, 2019, https://evnreport.com/raw
-unfiltered/rainbow-hysteria-how-lgbt-issues-became-a-mainstream-topic-of
-conversation/.

15. "Ex-Army General, Lawmaker Arrested," *Asbarez*, June 18, 2018, asbarez.com
/172874/ex-army-general-lawmaker-arrested/.

16. "Nine Queer Rights Activists Attacked by Mob in Armenia," *OC Media*, August 6,
2018, oc-media.org/nine-queer-rights-activists-attacked-by-mob-in-armenia/.

17. Stefania Sarrubba, "Armenian Villagers Tried to Lynch LGBTI People, Injured
Nine of Them," *Gay Star News*, August 4, 2018, https://www.gaystarnews.com/article
/armenian-villagers-tried-to-lynch-lgbti-people-injured-nine-of-them/.

18. Alex Cooper, "Following Mob Attack, LGBTQ Activists in Armenia 'Want Justice,'" NBC News, August 8, 2018, www.nbcnews.com/feature/nbc-out/following
-mob-attack-LGBTQq-activists-armenia-want-justice-n898821.

19. Kimberlé Crenshaw, "Demarginalizing the Intersection of Race and Sex: A Black
Feminist Critique of Antidiscrimination Doctrine, Feminist Theory and Antiracist
Politics," *University of Chicago Legal Forum* 1 (1989): article 8, 149.

20. Crenshaw, "Demarginalizing the Intersection," 151–152.

21. Crenshaw, "Demarginalizing the Intersection," 167.

22. Khandikian, "Rainbow Hysteria."

23. Ekaterina Fomina, "Armenia's Velvet Revolution Is Yet to Bring Change for the
Country's LGBTQ Community," *OpenDemocracy*, June 27, 2019, www
.opendemocracy.net/en/odr/non-sexual-revolution-armenia-en/.

24. Ani Mejlumyan, "Ahead of Elections, Armenia's Opposition Attacks LGBT
Rights." *Eurasianet*, October 31, 2018, https://eurasianet.org/ahead-of-elections
-armenias-opposition-attacks-lgbt-rights.

25. James Besanvalle, "LGBTI Christian Group Forced to Cancel Event in Armenia after Death Threats," *Gay Star News*, November 8, 2018, https://www.gaystarnews.com
/article/lgbti-christian-group-armenia/.

26. Khandikian, "Rainbow Hysteria."

27. Anna Nikoghosyan, "Can Transgender People Speak in Armenia?" *OpenDemocracy*, April 15, 2020, www.opendemocracy.net/en/odr/can-transgender-people-speak
-armenia/.

28. Nikoghosyan, "Can Transgender People Speak."

29. Saeed Kamali Dehghan, "Armenian MPs Call for Trans Activist to Be Burned
Alive after Historic Speech," *Guardian*, April 26, 2019, www.theguardian.com/global
-development/2019/apr/26/armenian-mps-call-for-trans-activist-to-be-burned
-alive-after-historic-speech-lilit-martirosyan.

30. Ani Mejlumyan, "Culture War Moves to the Top of Armenia's Political Agenda,"
Eurasianet, Nov. 14, 2019, http://eurasianet.org/culture-war-moves-to-the-top-of
-armenias-political-agenda.

31. Mejlumyan, "Culture War Moves."

32. "Country Ranking," Rainbow Europe, accessed October 13, 2020, http://rainbow -europe.org/country-ranking.

33. Pew Research Center, "5: Social Views and Morality," *Religious Belief and National Belonging in Central and Eastern Europe* (Pew Research Center, May 10, 2017), www.pewforum.org/2017/05/10/social-views-and-morality/.

34. Pink Armenia, "We Are Establishing the National Day to Fight for LGBTQ+ Rights in Armenia." Pink Armenia, July 30, 2020, www.pinkarmenia.org/en/news /national-day/#.XyR8wDUpC00.

Going Home Again

CHRIS BOHJALIAN

KAYSERI, Turkey—My wife and I are holding small candles, the yellow flames thin above the tapers, above a wrought-iron sand table at the Church of Saint Gregory the Illuminator in Kayseri. Kayseri is a Turkish city two hundred miles southeast of Ankara with a population nearing a million. It's not a part of Turkey where most American tourists venture. Usually when we think of Turkey and tourism, we envision the mosques of Istanbul or the beaches of Bodrum. We imagine the Roman ruins in Ephesus. I've never been to either Bodrum or Ephesus; the last time I was in Istanbul, it was for a friend's wedding. Instead, I journey to places like Kayseri. Why? Because I am Armenian and that's where my family once lived.

Saint Gregory's is one of a small handful of Armenian churches in Turkey outside of Istanbul that are not rubble or ruins, or have not been repurposed into a museum, mosque, or (in one case) fitness center. There is no longer an Armenian congregation in Kayseri, but sporadically—once or a twice a year—descendants of the church's parishioners who live in Istanbul journey here to worship. I'm not part of that Istanbul community, but my grandfather, Levon Nazareth Bohjalian, was born in Kayseri. It's likely that he was baptized in this church. It was built in 1856 and named after the man who was raised in this corner of Anatolia and who would bring Christianity to Armenia in the year 301. There is no priest in the city to let us in (virtually no Armenians live in Kayseri) but one of the locals knows someone who knows someone who knows the caretaker who has a key.

This is my third trip in three years with my friend Khatchig Mouradian, a professor at Columbia University and area specialist at the Library of Congress, to the great swath of Turkey that is Historic Armenia. The area stretches from the Black Sea to the Mediterranean, and from Ankara to Turkey's Syrian, Iraqi, Iranian, Armenian, and Georgian borders. It is the eastern half of Turkey. It is Anatolia. It is Cilicia. And until 1915, it was where the majority of the Armenians in the Ottoman Empire lived.

This year marked the centennial of the start of the Armenian Genocide: it was April 24, 1915, when the Armenian intellectuals, professionals, editors, and religious leaders in Constantinople were rounded up by the Ottoman authorities and almost all executed. During World War I, the Ottoman Empire would systematically annihilate one and a half million of its Armenian citizens, or three out of every four. Most Armenians alive today are descendants of those few survivors, including me. Both of my grandparents were survivors.

It is actually my great-grandfather, however, that I associate most with Kayseri. Nazaret Bedros Bohjalian, Levon's father, was a nineteenth-century troubadour and poet. Although he was born in Kayseri, he performed in such distant corners of the empire as Jerusalem and Constantinople, singing the poems he had penned. Based on one account of his life in an old Armenian history of Kayseri, I imagine him as a sort of Bruce Springsteen of the Anatolian Plains. He may not have had stadium-sized crowds or rock 'n' roll T-shirts, but it seems that he had enthusiastic audiences wherever he appeared. Among his works? A seventy-quatrain epic of the Hamidian Massacres—the prequel to the Armenian Genocide named after Sultan Abdul Hamid II, in which 250,000 Armenians were butchered. On November 18, 1895, the slaughter came to his city:

> They killed infidels with axes, daggers, and didn't ask who you were, whether merchant or coolie.
> They took the babies out of the wombs of their mothers, and those who witnessed lost their minds.

It is a wrenching eyewitness testimonial.

Armenian Footprints

Few Armenians remain in Turkey today, outside of the sixty thousand or so who live in Istanbul. You want to see the definition of ethnic cleansing? Visit Historic Armenia. You will find Islamized Armenians here and there, the descendants of the Armenians who were forced to become Muslim a century ago, and there is a tiny community of two hundred Armenians in Vakifli Koy, one of the six villages on the mountain of Musa Dagh on the Mediterranean Sea. They are descendants of the men and women Franz Werfel made famous in his epic novel of the Armenian resistance to the genocide in 1915, *The Forty Days of Musa Dagh*. Otherwise, it's rare to find an Armenian.

And yet our footprints are everywhere: Medieval churches. Ancient monasteries. Armenian lettering carved onto village walls or century-old doors. I've visited at least forty-five different Armenian churches and monasteries, most empty shells and some little more than foundations. Often, the ruins have piles of empty soda cans and water bottles, and black fire pits from recent campfires. Occasionally, there are deep holes where treasure hunters have dug up the floor in search of mythical Armenian gold. Usually, there is graffiti.

Sometimes the Kurds who live in the area now will share the horrors of how the Armenians were killed or deported, the stories passed down from generation to generation, and sometimes they will tell you that the Armenians simply moved away. They pick a year seemingly at random but always before 1915. We left, they insist, only because we wanted to be near our families in Aleppo, Syria, or Boston.

And now, of course, with the region so volatile, the Kurds will often share stories of more recent horrors. The day before I was in Sanliurfa, Turkey, this summer, ISIS suicide bombers detonated five trucks filled with explosives in Kobani, Syria, twenty miles from Sanliurfa as the crow flies, killing at least seventy Kurds. Two weeks later in nearby Suruc, Turkey, ISIS killed thirty-three young Kurdish volunteers—and injured well over one hundred—as they prepared to drive to Kobani to help rebuild the city.

Regardless of how you look at the history, however, the five hundred thousand Armenians who survived the genocide were never able to return home. It's why we are a diasporic people. Of the ten million Armenians in the world today, fewer than three million of us actually live in Armenia.

Family History

Which brings me back to Kayseri.

Which explains why I keep returning to Historic Armenia, despite the escalating violence.

It's my ancestral land.

In the mid-1920s, my grandfather traveled to Paris to meet Haigouhi Sherinian, and there they would fall in love and marry. In 1927, he brought her to the United States. The following year, he built the beautiful brick monolith in Tuckahoe, New York, where they would raise their children and reside for forty years.

My father grew up in a house that could be called exotic only by the standards of that particular suburb of New York City. Everyone spoke Armenian behind those brick walls. And so, like many daughters and sons of immigrants, my father chose to become as American as he possibly could. He even became that most iconic of mid-twentieth-century American business professionals, an ad man. A mad man. Think Don Draper. That's how extensive his reinvention was. And so other than the time I would spend with my grandparents, I did not grow up a part of the Armenian community or with a connection to my Armenian heritage. (The one exception? Our dining room. My Swedish mother figured out quickly that Armenian cuisine is delicious.)

Consequently, it was only at midlife that I felt a deep and relentless tug at my Armenian soul to return. This is, I have come to understand, the ground where the Bohjalians and the Sherinians once built their lives. My grandfather was the youngest of my great-grandfather's six children, and he was born only a few years before Nazaret Bedros would die in 1902. I will never know precisely which of the Bohjalians left Kayseri after the Hamidian Massacres in 1895 and which would be shot or marched into the desert to die a generation later. Was it within blocks of Saint Gregory's that my grandfather saw the Armenian men killed with axes and daggers? Was it on a nearby block that he witnessed the babies being cut from the wombs of their mothers? Did he himself lose a little of his own mind that day?

The fact is, Kayseri is a home that was taken from my family. It is that injustice—what my non-Armenian wife calls the "sheer unfairness of it"—that draws me back. It's my small way of saying to anyone who happens to notice, the Bohjalians are still here. Still around. You didn't quite wipe us out. I always feel acutely alive in Historic Armenia, as if some otherwise napping—untapped even—link in my DNA has been awakened and found its tether to the land.

Could I actually live there? Of course not. My last name alone would make me a pariah in parts of the region, and most of the time I am deeply proud to be an American. I have been (thank you very much) quite happily spoiled by the American way of life. It's really hard to find Ben & Jerry's or binge-watch *Breaking Bad* in Diyarbakir, Kayseri, or Van.

But I also can't imagine not returning to visit.

After my wife and I had murmured our small prayers at the church in Kayseri and placed the candles in the sand, she said to me, "You're breathing the same air your grandfather breathed as a little boy."

I nodded. She had put into words precisely why I was here. It's not coming home, precisely, but it is without question a homecoming.

Lost and Found

ALINE OHANESIAN

You are born longing for a past that was never yours,
for the smells and sounds of a place you've never visited,
unfamiliar even to your parents and grandparents.

We are a family of the dispossessed, they tell you,
as soon as you're old enough to make sense of the word "we."
Displacement is the only status quo they've known for generations,
from Adana and Aintep, to Cyprus and Kuwait, by way of Lebanon and Syria,
and finally, to the shores of Los Angeles.

They stare down at you, these people whom you love and who love you.
Remember, they tell you.
Never forget
this longing, this gift,
this culture and language and history and trauma and
—resilience.
Keep it safe. Alive. Guard it with everything you have. Don't let it perish.
It's a heavy burden, we know.
But don't worry. We'll be there to help you.
We'll construct schools and churches on this odar, foreign land.
We'll build a thriving community so robust
that your teachers, friends, coaches, and dance instructors
will all be Armenian.
They too will carry the same sacred longing.
You may be "other" here, on foreign soil,
But you will never be alone.

THE GREAT VOID they've planted in you is collective, shared mutually by everyone you know and love. This feeling of perpetual belonging and pride and forlornness and loss will always be with you. It will rise in your throat every time you hear the first notes of Djivan Gasparian's duduk. It will flow from your breast as you cradle your suckling newborn. It will swell inside you each time you encounter a fellow tribesman or woman on the streets of a new city. These men and women, scattered in all corners of the world, who share the unique joy and grief that comes with being Armenian, will invite you over for coffee and show you their adopted city. Every one of them will share the name of their ancestral village.

Pirkinik, Lezk, Soushants, Dortyol, Dikranagerd.

Names that can be found only on ancient maps, erased from history, wiped out like their inhabitants.

YOU WRAP YOURSELF UP in the warmth and comfort of this blanket of collective identity, grateful and content. Until one day, somewhere between adolescence and adulthood, this thing that's been with you since birth, more familiar than your given name, or that beauty mark on your big toe, begins to feel

H
E
A
V
Y

—and worn.

At Holy Martyrs School, your home away from home, the long-limbed, kind-eyed principal, whom you love and adore, the man who founded the first Armenian day school in the United States and ran it from 1964 to 1990, who would one day ask you to speak at his retirement party, visits your classroom once a month. "Tell me children," he says, even when most of you are inching toward the threshold of puberty.

"How many of you will marry an Armenian?"

Every hand goes up. Even the kid with the one odar parent.

"Now girls, how many of you will be good Armenian mothers?"

You want to raise your hand, to earn that twinkle he gets in his eye, but motherhood is not appealing. The mothers you know fluctuate between being ornamental and overlooked. Your own family is filled with immigrant and refugee women whose disrupted lives never afforded them an education.

You look around and spot the other girl who's kept her hand down: your best friend, whose unhappy childhood resembles your own.

"No matter," says your principal. "You girls can be Armenian language teachers."

You swallow your desires because that is what good Armenian girls do.

IN COLLEGE, for the first time in your entire life, you are not breathing, singing, and reading this collective cultural longing.

In fact, you begin to feel stifled by it.

This is followed by intense feelings of guilt and shame.

How ungrateful you are. How selfish.

Hasn't your community given you everything it could? What else do you want?

Amot. Shame on you.

You try to ignore the feeling, but it rears its ugly head in your personal life, your politics, and your art. You begin to wonder what life would be, *who* you would be, without this longing. And the question is intoxicating. It seduces you to an asphodel field somewhere on the border of assimilation.

All who wander are not lost, you tell yourself. A decade passes, and you wake up one morning and realize that you've built a home in the middle of that asphodel field. There is a swing set out back where your two sons play. You can hear them calling to one another in English. That's when you remember it: that all-encompassing feeling that used to sustain and consume you. And you miss is with every fiber and bone of your being.

You long for your lost longing.

And you take your children by the hand and embark on a journey. It will be long and arduous, but you are determined. The three of you go to plays, read books, march in protests, attend weddings and Saturday school.

It's not enough, you think to yourself. Your sons do their very best. They befriend the only other Armenian at their school, an awkward boy with whom they have nothing in common. They smile politely when you drive them back into the center of the community. "We feel like odars here," their eyes tell you.

There are no words for the pain and anguish you feel in that moment. You have failed them as a mother. You have failed as an Armenian. You are complicit in jermak chart, the white genocide, that self-inflicted wound every Armenian is warned about, the erasure that eradicates longing but also identity.

Demeter's darling girl, you've swallowed the pomegranate seeds. Like her, you'll be bound to the asphodel fields forever. One foot with your mother tribe, the other in the freedom of Hades. Your sons are not so lucky. The tribe can smell the "other" on them. You're determined to make them regurgitate the seeds of assimilation. This will require powerful magic, but you are a fighter, a survivor, an Armenian.

You lock yourself in a room and begin to conjure the smells, the images, the trauma and joy of your collective past. You cast your spell in words, the element of your preferred form of witchcraft. You spend ten years in that room. A decade, a small price to pay for your sins. Your spell has to be powerful enough to undo the damage you've done to yourself and those you love. There are days when you are tempted to give up the pursuit. Friends and loved ones tell you that no such magic exists. "You've done your best." "Life is short." "Let it go." But you don't let it go. You refuse to take another step toward the asphodel. You persevere.

And one day, unbelievably, the spell is bound in the form of a book, written in the language of your assimilators. You name your spell book *Orhan's Inheritance*. Orhan because it is the name of a great Turkish word conjurer, a storyteller whose work you respect. Inheritance because the thing you've been chasing and running away from, this harrowed past, belongs to the Turks as much as it belongs to you. You dedicate the book to your two sons.

ON THE DAY the book is released into the world, you are sitting in your car, in the parking lot of National Public Radio, preparing for your first interview. How will you ever explain the why and how of this book to a national audience? You feel small, ill equipped. You draw strength from the notes of Gasparian's *A Cold Wind Is Blowing* and you pray. You pray to your ancestors. To the one and a half million lost in the death marches. To the Bronze Age pagan winemakers gathered in the caves of Areni. Your prayer is a simple one. All the best prayers are. It consists of only two little words.

Use me.

Inside your breast, your heart whispers a different prayer in a different tongue. Nerreztek Enzee. Forgive me.

And they do. The ancestors add their magic to the spell. Your book becomes a publishing "success," whatever that means. It takes you to twenty-two cities in the United States and travels, translated, to fourteen different countries. You introduce your tribe and its history to audiences who are encountering it for the first time in Georgia and Alabama and Mystic, Connecticut. And you feel satisfied.

You do.

YEARS GO BY and your children, the two boys who were the inciting incident of this particular story, who have abandoned the swing set and sprouted hair on their chins and underarms, are busy. Very, very busy. Too busy with school and sports and hormones to ever read the spell book you crafted for them.

Your youngest, your baby, wears a size thirteen shoe and towers over you and his father. Soon, his older brother will leave your home for college. You wonder if you've taught him everything he needs to survive and thrive. Like the elders in Toumanyan's poem, you pray that he lives, but not like you. "Abrek Yereghek, paitz mez bes chabrek."[1] You teach him to cook and do laundry, to reach for joy whenever possible. You make sure he understands the value of a dollar and how to balance a checkbook. You teach him about the oppressed and his own privilege. And the summer before his departure, you take your sons on one final journey: to the source of all your lost longing, Hayastan. Armenia.

You hope that the sights and smells of the motherland, that foreign land, will seduce and intoxicate them in ways your words and sentences could not. You avoid the many prepackaged trips designed for diaspora members. You forgo the churches and monasteries, the genocide memorial, and a hundred other venues packed with nostalgic tourists. You know the way to their hearts. You take them instead to the forests of Tavush.

The trip requires a bilingual nature guide, two off-road vehicles, and plenty of grit. Your guide, a young man born in Iran but raised in Armenia, is no stranger to displacement. His love for this land is in no way metaphorical. He lovingly recites the name of every species of bird and plant and tree in at least three languages as he leads your family deep into the Ijevan forests. You trail behind your sons as they bond with him over food, music, and their love of Jeeps. He tells them how he used his small fleet of Jeeps to assist protestors in the Velvet Revolution. He picks wild dandelions and makes tea, curing your youngest of a stomachache. They introduce him to trap music and he laughs uncontrollably. The five of you arrive at a campsite called Lastiver, where two brothers, nature enthusiasts, have constructed several tree houses and a crudely made bar. Everything here is made by hand. You brace yourself for the impending cultural exchange, the language barrier, but it never comes. The men, Vahan and Hovanes, embrace your sons and lead them to the infamous caves, whose walls are covered in paintings made by Armenians of the Bronze Age or the Soviet Era. "Which is it?" you ask. "Does it matter?" they answer.

Many hours and miles later, the five of you descend into a picturesque gorge covered in lush green vegetation along the Khachaghpuir River. The name, a compound word, loosely translates to "cross spring," but you will forever think of it as the "fountain of intersections." Later your eldest will compare it to Tolkien's Middle Earth, only with more magic. The beauty of the place is almost painful. "This is my church," says your guide, though it feels like no church you've ever been to. Later, you sit on a log at the riverbank, watching your sons climb the large boulders at the foot of a waterfall. You take in their muddy calves, their large hands struggling for a good grip, their muscles straining against this expanse of ancestral land, and you allow yourself to exhale.

Time in the forest does what all the words in the world could never do. It allows your sons to make memories rooted in the soil. Their relationship to the mud and moss, the fog and trees, the flora and fauna, the forest dwellers has nothing to do with vengeance or loss. There is no language barrier here. The churning of the river, the sound of the wind sieving through the branches, the caw of birds need no translation. The undeveloped land in this magical, ancient corner of the world becomes beloved. A place that gives your sons adventure and sustenance. A place they could pour their love into. A place they want to revisit and protect.

Just before you leave Lastiver, you sit on a wooden chair suspended by a pair of rusty chains that hang from a tree whose branches extend out into the middle of the river. Your sons have convinced you to go zip-lining six thousand feet above the forest. This rusty chair, dangling a few dozen feet from the gargling river, is only practice. Every step you take from here on out will be guided by your sons and their love of this land. This trip no longer has anything to do with you and your antiquated notions of identity. This Armenia is their Armenia. Your older son pulls the swing all the way back, while his younger brother, who gets a perverse thrill from your fear of heights, begins recording.

"Ready?" asks your older son. "Ready," I say.

Note

1. This is a line from Hovaness Toumanyan's poem "Ancient Blessing." It translates to "Live, children. But not like us."

A Letter to My Great-Grandson

RAFFI JOE WARTANIAN

Contextual note: I wrote this essay in the voice of my great grandfather Mardiros Baloumian (1895–1983). I culled details about Mardiros's life from the books he wrote, interviews with his children, and photographs. Italicized sections are translations of his writing. A working digitized archive is available at https://mardirosbaloumian.wordpress.com.

DEAR RAFFI,

I died three years before you were born. I died while bathing in a shower that had no curtain. Just a nozzle sticking out of the wall. The toilet so close you could sit on it while rinsing the shampoo out of your hair. Suds bubbled in the nearby bucket that kept reserve water to compensate for the daily stoppage of Beirut's supply. I got dizzy, slipped, banged my head on the toilet, and that was it. Fast. Simple. Final.

I died in the shower at the end of the narrow hall, the walls so close together that, a decade later, you would climb them like a mountaineer intoxicated by the ascent. I knew the feeling. Knarig, my beloved daughter who became your doting grandmother, warned that your vertiginous escapades might damage the apartment she and her husband Melkon—so handsome, so stubborn, so loving of you and his seven other grandchildren—adored. You tried to resist, but the temptation was too great. You stuck out your arms and legs to shimmy up to the ceiling and waited for your older brother Shahé to scurry underneath. You would sometimes collapse upon him. And he would eventually collapse upon you.

It didn't take telepathy for Melkon to check on me in the bathroom. Though if necessary, telepathy could have been arranged. You see, I willed things into being just by thinking them. I still do. Right here. What do you think I'm doing inside your head?

By implementing the regulation of hypnotism and the rule of magnetism, I learned, I lived, and I made others live. I proved that when man becomes mentally spiritualized, he will subconsciously become the savior of his own life and that of others.

Melkon knocked on the locked door, his hands motor oil black from another day in his machine shop. No response. He jiggled the handle. "Hayreeg Mardiros?" he asked my bloating corpse, my eyes fixed on the whirling wall fan, mouth agape in a silent wail. This wasn't how I imagined the end, near a cockroach lingering under the sink. I imagined something different. Rose petals draped on my bed. My seven living children cradling me, singing in the soft pulse of candlelight as I released my final breath.

One more knock. Then he slammed his shoulder into the door. Melkon called for help. Voices, shouts, stamping boots. More shoulders thrown into the door. They kicked it. Kicked and kicked. The heavy wood splintered and cracked. They carried my corpse to the living room, where Knarig crumpled onto the sofa and wept. She vowed to never again lock the bathroom door. She vowed to honor my legacy, and she did: the family she raised with the same love I showed my children, the letters she wrote with the same imagination I infused into my own writing, and the needlework animals she created with the same creativity I cultivated. She must know how proud I am of her. Please, tell her.

I lived in the yellowing pages of the books I wrote—the trilogy *Man and His Inner World*, my memoir-manifesto *The Universal Man*, and the pamphlet *A Call to the United Nations*—kept on the bookshelf in your parents' den. The presence of my writings, published between 1978 and 1979 by Doniguian & Sons in Beirut, signaled that I still existed, somewhere, somehow, even if for you I was just a name, just the memory of a person you never met. I lived in those pages, sandwiched between the encyclopedias and the countless photo albums of your family's first years in the United States.

Your mother Yeran—the first of my twenty grandchildren—organized those forty photo albums with her trademark meticulousness. There were albums dedicated to her siblings' weddings, children's baptisms, vacations, graduations, and family reunions. I was proud of her for showing with photo albums what I articulated with words: a chronicling of life. Our projects belonged on the same bookshelf. Each of her photo albums boasted images, preserved in protective film, that told the story of your inheritance.

I. A red 1972 Dodge Challenger: your baba Ghevont's first car. He stood next to it, unrecognizable to you. Skinnier than you ever knew him. The way I knew him: his jaw square and sharp. His eyes dark and piercing.

II. South Baltimore General Hospital: your birthplace. A brown-brick building with white trim presiding over the Patapsco River. The hospital where, in 1974, Ghevont accepted his first job in America to serve as a rotating intern.

III. Antelias, Lebanon: Yeran in her wedding dress and Ghevont in his tuxedo on their wedding day, May 7, 1978. They stand in profile, surrounded by our beloved family and friends at the grand entrance of the Saint Gregory the Illuminator cathedral. This was the center of our ancient church, the Holy See of Cilicia, which spent millennia on our ancestral lands until the forced relocation caused by the genocide.

IV. Catonsville, Maryland: a modest two-story house where, weeks after the wedding, Yeran and Ghevont moved.

V. Yeran standing in the house's unfurnished living room, dreaming of the day she could return to her beloved Beirut after the civil war ended. That was the agreement she and Ghevont struck: a few years in Baltimore to finish his medical internship, then back home to Beirut. Lebanon, our adopted nation of cedars and Phoenicians, did not comply.

Each April, as the anniversary of the genocide approached, Yeran or Knarig would pull one of my books off the shelf. They dutifully dusted the cover and told you that I survived indescribable horrors. Knarig's voice trembled as she spoke of me, recalling my tears and vivacity. They told you I lost my family. They told you I saw nightmares. They told you of the words I wrote.

I lived through those times with the constant threat of death. Every step of the way, I witnessed the tragedy and the horrors of the Armenian massacres. I saw hell incarnate on Earth, more than what Dante could depict. To appease my tortured soul, I deemed it right to jot down my painful memories and convey them to you to be preserved in your archives as the documents of a surviving eyewitness to the Armenian massacres.

My words became my legacy and my prison. They gave me a voice, yet silenced me. I was more than a genocide survivor, yet that became my known identity. Of course, I wanted readers to know what I had witnessed starting at the age of twenty, and to rectify the crimes committed. Still, I wanted them to reckon with the full scope of my literary production, which, in addition to genocide testimony, also explored hypnotism, magnetism, and manifestos for a better world. Instead, they dismissed my loftier passages, preferring instead to only focus on the survival narrative.

I wrote in Արևմտահայերէն,[1] my native Western Armenian tongue, a language the UN would declare endangered twenty-seven years after my death. (Don't get me started on the UN.) Several attempts to translate my words were undertaken, all of which were abandoned. Perhaps they couldn't choose which of the many languages from our family's migratory path to use: عربي ,Türkçe, français, or English. The publication of my words in Western Armenian seemed sufficient, even if they went mostly unread or misunderstood. They were, at least, *there*. A comforting presence. A link to the past. Proof of origin. But you weren't satisfied with the half-complete attempts to translate my words. You wanted to encounter the story from the source and read every last word. You considered my experience essential to grasping your family's past as a path to defining your present and future. I never promised to answer any of your questions, yet you still turned to me. Sometimes you regretted it, especially during my denser flourishes.

Sure, some of the words looked long, but they were just compounds. Like քնաշրջիկամտալուսաւորուածութեանը,[2] a thirty-one-letter masterpiece. The first chunk, քնաշրջիկ, means "sleepwalking path," and լուսաւորուածութեանը means "the illumination of." You weren't quite able to account for the other four letters in the middle of the word, ամտա, so you settled with "the illumination of a sleepwalking path." A noble attempt, or maybe you just misread the word.

Knarig likewise appreciated my inventive approach to language. Perhaps because she knew me best. Perhaps because she was the first person I ever hypnotized. We were in our home: a two-room tin shack in the Latakia refugee camp of Armenian Genocide survivors. I tiptoed to her crib, took a deep breath, and raised my hands over her sleeping body.

With self-confidence and the conviction that I could replicate the wisdom and might of the Earth's creator, I mentally willed my one-year-old-daughter Knarig, who was sleeping in her crib, to open her eyes, say "Mama," and then return to sleep. As a hypnotist, I miraculously transformed to reality what I had willed mentally.

I dashed out of the home and hastened down a dirt road. I studied my hands, tools once used to bury my fellow Armenians transformed into transmitters of a supernatural life force. Rats rambled across the street dotted by tents and shacks of Armenian neighbors from Hajin and Kharpert, and even a few from my hometown of Zara. I reached the top of a nearby hill and looked out toward the Mediterranean, the briny air in sharp relief under the dark of night.

I studied the faces of people walking by and became hyper-aware of the quality of each man's inner nature and personality. By proving the accuracy of my judgments, I felt spiritually gratified and felt myself becoming divine.

Months earlier, at a meeting in central Latakia, a hypnotist had just demonstrated his prowess before a group of men and children. Carrying my camera after a day of photographing beachgoers, I approached the hypnotist and asked if he might offer lessons. The hypnotist—perhaps a sage, perhaps a snob put off by the sight of an Armenian refugee—refused, but he did provide one tip: read François Victor Foveau de Courmelles's *L'Hypnotisme*.

Lacking facility in French did not stop me. As a boy in Zara, I had heard the language in passing, a symbol of an opulent, distant West. The people of Zara spoke in Armenian and Turkish. Beyond cosmopolitan Istanbul, French had little utility for those of us living on our indigenous lands occupied by the Ottomans. But France's mandate over Syria and Lebanon, forged in 1923, rendered français a gateway to opportunity and knowledge that seemed abundant in Europe.

I found a bookshop and ordered a French-Armenian dictionary along with *L'Hypnotisme*, which arrived in thirteen days. On the first read, I focused on grasping words and phrases. *La transe* translated to զմայլվածութիւն,[3] the word for "trance." *Le rêve* translated to երազ,[4] the word for "dream." *La sagesse* translated to իմաստութիւն,[5] the word for "wisdom."

On my second and third read, I began assimilating the concepts necessary to take up the practice. The theory was no longer the abstract stuff of books. It lived within me. It originated in my mind, from the electric spark of a synaptic cleft to the energy emanating from my fingers. Hypnotism united me with a supernatural life force that, I believed, all humans possessed but few had the discipline to access.

Since that day, I applied the rule of hypnotism and the law of magnetism to unveil realities that are hidden from the consciousness of human beings.

As I grew older and began to write, I commanded my words to hypnotize readers. Those who were open and patient enough to sit with my text would transport to a sacred dimension. But not everyone showed patience. I was stunned when your older sister, my darling first great-grandchild, skipped translating page 27 of *The Universal Man*. In the critical passage where I described my training in the foundations of hypnotism with Doctor Kosta Anastasian, she wrote that my work "goes off into the incomprehensible hypnosis jargon." The nerve. Even Ghevont, with his advanced training in Armenian literature, tossed *The Universal Man* aside in frustration. "This doesn't make any sense," he proclaimed. For all his intellect, I was surprised by this lack of discipline.

How I would have objected if I had been present for such dismissals. Of course, objecting to those translating your words is a delicate task. One must simultaneously provide encouragement and guilt, a classic Armenian recipe. First, I would have offered them water infused with cucumber and orange slices. This would sharpen the mind. Second, I would have treated them to their favorite sweets. As you know, our family loves sugar and honey. (Good thing my surname includes *bal*, the Turkish word for honey.) Then, in the comfort of these flavors, I would have pushed for greater effort. But in my absence, there remained only my words, unassuming on the page, and the memory of me, fainter with each passing second.

I suppose it's easier to dismiss a man after he's dead. To only hold on to the parts one wants to remember and forget the rest. Your contemporaries came close to understanding how my survival inspired an infatuation with the occult, but they quit when the work demanded more than they could give. Your contemporaries wanted to know of the blood and gore. Trauma and resilience. In your violent society, blood and sex sell, as do tidy classifications of black and white, good against evil, Muslim against Christian, Turk versus Armenian. The story of the Armenian Genocide met those requirements, but what got lost was the account of my life beyond the trauma. The struggle of a return to normalcy; the impossible pursuit of it. The search for meaning in the mundane as days flowed into weeks, and months melted into years.

Normalcy never came. In 1975, Lebanon descended into civil war as I entered my eighth decade of corporeal existence. The fortune I earned constructing roads around the country was not enough to protect me or my family. Barouyr, my only son, was shot in an ambush. Palestinian militias overtook my home in Gemmayzeh. In our neighborhood of narrow streets, the sweet scent of jasmine flowers was obscured by the stink of gunpowder.

I moved in with Knarig and Melkon in their fifth-floor apartment nearby in Geitawi. The view from the salon balcony was as stunning as the clouds of smoke rising over the city. Snow-capped mountains sloped into a Mediterranean Sea littered with cruisers. Armenian church steeples intermingled with pink, blue, and white apartment buildings. It felt like home.

Visits to the building's bunker became a recurrent ritual thanks to bombardments by Syria or Israel or Iran or America. Flickering lights. Cans of olives. Skittering rats. This was safety. A dampness that reminded me of the thirteen winter days, decades ago, that I spent in a cave after running for my life. The unnervingly familiar stench of bodies wafted from the streets. I tried to not smell. I tried to not see. I tried to not remember the slap of limp limbs against my own as I buried bodies under the threatening stare of my master. I was four years a slave on the "farm."

This farm was called "Kharaj." In reality, it was not a farm. It was a concentration camp of Armenian deportees who were collected and sent to the site of their final extermination: the Euphrates River or Der-El-Zor. Those who were unable to walk were massacred on the spot.

Every afternoon, caravans of Armenian deportees, driven by bloodthirsty Turkish irregulars, arrived at this farm beaten by rifle butts and whips. Roadsides were strewn with the corpses of those who had already died of hunger, thirst, exhaustion, and disease.

As soon as a new caravan of Armenian deportees arrived, there emerged professional butchers of all kinds. Criminals, gangs, soldiers, officers, slave auctioneers, and harem-keepers clustered around the caravan like hungry jackals ready to devour their prey. First, beautiful women and maidens were chosen. Some of them were taken away. Others were stripped of their clothes, raped in shout-filled orgies, and then slaughtered monstrously. Some others were auctioned for the Turkish harems. Meanwhile they took the men away and disposed of them. Infants and breastfeeding babies were torn from their mothers and pierced by bayonets. Some mothers, at the sight of these horrors, strangled their babies with their own hands. Armenian priests had their eyes gouged out with red-hot branding irons. Old men's beards were flayed, and their hair torn from their scalps. Monsters, hired by the interior minister Talaat, poured petrol over crowds of Armenians and burned them alive. Others dug communal graves and buried their victims alive. All these barbarous atrocities were committed by hired criminals dressed in Turkish soldiers' uniforms, paid and encouraged by Talaat and company.

The words flowed from my firing neurons to my hands. I pressed the circular typing keys with hand-drawn Հայերէն[6] letters taped above the original Кирилица. When I felt weak, I called in my grandson Viken, grandchild number five of twenty, to type as I dictated.

The ratatat of fingers on a typewriter. The patter of rifle fire from the Beirut street below. The sounds reminded me of bullets cracking in the killing fields of Anatolia, where, many years earlier, I discovered the source of my salvation.

I was traveling with a group of Armenians from the city of Karin back to my home village of Zara. We walked for a week through forests and plains, along rivers and lakes, past mountains dotted with trees. As we approached our destination, a group of Turkish soldiers appeared on horseback and began to fire their weapons at us.

In this one hour, death was inescapable for everybody. For the first time, I was in a situation where I could be shot by a gun and lacked any protection. I shivered from the threat of bullets. In despair, I started to pray in my mind, asking God to protect me. My shivering stopped after thirty minutes. I don't know why, but suddenly, I felt my life was in no danger. Bullets were still flying all around me, yet I noticed a sense of inner security and knew no bullet would touch me. I sat and ate bread, unafraid of the shootings.

Judging by that day's events, I am convinced that my physical and psychological self-defense arose from my emerging abilities in hypnotism and magnetism, which dispersed bullets from the soldiers. I was freed from that violence. This event proved to me that I was producing a flowing inner power that surrounded me with a deep belief that was protective in ways similar to the sun's rays, which gave light and heat like an electrical current emanating from metals.

When I told people this story, when they saw the look in my eyes as I spoke, it made perfect sense. That's the power of hypnosis. There's so much one can transmit with just the eyes. A glance. A glare. A gaze.

But words on a page were easier to dismiss. I watched readers scratch their heads and ask, "Is he suggesting that he survived through prayer to God and his powers in hypnotism and magnetism? If so, then why didn't he use those powers to prevent more damage, or save others? And where is the evidence for all of this?" Poor souls. Trapped in the confines of empirical knowledge. This has always been the flaw of the unfaithful. They've lost touch with what it means to *believe*. To recognize and pursue aspects of reality just beyond our sensory grasp. To perceive the magic of the seemingly imperceptible. To embrace our need for systems of thought that transcend the problematic status quo.

Don't become like them, Raffi. They, with their quarrels and possessions, have not heeded my words. But you are beginning the journey.

Keep seeking. Keep reading. Keep writing. Keep creating.

Close your eyes. Hold out your hands. Speak. Live. Write. Die. And live again.

Your loving great-grandfather,
Mardiros

Notes

1. Transliteration: Arevmdahayeren.
2. Transliteration: knashrchigamdalousavorvadzutyane.
3. Transliteration: zmaylavadzutyoun.
4. Transliteration: yeraz.
5. Transliteration: imasdutyoun.
6. Transliteration: Hayeren.

Open Wounds

ANNA GAZMARIAN

AT FIRST GLANCE, the bone fragments on display at the Armenian Museum of America in Watertown, Massachusetts, appeared like fragments of driftwood riddled with holes formed by shipworms. The ligaments were mixed with blades of dried grass. I sent a photo to my archivist friend; she could not believe the poor quality of the preservation. The bottom of the case was painted the color of the Syrian Desert, where an Armenian couple found the bones on a pilgrimage in 1996. The bones belonged to an Armenian who attempted to flee the death marches of the Deir ez-Zor camps, concentration camps set up in the heart of the Syrian Desert. Crouching to the ground, I pressed my nose to the glass as I searched for grains of sand.

Next to the bones, a tunic recovered from a dead Armenian child was displayed like a body floating on the Dead Sea. The tailored pants and shirt had been uncovered in the Syrian Desert by an American missionary, Helen Gutterson, while searching for Armenian survivors. Only traces of them were found. I thought of my great-grandmother, Manoushag, along with her brother and father, who were brought to the same desert and shot by Young Turks. Their bodies, I assume, were also left to rot in the barren land. Upon presenting the clothes to the museum, Gutterson instructed it to keep them for future generations, lest people forget. As I view photos of Syrian refugees fleeing their land on international news, I cannot help but wonder if forgetfulness is at the root of why history continues to repeat.

On my twenty-minute bus ride back to Boston from Watertown, an open bottle of Diet Coke spilled in my purse and made the notes I wrote at the museum illegible. My husband, David, met me for dinner at an overpriced French restaurant recommended by his new coworkers. He had recently started a consulting job in Boston, working in a trailer between a morgue and methadone clinic while Mass General was being expanded. David covered his mouth with the palm of his hand to conceal laughter as he watched me use my phone to translate the menu in search of American fries saturated in grease. There were none. The waiter encouraged me to be adventurous and order snails. I fought against asking David to go to a burger restaurant across the street for fries and settled for pasta.

After we ordered, I pulled up a photo of the bones from the museum exhibit and handed David my phone without providing any context, as if he should know that he was being shown proof of the Armenian Genocide. Our waiter peered over David's shoulder at the photo and spilled water on the tablecloth. David continued to tear off pieces of the bread without making comments or asking questions about the four hours I spent at the museum. By his silence, I knew that he was worried. He was staring at his shoes instead of making eye contact with me. He kept moving his lips as if he was about to say something, but he was at a loss for words.

The more entrenched I had become in depression, the more I had turned to learning about my ancestors, specifically Manoushag. After six years of attempting various antidepressants and struggling to connect with various therapists, I had found a desire to direct my sadness to something outside myself and bigger than my own experiences. Eradicating depression with mindfulness, meditation, or breathing techniques led by therapists in overcrowded offices filled with plants and motivational posters seemed hopeless. Reliving my history felt redundant and pointless. But gazing at gaping wounds of others never did.

I had not traveled to Boston with David simply to wander through exhibits and memorials dedicated to the atrocities that Armenians have endured for centuries, though I had a history of choosing travel destinations based on their proximity to Armenian communities. Our trip centered on an appointment for my fifth psychiatric evaluation. Dr. Nassir Ghaemi shared my obsession with studying and learning from the past, which drew me to his research about bipolar disorder. His research concluded that bipolar patients are often misdiagnosed with ADHD and prescribed stimulants, which can exacerbate mood destabilization. I had taken Vyvanse and Adderall since fourth grade and held out hope that he was right. Perhaps examining my own history would lead to some type of cure or answer to why no amount of medication decreased my depression for an extended period of time.

In his book *First-Rate Madness*, Ghaemi studies the lives of Abraham Lincoln, John F. Kennedy, Gandhi, and Martin Luther King Jr. to argue that the best leaders from history are also the ones who struggled with symptoms of mental illness. His book did not receive acclaim, nor did I necessarily believe his reasoning. Reviewers critiqued Ghaemi for his sweeping generalizations, which was not surprising. Most psychiatrists I have worked with generalize the experiences of mental illness. My depressive and manic episodes never led to dramatic revelations or strong leadership skills like Ghaemi described. This romanticized depiction overlooks the loss of time and opportunities that symptoms take away. Recovery seemed formulated by the medical community as a matter of maintaining coping skills. But in reality, you can do everything right and still relapse. This is a lesson that I continue to relearn. The book neither gave me hope nor made me believe in his correlation. But his fascination with history interested me enough to schedule an appointment with him in Boston. I had not visited the city since I was eighteen and worried what memories the trip might trigger.

When psychiatrists or therapists ask about my last memories of being mentally stable, I describe Boston in wintertime. I was drawn to how the historical monuments blend in with the modern skyscrapers. The past and present blended together. Even the way that Dunkin' Donuts was practically on every corner for no apparent reason appealed to me. I visited over winter break after my first semester of college to learn about different art nonprofit programs in the city. There are five years' worth of photos missing from my computer. I deleted them—pictures from my trip to Boston with David included—because they reminded me of who I was before my diagnosis.

Years later, I regret this decision, because there are pieces of my psyche I cannot piece together from that time period. During my trip in December 2010, I was assigned to paint the walls of a psych ward that inspired the movie *Shutter Island*. Before we arrived, I expected to hear patients screaming incoherently from rooms around us while medical professionals rushed to subdue them. But that afternoon, the only sound came from our brushes as we dipped them in silver cans that appeared several years old. We used various shades of beige to cover the chalk-white hallway that lacked windows and artwork. As I leaned over with a small brush to paint around the crown molding, I stopped whenever nurses passed by with patients. At one point, a girl who appeared my age walked by while nervously chipping at her metallic nail posh. As she looked forward without making eye contact with any us, I studied her makeup-free face for some traces of insanity like what I saw in the movies. I did not feel empathy for the patients, just as I did not feel empathy for the student in my international security class who told me she was bipolar months before I was given the same diagnosis. Every day in class, I sat quietly to avoid the kind of manic outburst I saw on television. But that never occurred from her. I felt fear about a type of pain that I did not want to fully understand or experience. I believed that if she tried harder, perhaps she could be healed.

In 2011, during the second semester of my freshman year, I got a D in an elective on the Alps, a class I took because the only other elective available explored the history of armchairs and was taught by a Swedish professor with an office filled with Ikea furniture. I turned in my final paper about Hitler living in the Alps three weeks late without providing any works cited. It was not because I did not care; rather, I had stared at a blank Word document for weeks without being able to properly form a written sentence. That May, a week after I slept through my public policy final exams, which I never made up, I moved to Boston for an internship. Looking back, I believed that returning to the last place I remembered feeling healthy could heal me or provide answers.

A family-owned market that smelled like spoiled meat and ignored expiration dates was the only place in a several-mile radius to buy groceries. The laundromat staff at Wash N Dry laughed, as I could never tell the difference between the dryers that were broken and the ones that took less than two hours to dry a load of laundry. I never brought enough quarters; the colors of my clothes bled together. Back then, I wore more than one color each day. By the time I got back to the house, my clothes smelled like smoke from pedestrians. The landlord said this was part of city life. The most popular restaurant near where I lived was a recently renovated McDonalds that always managed to have a line out the door regardless of the time of day.

I interned with a nonprofit advocating for fair trade even though I did not support their activism. I accepted the internship after the founder mentioned how every employee was expected to work at the annual ice cream festival downtown in exchange for an all-you-can-eat ice cream festival pass. I served Ben & Jerry's at a booth across from a table selling organic hand soap. Every hour or so, I used a fresh spoon to sample the flavors, including the newest, with salty caramel and chocolate-covered potato chips, which was discontinued after a year.

My boss fired me a week after the ice cream festival for obvious reasons. From Back Bay station, I started ignoring my morning routine of switching from the Green Line T to the Red Line train for morning meetings. I snuck into Harvard's library pretending to be a student and felt pride whenever parents asked for directions to the academic buildings they envisioned their children attending. I wrote my number on pieces of paper and planned to hand them out to attractive men on the subway.

But I was too depressed to be attracted to anyone. I couldn't talk myself into falling in love. My blog, with two followers, featured photos taken in trendy coffee shops, ceramic mugs filled with more artificial flavoring than espresso, captioned with Bible verses about finding joy in suffering. I was miserable, mostly for not having a reason to blame for my misery other than missing brain chemicals. I walked for hours until the bottoms of my feet blistered or until my iPod—filled with unrequited-love songs—died, never paying attention to maps or my surroundings, only the pace of my walking and the occasional car accident.

On those nights after midnight when I walked in alleyways with sirens ringing, I had faith that someone else could cause me harm so that I would not have to do it to myself. This was my own form of self-destruction. I told my mom that a man sitting in a carpet cleaner grabbed my hand on my walk back from the bus station. Still, I cannot remember if this was true or simply a cry for help. I knew my mind was getting sick. I needed something to point to as a cause for my pain. None of the reasons I formulated seemed good enough.

BEFORE MY APPOINTMENT with Dr. Ghaemi, I visited the Armenian Museum for a second time. A woman wept a few exhibits over from the bench where I sat above the air-conditioning vent to cool off. Her weeping drowned out the sound of cars passing outside at a steady pace down the one-way road. Every time I heard the annoying click of her phone camera, I imagined her connection to the exhibits she passed by. As I looked through a box of Armenian history books in the gift shop, museum staff told me that the majority of visitors had relatives who survived the genocide. I skimmed through history books written in Armenian and Arabic. Occasionally, when I had seen what I was looking for, I nodded as if I were a scholar conducting a research project. I pretended to understand what appeared to be hieroglyphics or scribbles. Perhaps like me, this woman found she was haunted by a trauma she did not believe was hers to carry. Or unlike me, she accepted that she would carry it for the sake of her relatives and their memory.

I looked at photos of World War I propaganda, drawings of women advocating for aid for Armenian and Syrian relief that put Rosie the Riveter to shame. I wanted evidence, something to point to for what they endured. There was a connection between me and the weeping woman clicking her camera again and again; we shared an obsession with the past. For selfish reasons, I lacked the willpower to look away from the suffering that my distant ancestors had endured; studying the wounds of survivors distracted me from studying my own.

IN JUNE 2015, three months into marriage, my depression returned without giving a warning. It came back with the same force that had caused me to drop out of college three times before graduating. There were no traumatic life events to explain it. I skipped my temp job, where I scanned documents all day at an insurance agency to save up for our rent in Fairfax, where I planned to attend graduate school. I sat in bed instead and listened to the recording of Manoushag describing how she survived genocide. I had a similar pattern in college. For days, I left my dorm room only for office hours and to purchase blueberry waffles and McIntosh apples to last as meals for the week. My dorm room was covered with black-and-white photographs of Manoushag's village that were sent to me by a historian. Above my bed, I hung a photo of Manoushag taken days after she arrived in the States. She had a short pixie cut given to her at Ellis Island that matched my own hairstyle. Every weekend, I spent hours in the library basement with a stack of books about Armenian history.

I can see now that part of what originally drove me to study my ancestors was that I could identify with the sorrow that Armenians experience in having their history continually denied and ignored. From growing up in an evangelical community that questioned the legitimacy of mental illness, I understood the pain of having people question the very existence of what you have endured. The burden of feeling like you have to prove the legitimacy of your wounds was something that I felt on a daily basis. On Armenian Genocide Remembrance Day, April 24, I remember scrolling through news articles in the library that featured photographs of Armenians holding signs that read, "Our wounds are still open." Pictures of this sign infiltrated Times Square and downtown Los Angeles as thousands of people took to the streets to demand that their history be acknowledged. When I saw these photos, I could not help but connect them to my own wounds and what it would take for my own healing.

Dr. Ghaemi's windowless office was filled with portraits of Lincoln, MLK, Kennedy, and other male historical figures that he believed shared my bipolar diagnosis. None of the figures he writes about are women. A med student sat in a corner wearing a blue lab coat designating his social status at the hospital and asked if he could sit in on our consultation to take notes. I felt sympathy for him in knowing that my case was nothing special. I never did especially destructive or abnormal things while manic. I never abused substances. I never had any hospitalizations. My suicide attempts mirrored science experiments of mixing drugs, but I never took enough.

Before Dr. Ghaemi introduced himself to David and me, he answered a phone call from his wife, who asked him how to turn on their home air conditioner. When I gave him a copy of my list of medications, thirteen in total, he laughed and called them garbage. My shoulders sank deeper into the faux leather chair. The majority of the appointment involved him asking me questions about my medical history, as if genealogy could provide answers. While asking questions about the psychiatric history of my family, he drew a diagram to draw connections between me and the people who share my blood, but throughout our time together, the diagram remained empty. Whenever I listened to Manoushag's tape, I copied down her words in hopes of finding similar sentiments expressed by me. Instead, I hear her say, regarding what she endured, "I remember having no feeling."

I read in Dr. Ghaemi's notes later that he thought of me as a reliable historian. My depressive symptoms often altered reality. He attempted to explain his research in understandable terms and reported that based on my symptoms, the ADHD diagnosis that I received fifteen years prior was incorrect. He provided a prescription of lithium and reviewed several paragraphs' worth of side effects. He suggested that I quit taking my other medications and resign from my job to prepare for withdrawal symptoms that would last for months. Essentially, I was asked to start over from the beginning.

He described symptoms like increased depression, anxiety, and lack of energy. His recommendation confirmed what had been worrying me for weeks: I was not ready for school; perhaps my dreams were unrealistic. Looking over at David, Dr. Ghaemi told him to find a job that did not involve traveling so that he could be at home with me. Sitting there, I did not know if I should trust him, but there were no other options. David and I unanimously agreed with Dr. Ghaemi's assessment because in that moment, he appeared to have answers that we desperately wanted.

While David and I drove back to the hotel in silence, I thought of Manoushag sailing on the bottom of a ship, where she was forced to drink ocean water until reaching Ellis Island. On land deemed holy, she waited to be poked and prodded by doctors, to be told whether she would have the chance to start over. Believing that my ancestors' resilience is genetic was enough for me to trust that I could start over, too, that I could survive. I pictured her portrait that hung above my dorm room bed, which she took days after coming to America—her round nose looked no different than mine.

Բառերը—the Words

J. P. DER BOGHOSSIAN

"DO YOU KNOW that Armenia is not how we even say Armenia in Armenian?" I said, slurring my words to some gay friends at a hookah lounge, doling out stories about my Armenian family. "It's Hayastan."

"How do you pronounce it?

"High-uh-STAHN."

"All those 'stan' countries are so backwards," one friend said, patting my knee. Afghani*stan*. Paki*stan*. Haya*stan*. "You're better off living here," he continued, in the same tone of voice that I imagined a kind editor would use as she advised a writer to put the manuscript away. There's nothing there. Let it go. But I didn't. I wanted the right words, written in the right way, to describe what was happening to me in the ambiguous spaces of conjunctions and hyphens, a "Queer-*and*-Armenian American."

JOSHUA HAGLUND stumbled out of his Yerevan apartment, beaten, stabbed. In the courtyard of his apartment building, in the city center of the Armenian capital, he collapsed. His blood pooled underneath him, thick, hot. He pleaded for help. Elmira Harutiunian called the police and ran to his side. He was murmuring, and all she knew how to say in English was, "What is your name?" He pulled out his ID. As they waited for the ambulance, his thoughts, then his breath, then his eyes succumbed.

Haglund, a Minnesota native, had been teaching English at the Yerevan Brusov State University of Languages and Social Sciences. He was the first-reported American to be murdered in Armenia. Five months after

Haglund's murder, deprived of fundamental information about the case, his family traveled to Armenia seeking a police report, an autopsy, anything. Haglund was an out gay man, and his family feared he was killed for it. Years later, they still had no answers. They worked with their congresswoman to draft legislation to compel Armenia to investigate. They retained new lawyers. Their investigation led them to alleging that the police had ignored and covered up key evidence. Rather than pursue that evidence, the police instead chose to arrest Haglund's gay friends before intimidating and torturing them to create fear in the queer community. His murder remains unsolved.

THE GAY RIGHTS ACTIVIST Vrezh Varzhapetyan walked down a Yerevan street as three men cursed him, hurling homophobic slurs. Then, they chased him. They demanded to know if he was Armenian. When he said yes, they punched him in the mouth and nose, again and again. "You have no right to call yourself Armenian!" they yelled, beating him.

Despite calls for justice, despite multiple surveillance cameras on the street, no one was arrested. When Varzhapetyan gave his statement to the police, an officer told him, "Gays are not allowed or loved in this country."

WHEN I ATTENDED COLLEGE in Los Angeles, I concocted a hypothesis that I would attract more boys on various hookup and dating websites if I identified as Middle Eastern instead of white. My father, Bob, was American, of English and German descent. My mother, Myriam, was Armenian. And Armenia, I pointed out, was in West Asia / the Middle East, not Europe. My hypothesis was a numbers game. The more boys I met, the better my odds of finding one who might understand the complicated mess I was. I had seen my "white" numbers. Maybe "Middle Eastern" would be higher. Besides, I wasn't always passing for white on campus. There was a constant scrutiny from students and instructors: "What is your real name?" "You must be Jewish, right?" "Excuse me, are you Palestinian?" "Aren't you from India? You're always hanging out with Arati and she's Indian."

Even in Northern Michigan, where I graduated high school, the locals would ask, "Where are you from? You have an accent and I can't quite place it." I figured it was the combination of my Middle Eastern face and my gay accent, which was also scrutinized. *You don't sound stereotypically gay, but you don't sound like the guys from here.* I would watch their blue eyes squint, mouths frown, and arms cross in confusion when I told them I was born in their hospital and graduated from their schools. If I went on to explain that I was a hyphenated American, that my family were refugees to France during the Armenian Genocide, that I was a dual citizen, then their eyes relaxed, mouths grinned, and arms opened. I affirmed that difference came to, not from, Northern Michigan.

My Armenian family claimed me as their own because they thought, *He looks Armenian.* As a child, a tingle would zip down my spine as my Armenian grandmother cupped my face with both of her hands, a throb of recognition in her eyes, a blood bond.

When I considered the racial categories of my dating profile settings, I saw ambiguity. Which was more accurate? With a click of my mouse I could change my race. It was as simple and as complicated as that. The experiment began. With my white profile, I received at least one or two messages a week, sometimes three or four. With a Middle Eastern one, I figured I would receive twice that many.

Every night I checked the results, sitting in my briefs and T-shirt, leaning into the computer, legs tucked underneath my chair, feet hooked on the rung, my wiry frame curved into a question mark. I would log in and wait for my messages to load. But there weren't any. I would check another site. No messages. Another site. Nothing.

It continued like that for a couple of weeks. Maybe it was the new reality of a post-9/11 world. But to be fair, I also skipped past the Middle Eastern boys as I drafted my own roster of recruits, evaluating each white boy's potential by his weight, height, physicality. I did consider the pouty stare of a Middle Eastern boy, the way he lifted his shirt to show his abs and how he displayed a profile picture with his arm draped around a woman's neck, as if to say *I'm gay, but not that gay.* I would wonder if the Middle Eastern boys were Armenian. That question would push my chest back from the computer and unhook my feet from the chair. I would run my hands down my bare thighs and huff blasts of air through my nose, not unlike a deer when it suspects trouble. A queer Armenian? No one in my family was. When we hosted Armenian friends, neighbors, and extended family, none of them were either. And neither were their children, nor the friends of their children.

I considered whether it would have been a comfort to discover another queer Armenian boy. Wouldn't it have been a relief to pull off my shirt and show him my scars and not have to explain the emotional and spiritual abuse? To watch him pull off his own shirt and show me all those same scars in all the same places. Wouldn't it have been a reprieve not to need words and instead have the quiet solace of shared experience?

At the thought, I would suck my teeth and pull on the curly black hairs on my thigh. With my thumb, I would press red ovals onto my skin and scratch red lines from my knee up to the edge of my briefs. If he had suffered the same, then that would be a pattern. I didn't know how to cope as it was. I couldn't risk attracting more threats.

After two weeks of empty inboxes, I had enough and shut down my experiment. It seemed that for the white American boys, who had ignored my messages, "Middle Eastern" was incommunicable. It was preferable when I was "white of Middle Eastern descent," maybe because "of descent" suggested the past, something lost, or taken, or melted away.

I turned off the lights knowing I also felt that Armenian boys were incommunicable. I crept into bed, pulled the blankets up to my chin, closed my eyes, gripped my sex, and conjured up the nude body of one of those American boys. Tall. Curly red hair. Milk-white skin. Thick arms that could claim me, pick me up, throw me over his shoulder, swat my rear end, scold me for playing a dangerous game, then carry me back to where I belonged—away from the Armenians.

"WHO WILL SAVE THIS BOY?" My pastor appealed to his three-hundred-person congregation. My adolescent body sat perched on a stool next to his pulpit. The pastor had chosen me as his symbol of the universal boy, innocent, vulnerable. He swung his hand in the air, doubling down on his challenge. "Who will save this boy from the temptations of this world? Drugs, alcohol, lust, pornography, and *deviance*. Who will stand for him?"

I squirmed; my eyes bugged. There was a ripple of stifled laughter from some young men. Out of all the boys in the youth group, why had the pastor plucked me out? Was my femininity his subtext? Bob rose from his pew and I writhed. This had been preplanned. The pastor plastered his words on me. A public lesson in front of God: the next time you think of lust, pornography, and deviance, think of me. Script in hand, Bob declared, "I will stand for him."

Before my college graduation, Bob scrutinized my conversation with a college instructor, a fey gay man who hugged me and offered a few words of encouragement. Bob had not heard our exchange, but he read the body language of an obvious queer man touching his son. Afterward, we had our first direct conversation on the subject. It was brief. "It took everything in me not to punch him just now."

🌼🌼🌼

AT A WORK CONFERENCE in Washington, DC, I decided I might be ready to look for other queer Armenians. I was thirty-four, after all. I propped myself up on the hotel bed and typed two words into Google: gay Armenians. I braced myself for hostility and the possibility of a rogue LGBTQ-friendly op-ed, published in an American newspaper since the Armenian newspapers would have rejected it.

The first result was the *Hye-Phen Magazine*, an online publication founded and written by queer Armenians. Next, there was an op-ed by Kyle Khandikian in the *Armenian Weekly* newspaper. Then, there was the website for the Los Angeles–based Gay and Lesbian Armenian Society (GALAS). I rolled my eyes. Where was GALAS when I lived there? I clicked through their website and Facebook page. There were photos of grinning queer Armenians. GALAS hosted social events, speakers, fundraisers. They had links to culturally competent health services for LGBTQ Armenians.

I pushed the laptop off me. *Where was GALAS when I lived there?* I grabbed the remote and flipped through the television channels. I walked to the vending machines. With my index finger I stabbed the buttons. The strawberry Pop-Tarts dropped. I punched my hand through the slot door, harder than intended. Package in hand, I stared down the empty hallway.

Why hadn't they rescued me? It was a childish complaint. But potent. If they were organized, then why didn't they come find me? Why hadn't they been like the wizards of Ursula K. Le Guin's *Earthsea*? The possessors of secret knowledge, seeking out gifted boys, spiriting them away to the island of Roke to learn a magic based on knowing the true words, the true names, of all the living things in the world so that they can reestablish balance to the universe.

I meandered back to my room, sat on the edge of the bed, and watched an episode of *Girls*. I couldn't tell if I was angrier with GALAS or with myself for hiding so well that the idea of a queer Armenian organization was a bridge too far for my imagination. I broke the strawberry Pop-Tarts into pieces, grinding them in my mouth into a thick paste. It was difficult to swallow.

I HAD CHATTED with him on Match.com for months, and we decided it was time to meet. He lived in Lansing, Michigan, and I was living in Traverse City. I told him I would rent a car to drive to meet him halfway. On the prearranged morning, at the rental car agency, as I was scrawling my name on the rental agreement, he messaged me.

"It's raining out and I don't feel comfortable driving."

"That's okay, I'll drive to Lansing."

"Don't, I can't meet."

The agent handed me the keys. I was too embarrassed to cancel. I rambled around Leelanau County for a few hours before my anger kicked in. He wasn't the only person I had been talking with online about a relationship. There were Jim and Gordy in Minnesota. I had been stalling with them because I didn't know what a polyamorous relationship was. But there was an attraction. And they had been asking me to visit. I returned the rental car and charged home to email them. "Let's talk details." I had no point of reference for polyamory, but Jim and Gordy were kind, and they were real. We believed in the same things. They understood what a relationship was because they had been together for almost forty years. They wanted to build a life. With me. Maybe "polyamorous" was a word I had been waiting for.

JIM, GORDY, AND I traveled to Los Angeles. We had been together for five years, and we had all lived in L.A. at various points in our lives, so we planned a vacation to visit Jim's sisters and to share with each other the various landmarks of our old lives: homes, colleges, jobs. I took the opportunity to arrange a meeting with Armen, the president of GALAS.

We slogged our way through traffic toward Glendale and the Paradise Pastry and Café. There, I couldn't help streaking my fingerprints all over the pristine glass displays, mesmerized by the rows and rows of Armenian pastries. I ordered a variety plate of baklava, nazook, and gata.

Armen sat in the far corner of the café. Long, curly brown hair pulled up into a bun. Chiseled jaw. Impeccable white teeth. Brown skin. The top button of his shirt undone, his chest showing. I tugged on the hem of my olive-green polo. Why hadn't I dressed up for this?

There was a debacle with the introductions. I thought I had introduced Jim and Gordy as my partners, but later Armen asked which of Jim and Gordy was my dad, a not uncommon situation given they were twenty-three and twenty-four years older than me, respectively. I clarified they were my partners. He looked puzzled. I let it slide. I was not there to discuss intergenerational polyamory.

We talked about the founding of GALAS. There was something about new changes that Armen had worked on as president and upcoming plans. He asked if there were any Armenians in Minnesota and was surprised when I said a few hundred, plus a church and cultural organization, of which I was on the board. Throughout, I knew this was a unique moment, meeting and talking for the first time to a queer Armenian, one who led a queer Armenian organization. I wanted to lean in and ask Armen inappropriate questions like when was the exact moment he knew he was gay? When did he first come out and to whom? How did he tell his family? How bad was it? Myriam had dissolved into tears in a restaurant and was so upset the poor Midwestern waitress had no idea what to do and abandoned us at the table. What specific symptoms of anxiety and depression did he have? Were they the same as mine? Did he have the nightmares too? What about the intrusive thoughts during sex? Did he see the dark shapes in his windows at night? How long had he been in therapy, and how many therapists had he gone through before he had found a good one?

But the conversation was what it should have been: cordial and diplomatic. Then, it was over. We stood, shook hands. Armen left. I watched him walk to his car, taking with him his answers to the questions I felt I couldn't ask. I still had a block. I chose to be polite, rather than ask, *Hey, would you be cool chatting on Facebook?* Jim and Gordy looked at me. What next?

If I had a block, then I would find my answers in books. I would find all the books written by queer Armenians. I would find all the books with queer Armenian characters. I would find every word a queer Armenian had ever written down.

"DON'T TELL ANYONE YOU'RE GAY," Myriam demanded. I dropped my suitcase and myself onto the guest bed of my grandmother's apartment. It had taken two planes and two trains to haul me from Minnesota to Valence, France, for a visit with my extended Armenian family. Myriam rose to her full height, all five feet and one inch of it, to claim her maternal power of censorship. "I already have enough shit to deal with."

"They have such power over you," said Adam, my therapist. He observed that I kept turning Bob and Myriam into villains, that I kept saying my body wasn't mine, that they "owned" it. He said to me that there were laws to protect me in Minnesota and that I was in a loving relationship with Jim and Gordy and that I have a job that will protect me if they showed up there and that I could use him to mediate conversations.

The point, he said, of eye movement desensitization and reprocessing (EMDR) therapy was to get some distance. He said it was possible they were bad people. The world is a dangerous place, and there are villains out there. But, he asked me, how can we not give them so much power? Not to excuse their behavior or dismiss the idea that they should be responsible for their actions, but to use EMDR to understand the context, to see that what they did wasn't about me. As I stared out a window, he hung these words onto my silence: "How can we live with our wounds and not have them govern us?"

MY LIBRARY of queer Armenian books sits below my shelves of queer literature and above my shelves of Armenian literature. The book spines are colorful: electric yellow, lime green, teal, royal purple, black, and fire engine red. The words that pop out at you are "Pride," "Men on Men," "Lion Woman," "Me as Her," "Queered," "Balls."

I believe I have one of the most comprehensive libraries of queer Armenian books. There could be others, like ancient Armenian coins buried in the earth, unknown until I dig them up. Even as I write this, with help from others, I still find new ones.

It took a few years to assemble. I started with Google and used all these search terms in every combination: "book," "novel," "gay," "lesbian," "bisexual," "transgender," "LGBT," "Armenian," "Armenians," "Armenia." That led me to blogs, websites, zines, Twitter, Instagram, and the like. I came across the names of queer Armenian organizations and online publications, two of which, *Unzipped: Gay Armenia* and the *Hye-Phen Magazine*, provided a crucial trove of reviews and book lists. I discovered websites that had ceased to exist, and I tracked down their URLs to use the Internet Archive Wayback Machine to look at archives of their pages. Amazon and Barnes and Noble were other obvious search engines, but I also needed AbeBooks, Better World Books, Book Depository, Alibris, Thrift Books, and Half Price Books.

I created a list of Armenian bookstores. If they didn't have a website I could search, or a website at all, I crossed them off my list. I used my academic credentials to gain access to major university libraries. I made a list of Armenian newspapers and news organizations and searched their internet archives.

There were problems. My search process provided me with books, but what about the authors' identities? Some didn't list their sexual orientation or gender identity in their bios. Some didn't have bios at all.

There was censorship. An Azeri author wrote a novel about a love story between an Armenian man and an Azeri man. The book had been banned in Azerbaijan, and that was the only reason I found out about it. The ban led to international headlines. The author, Ali Akbar (an alias), succeeded in printing a few hundred copies but had to sell them out of his car. I scoured the internet for a couple of years, a constant check to see if one would turn up. I found out that while there was no English translation, there was a Dutch translation (not helpful since I don't know Dutch). Two years into my search, convinced there was an English copy, I found a website that had a PDF copy in Azeri. I downloaded it, and Google Translate gave me a readable, if not accurate, translation.

There was an ethical question. Many of the books had only one, or two, or no copies left for purchase. One of these books I could find in a major university library. Now, I could borrow that book and then never return it, skipping out on the fines and fees, giving up my rights to interlibrary loans forever. Or I could keep the book and prepare to pay a couple hundred dollars of fines and fees.

Does a university have the right to keep me, a queer Armenian, from owning a queer Armenian book? But what right do I have to steal it? Whom do these books belong to? Who *should* own them? These words are beyond rare. It is possible to read thousands of pages of mainstream Armenian writers and never read about a queer Armenian. In fiction, nonfiction, or poetry. Our fiction writers can't seem to imagine such a character. But if the book sits on my bookshelf, then no one would have access to it. Whose rights to ownership would do the least harm? Mine or the university's?

Also, there was a question of expansion. I found novelists, memoirists, poets, academics, anthology editors, journalists, screenwriters, and essayists: Kamee Abrahamian, Nancy Agabian, Arpi Adamyan, Sophia Armen, Armen of Armenia, Rosie Vartyter Aroush, Mika Artyan, Art Arutunyan, Christopher Atamian, Shushan Avagyan, Arlene Voski Avakian, Bob Avian, Nyri Bakkalian, Michael Barakiva, Maral Bavakan, Eve Beglarian, Chaz Bono, Melissa Boyajian, Gregory Casparian, Haig Chahinian, Yeghishe Charents, Chris Edwards, Veken Gueyikian, Jarrod Hayes, Olivia Khandikian, David Kherdian, Alex Ikke-Tuppel, David Matthew-Barnes, Armistead Maupin, Aram Mrjoian, Sevan Mujukian, James Nagarian, Armen Ohanian, Pouria Heidary Oureh, Nelli Sargsyan, Movses Shakarian, Tamar Shirinian, Emma Shooshan, Natalie Shirinian, George Stambolian, lusine talalyan, Vahan Tekeyan, Alexandre Vidal Porto, Hrag Vartanian.[1]

When I read through my library, I think I have all the words I will ever need to describe the conjunctions and hyphens linking queer and Armenian and American, and yet I never seem to have enough. I can stand as a keynote speaker in front of an audience of five hundred and declare that I am queer and living in a long-term intergenerational polyamorous relationship, but I crumple into a silent victim when forced to talk to any family member. I expanded my sense of self and humanity by creating the library, but it reminds me every day that my humanity can't even fill an entire bookshelf. I lean into the resilience I learned from the Armenian community to survive the Armenian community.

Part of the library describes my conjunctions and hyphens as binaries, or seesaws. To achieve a sense of balance I must stand in the center. If I were to settle into a seat on either side, claiming an identity, then I would just end up crouched on the ground watching my other identity hang in the air.

Another part of the library illustrates that in the slim space of my conjunction, and in the small stroke of my hyphen, I have oceans of words, waves of confusions and attractions and defiance and shame and love and yearnings. My hyphen is as metaphorical and literal as the Atlantic Ocean.

But because of the library, I read words like queer and Armenian and American as high-energy particle beams that we hurl into the conjunctions and hyphens of our lives, like a hadron collider, blasting them through the corridors at dizzying speeds, smashing into each other, with a malevolent, or banal, or desperate intent to observe the Big Bang, witnessing how these words burst into terrifying new atoms and galaxies and stars, yes, terrifying and merciful new gods, and life, please, be merciful, with all of us tugged by the inescapable gravity of new planets pulling us back to the irrepressible first words ever written in classical Armenian: to know wisdom and instruction; to perceive the words of understanding.

Note

1. Many books by these writers are included in the reading list at the end of this anthology. The full library can be found at queerarmenianlibrary.com.

The Road to Belonging

RAFFY BOUDJIKANIAN

SQUINT A LITTLE as you travel along Alberta's highways, surrounded by the flat farmers' fields that helped earn the Canadian province and its two neighbors to the east the designation of the Prairies, and you could think you were somewhere in Armenia.

The dry weather echoes the Caucasus country's own, too, pleasant in the summer. Outdoor jogs and long walks won't often leave maps of sweat stains on your clothes. The topographical similarities especially hit home when you're farther in the south, as the looming shadows of the Rockies remind you of the occasional mountains and ranges in Armenia, or the ones that are not quite there, such as Ararat, just across the border in Turkey.

But today's trip won't take me anywhere near those elevations. It's June 2, 2018, and I'm on a bus traveling from where I live, Edmonton, in the north, to a smaller city a one hundred–minute drive south, Red Deer.

It's Alberta's annual Armenian Festival, and Edmonton does not have a sizeable enough Armenian diaspora community for it. Neither does Calgary, the province's most populous city, so organizers hold the event in Red Deer, a sort of geographical halfway point between the two larger locations, hoping to attract Armenians from both hubs.

Once the bus pulls over at a hotel parking lot in Red Deer, I hop off and summon an Uber to get me to the actual place, a community hall rented out for the occasion.

The driver has never heard of it and punches in the address on Google Maps.

He's not the least bit curious about what kind of event I'm going to, nor who I'm meeting.

It's fine I suppose. Somehow, I'm just not feeling the intellectual labor of explaining what an Armenian is to him.

Before moving to Alberta in 2016, I had never really lived anywhere in my life that did not have a big Armenian community. That year, official Canadian government figures pegged the number of Calgary Armenians at 1,010.

In Edmonton, the number was lower: 620.

Until then, I had lived most of my life in Montreal, Quebec, which, with over 26,000 Armenians, edged out Toronto as having Canada's largest Armenian diaspora population.

It is March 1991, close to Easter. I'm almost seven years old, sitting in one of two taxicabs shuttling me and my family from Montréal-Dorval International Airport to my aunt's house, on our first visit to Canada, the country that will become our new home.

My remaining immediate family are all in the next car, along with our luggage. Other than the driver, I'm alone with my aunt, whom I have never met before.

She makes conversation, and I don't recall providing much in the way of scintillating repartee.

She must have me pegged for a shy little boy, which, to be fair, I was.

But I'm also mesmerized by what I can see outside my window.

Along the entire stretch of Highway 40, sets of streetlights brightening the way.

In the Beirut of the 1980s, where and when I was born, it was not uncommon to spend most of the day experiencing power outages. How much electricity does Canada have, that it can just . . . afford to keep the entire autoroute illuminated?

The sheer vanity of it both impresses and vaguely upsets me, in a way seven-year-old me would likely struggle to articulate. Later, at my aunt's place, the wonders continue. The hot-water tap actually releases hot water on command. The cold water is potable.

The Armenian community in Montreal is younger and smaller than the one in Beirut, which is one of the oldest and biggest outside Armenia proper, but it is also by and large wealthier. So, whom did I have more in common with after spending the rest of my childhood in Montreal? Armenians in Beirut, or Canadians?

IT IS 1998, and seven years after crossing the world from east to west, I've been on a journey a couple of days long going back the other way.

From Montreal to Frankfurt, and Frankfurt to Yerevan, Armenia. I've been traveling without my family this time, part of an organized trip with the Homenetmen Armenian Scouts Montreal chapter.

The idea is chapters from across the world gather in Armenia for a two-week summer camp. We call it a jamboree, officially. The title's meant to differentiate from the smaller, more traditional annual summer camps in our own backyards. Finding the cheapest airfare possible for this large of a group has meant that old favorite of international travel: a long layover somewhere at a midway point.

In this case, that somewhere is Frankfurt International Airport. Which, in part, is cool. I get to add one more to the list of countries I've visited. Unfortunately, it also means we're there for just about twelve hours.

Some of the others have entertained themselves playing soccer in the passenger waiting area. It's a Cup year, and such a commercial starring the Brazilian team is just too fun an imitation to pass up.

Well, for most of us. Armenians have a kind of obsession with soccer. It's not as if our national team has ever cut a large profile on the world stage, but we remain ever hopeful. I'm not part of the Homenetmen soccer team, though many of my friends in the scouts do play. The other difference between me and them is they're actually good at it.

By the time we get to Armenia, it's early in the morning on a hot August day, and I'm spent. Right there on the tarmac, one of my friends decides it is time to show his lifelong appreciation of Armenia immediately. "I'm going to get down on my knees and kiss the ground," he says.

I tell him I won't be doing that, because I think it's unhygienic.

He dismisses my unpatriotic concern, kneels, and performs his ritual of loyalty.

I watch him and wonder if I'm at fault, for not being Armenian enough.

BACK TO 2018.

We arrive at the community center.

The driver lets me out.

I walk into the hall.

I know only a couple among the fifty or so people present, but it is also familiar. I recognize the meals everyone has brought for the potluck, the notes of the folkloric music playing on speakers in the background. A friend, M, waves me over to sit at her table, one of the first Armenians I had met upon moving out West. I had messaged a Facebook group after arriving in Calgary, wanting to connect with other Armenians. M was the administrator, suggesting we meet for coffee. Once we did, within five minutes she had realized that she knew my parents and established that we were family friends.

Not exactly a refutation of an old cliché about how "all Armenians know each other," but amusing, nonetheless.

IT IS FALL 1991. I'm at my new school, which, with elementary through high school classes, will be a regular, all-encompassing part of my life for the next eleven years. Montreal's largest Armenian educational institution, Sourp Hagop.

I'd attended Armenian school in Beirut as well, but there is nothing like other kids to make sure you know you're different.

I spent the first couple of years obsessively trying to fit in, with half-hearted explanations and defense of why being Armenian from Beirut was cool.

On one such occasion, we received a not-quite-show-and-tell assignment. The idea was to hide some object in a bag and walk it around the classroom, letting the other students guess what you've got while you provide clues. They feel the mystery item through the folds of plastic. I'm excited, convinced what I've brought is doubtlessly the coolest possible thing these Canadian children have ever seen. Mind-blowing. Exotic. It'll win me all the friends at recess I've been severely lacking.

"This is something my brother and I used to collect all the time on our balcony in Beirut," I say, as my classmates poke and prod at the bag's contents.

They do not get it.

"We'd need to do it in the mornings," I go on, adding the objects would typically not materialize until sometime in the evening or at night.

They are still clueless.

I am so proud of my cleverness.

"See, it would be too dangerous for us to go out at night, because of all the firefights around our building; it was during the war."

(There were UN peacekeepers stationed in the hotel to the right of our apartment and a faction of militia in the field across the street.)

I worry I've now provided too much in the way of hints. Surely one of them will get it.

Nope. Still nothing.

"It's a bullet case," I say, excited, at the end of my presentation. I brandish the slug triumphantly out of the bag.

The stares that greet me are either blank or horrified.

In Lebanon, it was about as normal as possible for children to collect spent bullet cases.

Here, what's normal is to collect shiny trading cards depicting hockey players.

1998.

Our trip with the scouts in Armenia has taken us through the ruins of centuries-old monasteries, on rocky roads surrounded by arid fields and rigid cliffs.

Armenian is the first language I ever learned, but the residents of Armenia speak a different dialect, what we call arevelahayeren, or Eastern Armenian.

It's hardly difficult to understand. Some words don't quite mean the same thing, or verb conjugations don't quite end the same way. Letters and sounds slip and slide and roll off tongues just a little differently.

But really, all you have to do is focus when someone is speaking, maybe ask them to repeat themselves, and odds are you'll get it.

Still, it is just one more reminder that though Armenia is home, it's also not.

I wasn't born here, and my ancestors were from the part of the ancient Armenian homeland that was swallowed up by Turkey, far to the east of where I was standing.

We visit the Sardarapat Memorial, a short, twelve-minute drive away from the border with Turkey, built as a monument to one of Armenia's battles for independence in 1918, just three years after the genocide began.

Sardarapat is a simple structure.

Ahead of a red wall, two gigantic red bulls face each other, a bell tower between their stares.

A dozen bells ring on it.

I am moved to tears when I hear their melancholy chime in the soft wind.

It seems silly.

I've never seen this place before, except in schoolbooks teaching us Armenian history.

Somehow that sound calls to me as much as anything can.

I am home, it tells me.

I fall just short of kissing the ground.

2018.

The organizer of the event had asked me to bring a copy of my recently published book to talk to people about it if asked. I leave it on a table to the side, along with some other stuff produced by different artists and writers.

One of them is a blue-white slab of a sculpture, about the size of my hand and the weight of a child's football.

It's got two peaks, one tinier than the other, depicting, of course, Ararat. The name of the legendary mountain is carved in Latin letters on the side, in case you don't clue in.

The author comes and introduces himself to me.

He then offers a trade, his work for mine.

I'm not terribly enthusiastic. It's one of my last author copies of my book, and the only one that's not promised to a relative.

Then again, I'm one of the few Armenians I know who does not have some kind of art showing off Ararat in their household. Maybe it's about time that changed.

I'm not a big fan of cliché, but Ararat's a powerful one, and it became that way for a reason.

That Turkish-Armenian border? The mountain's right on the other side of it, been that way since 1921, when treaties were drawn deciding what part of Armenia would go to the Soviet Union and what part would remain in the nascent nation-state of Turkey, six years after the Armenian Genocide began.

Ever since then, the mountain has come to represent all of that Armenian history, the lost lives and lost land. It's not a small mountain, but that's a large burden for any shoulders to bear.

I accept the trade.

IT'S APRIL 1993. I'm in third grade, eight years old.

Our Armenian language teacher sets aside a long period of class time to give us a historical lesson on the genocide of 1915.

Decades later, I would ponder about how normal this all seemed growing up, but for now the thought does not cross my mind. Of course, you need to learn what happened to your ancestors. As with most children in the classroom, I'm already aware of my own family's personal story, at least parts of it, anyway.

I had been only four years old when my dad first spoke to me about the genocide, in vaguely general terms, after I'd caught him reading a book about the events, its black cover decorated in skulls.

This, too, is a quintessential part of the Armenian diaspora, largely the reason why diasporic communities exist in their current form.

But, is it the only reason?

Does it have to be the only reason?

It's 2002, and I'm attending my first concert, at age eighteen, with three friends.

The headliners? System of a Down. The Armenian American industrial metal quartet has just reached what many fans would consider the height of their popularity with their second album, *Toxicity*. I unabashedly call them my favorite musicians and insist it's only because they're so talented, having little to do with their ethnicity. And look, see? There's something clearly related to the Armenian diaspora that I love and has nothing to do with the genocide.

Other than maybe a couple of their angriest anthems, which are also some of my favorites.

One of my friends unfurls a small Armenian flag he's brought with him to brandish over the swelling crowds of the mosh pit.

I'm not normally into overt displays of patriotism, but I get defensive when another ticket holder walks by us and tells him to put his Spanish emblem away.

"It's Armenian," my friends and I explain.

"Armenian?" the concertgoer asks. "They're not Spanish?" he continues, pointing at the soon-to-be-occupied stage.

"No, they're Armenian."

Bewildered, the flag-hater vanishes from our sight with no further arguments.

1915.

To tell the full tale of all the branches of the two sides of my family, shaken or burnt until all the leaves fell loose or turned to ash, would take more space than the pages of this essay allow.

My dad's side of the clan, the Boudjikanians, used to live in Kharpert, a fortress-town in what is now eastern Turkey, then a largely Armenian-inhabited part of the Ottoman Empire.

My paternal great-grandfather, Hovhanness Boudjikanian, was a philosophy teacher at Euphrates College, an institution run by American missionaries. His full title was something like "Professor of Mental and Moral Sciences," which I love because it reminds me of Dr. Strange's "Master of the Mystic Arts," and, just like the Marvel character, Hovhanness sported a moustache.

When the Turks began rounding up the Armenian intellectuals, prior to the deportations themselves, they came knocking on Hovhanness's door.

His son, my grandfather, seven at the time, wrote about the events later on. He said his father had been in the middle of a morning shave when the gendarmes arrived. They told the rest of the family he was going away for only a short while, that he would be back quickly. The setup was that Hovhanness was a dangerous subversive, hiding weapons and artillery.

Their entire basis for this was a speech Hovhanness had delivered years earlier, praising Armenians for holding on to their identity though they were part of a larger empire, words spoken on a twin anniversary commemorating both the Armenian alphabet and the first book printed in the Armenian language (though the events were centuries apart— AD 405 and 1512—and of course technically not quite aligned for a twin anniversary).

Hovhanness was returned home in the evening.

The officers also searched my family's entire belongings, pretending they were looking for bombs. My grandfather described one lifting a hen above its nest to check if any explosives were among the eggs.

They took the professor away a second time. And he never returned again.

My grandfather, Armen, got to see him once more, inside a Turkish prison.

There, through the bars of a cell, the man told his seven-year-old boy that he needed to be kind, take care of his brothers and sisters, and pray for him.

In his writing, Armen explains that prisoners were tortured for the next several days, Hovhanness screaming, "What gives you the right?" to his jailers.

"You were saying, 'Let's live as Armenians, let's die as Armenians,'" a guard responded, throwing back at him one of the passages from Hovhanness's speech.

Days later, Hovhanness's mother, Armen's grandmother, made an attempt to see him in prison but was denied. Instead, a gendarme presented her with his blood-stained clothes, telling her to go wash them.

My grandfather and his immediate family eventually managed to escape the genocide, thanks to the help of a German missionary.

They wound up in Beirut in 1922.

The same city where my mom's ancestors, the Keuroghlians, had eventually escaped to from where they lived, Marash, also in eastern Turkey.

It's not that strange a coincidence, really. The world is a small place, and proper refuge for escapees of a genocide in the early twentieth century, ones who had long since not been masters of their own country and looking for something with at least a vague sense of familiarity, narrows down the options further still.

Lebanon was already home to a significant proportion of Armenians prior to the genocide, and with its significant Christian population and relative proximity to the homeland, it must have been an appealing beacon for more of them at the time.

In fact, the Keuroghlians' initial escape from Marash in 1915 was to Damascus, Syria. That's where my mom's father and mother met. They eventually made their way to the outskirts of Beirut, and then on to the Lebanese capital.

My mom reports that her father, Vahram Keuroghlian, who was already a man in his twenties when the massacres started in 1915, wanted to play a leadership role for other exiled diaspora Armenians in Lebanon. He and his brother Soghomon committed themselves to helping run activities at the local Armenian Apostolic church.

This included financially sponsoring renovations inside the hall of the building.

Walk into the Armenian Apostolic Church of Karasoun Mangants (Forty Martyrs) in the Nor Marash neighborhood today, and you will still see an altar bearing Vahram and Soghomon's names, along with those of their other two brothers, Haroutyoun and Hagop. But Vahram was not frequently at Sunday mass. Often, his wife, my grandmother, would attend while he stayed home for the day.

My mother's explanation is that he just may not have been a deeply religious man, but, as with many Armenians, he felt a sense of responsibility toward the community, and with no independent Armenian nation to speak of during his lifetime, felt the cross was one of the few authorities to support.

It is 2002.

My second trip to Armenia, again with the scouts.

It happens to be a year after the 1700th anniversary of Armenians adopting Christianity as an official religion, making us the oldest Christian nation in the world.

Evidence of this is scattered all over the country, as well as what is now part of Turkey. Churches and monasteries dot both landscapes, mostly in ruins in the latter, as old as the entire history of younger countries.

For the second time in my life, I visit the Sourp Asdvadzadzin (Holy Mother of God) monastery. The initial bones of this structure are 1,378 years old, and our history suggests it obtained a symbolic status earlier, in the last years of the third century AD.

The site houses what Armenians call Khor Virap, or Deep Pit.

Think of it as a prison akin to the Oubliettes of France, though it was so small there was not much room for more than one prisoner at a time.

The pit is a place of pilgrimage and veneration for Armenians, and a tourist attraction, for the most important convict it held was none other than Saint Gregory the Illuminator, considered the official founder of Christianity for our people.

I was ten years old when I first heard his story, stuff that would surely make Shakespeare or Dumas weep in excitement at the idea of an adaptation. It was June 1994, I was in Armenian History class, and our teacher explained that the Armenian king, Khosrov II, was in pitched battle with the neighboring Sasanian Empire of Persia.

Khosrov II lost, and the Sasanians invaded. The Armenian king's death came at the hands of his cousin, Anak, who had grown up in Persia. Khosrov's clan would have its bloody vengeance too. The only known escapees on the Armenian side? His son, a young boy named Tiridates III, who was smuggled away to Rome for safekeeping, and Tiridates's sister Khosrovidukht (which actually means Daughter of Khosrov), who was taken to Caesarea (modern Kayseri in Turkey). Coincidentally, Anak's only known surviving offspring, his young son, named Gregory, was also taken there.

That on its own was quite enough for me to be dying to know what was next, and so when our teacher told us we would learn the next part of this only when we returned to school in September, I was practically enraged. First my TV show seasons ended in unbearable suspense, then schoolwork followed suit.

When we returned to class in fall '94, I was all ears for the rest.

Tiridates grew up in Rome on tales of his homeland and royal birthright. He was encouraged by the empire to return and retake his throne, supplied with an army to that effect.

On his travels, in Caesarea he reunited with his sister and met Gregory, who quickly earned his trust and became his right-hand man in the battle to reclaim Armenia.

It was only once that was all settled, in AD 287, when he was the new king of the Armenian kingdom, that Tiridates learned two shocking truths about Gregory: that he was the son of the man who had assassinated his father and that he was a secret Christian.

Furious, Tiridates had Gregory thrown into Khor Virap for life.

What the king did not find out was that his sister was also a secret Christian, with deep sympathies for Gregory's plight.

Here is where official history and the embellishments of legend mix and match. Khosrovidukht, moved by her faith and deep pity for Gregory, supposedly visited him every day in secret to toss food down into the abyss where he was kept. She never quite knew if it reached him, never quite knew if he was alive.

That she did this is not too difficult to picture if you go to the site now.

But of course, now, there is a stepladder taking you through the narrow crevasse to the bottom, and all of it is carefully lit for you to see.

At any rate, lore has it that over the following decade, Tiridates slowly began to lose his wit. This reached its zenith when a group of virgin nuns visited Armenia and the king fell madly in love with one of them, Hripsime.

With his advances rebuffed, he grew furious (guess it was a bit of a theme with him) and had all of the nuns tortured and killed. Ancient texts then describe him becoming like a wild animal, fleeing into the woodlands, incurable.

In AD 301, Khosrovidukht had a dream in which she saw that Gregory was still alive, and the only person capable of healing Tiridates, by converting him to Christianity.

She convinced a group of noblemen to go down into the pit and verify the prisoner's state. Once they found him, they moved him out, cleaned and bathed him, then brought him in front of the mad king.

Walk into a number of Armenian churches and you can see a painted fresco of what happened next: Gregory laid his hands on Tiridates's forehead, and the monarch was healed at his touch.

So awed was Tiridates by all this that he was then supposedly convinced to completely abandon Zoroastrianism, the Armenians' religion back then, and embrace Christianity.

There are more practical explanations, of course. Those visiting nuns? They were from Rome, slowly but surely turning toward Christianity as an official religion. It is likely Tiridates and his court saw this coming and wanted to be not only in lockstep with the big, powerful empire but also ahead of the curve.

History does not make it clear exactly how repentant Tiridates was for all of his actions, but he did let Gregory lead the charge on converting the nation. Visit the Vatican today and you can see a nearly eighteen-foot-high statue of Saint Gregory on the grounds.

As for the women Tiridates had slaughtered, a monastery was named after Hripsime in Armenia in the seventh century, and another was named after Gayane, the leader of the nuns, again in that same era. But that was hundreds of years after the king was alive, clearly a decision he had no hand in at all.

Having read this story now, can you not just hear the *Gladiator*-esque Lisa Gerrard and Hans Zimmer musical score accompanying a similarly sweeping swords-and-sandals Hollywood epic dramatizing these events?

Why is it the only thing most people think about when they hear the name Armenia (if they've heard it before) has to be the genocide? Why can't there be any room for discourse about this other tumultuous period of history? Or, really, any time in the three millennia Armenians have existed?

Of course, it's almost impossible to avoid reflecting on the G-word when you visit the chapel built around Saint Gregory's prison pit.

Right across a yellow field, clear as day when it's bright and summery, on the other side of the border, rises Ararat.

1997.

I'm thirteen.

It's been a troubling few months. My maternal grandmother, Anna, is nearing death.

She had stayed with various members of the family, including us, until she absolutely required hospitalization. We try to visit her as often as possible, and she remains lucid until the end, always recognizing us.

I feel bad for her neighbor in the hospital room, another older woman whose memory has clearly begun to fade. She often speaks to me when my mother and I visit grandma and occasionally appears to mistake me for one of her own family members.

Sometimes she calls me Nick, and I can only imagine that's because she misreads the letters on the Nike jacket I occasionally wear.

One day, she's just not there when we visit. I don't have the heart to ask a nurse what happened.

A few more weeks pass.

My parents return from a visit I had not accompanied them on. It must have been during a weekend, because as I recall it, it is in the middle of the day and I am home.

They look at me and say they have bad news.

Grandma's passed away.

I'm hit with a certain numbness, then start crying.

Anna was not my first grandparent who died. I had never met her husband, Vahram, who was gone long before I was born.

My paternal grandmother, Maritsa, died when I was so young my parents could not explain the concept to me.

But Anna's death was the first to hit me at an age when I could really understand what it means.

She had bounced me on her knees when I was a child.

My siblings and I had at first despaired, then laughed when she had ruined our knock-off Atari console by wiping it with a wet cloth to get rid of the dust amassing on it.

She had left for America, another aunt's house, when we were still in Beirut, but then we had been delighted to catch up with her when she came to Canada, around the same time we moved there.

She traveled between the two North American countries for the next few years, to see all her children and grandchildren that she could.

Imagine fleeing the planned annihilation of your people, then Lebanon, torn by war, then spending the last years of your eight decades and change flitting between two Western nations so different from what you have known your whole life simply because your kids and their families did not all end up at the same place (to say nothing of the branch that went to the other end of the world, Australia).

That's what being a diaspora Armenian meant to Anna.

And losing her was thus not just losing a grandmother; it was losing one of the last two direct ancestors who survived the genocide, against all odds.

The very last, my dad's father, Armen, would pass away two years later, back in Beirut, which he never left.

Grandmother's funeral is at Sourp Hagop, the church adjacent to my school.

It is in the middle of a weekday. Though the two buildings are a five-minute walk from each other, my principal is nervous about my crossing the street. He drives me over, where I join my family.

I glumly listen to the words of the priest eulogizing her.

Above us are Tiridates and Saint Gregory, watching over everything from their painted fresco.

2018.

As various families at Alberta's Armenian Festival eat and drink, music continues to blare through the sound system, and speakers attempt to entertain the guests with droll anecdotes or singing.

My friend M takes videos and posts them live to Facebook.

It's not exactly the most remarkable event in the world. Which of course has hardly stopped anyone before from throwing live video on social media feeds.

But we're obsessed, aren't we?

We want to, we need to, show the world we've survived so much and can come together and celebrate this, even if it's as small a venue as some fifty people gathering in a no-name community center in what is only the thirty-first most populous city in Canada.

2007.

Plenty of trepidation and excitement in the air as we prepare for my sister's wedding.

All those families and their branches, scattered by the genocide and the war to all the winds?

Most of them are in Canada for the occasion.

I lose track of the number of times I drive to the airport to pick up relatives. Aunts from Beirut and Paris. Cousins from Lyon and Los Angeles. Some just drive along the highway from Toronto. One of the later arrivals is a cousin from America and his family. I've known him since the Beirut days, but they had moved to Paris and then California.

Unfortunately, even though they make it right on time for the wedding, their luggage does not.

In a panic, I take him and his son to a clothing store where I was formerly employed and luckily still know most of the staff.

We engage in a friendly haggle and barter about prices and tailoring and manage to get them suited up for the ceremony. At the register, a cashier looks me up and down; I'm all dressed up in a tuxedo already. "You're not the groom?" she asks.

"No," I say.

"When's the wedding?"

"In a few hours," I let out, mildly panicked.

My cousin would later make a joke about the connections I called on to get them ready. "It's like being back in Bourj Hammoud," he would say, referring to the primarily Armenian neighborhood in Beirut where seemingly everyone knows each other.

2000.

I'm sixteen, in grade 10.

Just about old enough now that I've started vocalizing thoughts about wanting to make a living out of writing or journalism.

It's not exactly a popular vocation among ethnic Armenians.

Now don't get me wrong. Statues immortalizing our writers are all over Armenia, villages and small cities named after them as well.

Growing up, in school we're made to learn the names, biographical details, and works of the Armenian literary canon, but because of the G-word, because so many diaspora families started from scratch after the events of 1915, and in some cases again after moving farther west from tensions and conflict in the Middle East, the financial precarities of a career in arts or communications are particularly frowned upon.

At one point, I tell a school official I am leaning toward a higher education studying communications.

"Oh, but don't you need to be a good writer for that?" they answer with a wink and a smile.

I'm still unsure if the implication was that the school was incapable of shaping me for it, or if it had been, that my skills were wanting.

Still, with the realization that this is the path I am looking forward to, I also begin to pay increasing attention to the world of politics, encouraged by my parents.

One night, my mother and I attend the Armenian community center to take in a speech from a visiting politician.

They speak mostly French but open up the remarks with a "parev," or "hello" in Armenian.

Some in the audience laugh.

I cringe.

I'm a little young and naive to know that the speaker had engaged a writer to carefully craft that ethnic-friendly greeting and asked them to rehearse it before deploying it to the rapt applause of potential voters, but my gut screams that it is insincere, nevertheless.

The real cringe, though, comes later.

When the speaker empathizes with genocide survivors by comparing the mass killings to language frictions in Quebec between francophones and anglophones.

See, we struggle not to define ourselves by it to the world, but at times it's all the world wants to define us by, anyway.

2018.

Again, in the midst of nearly total strangers, someone picks me out as an acquaintance and approaches me at the festival. I'm embarrassed to admit it takes me a few minutes to catch on to him and see he's correct.

He's a friend of my brother whom I had met around a decade before at the airport in Montreal.

He and his family had moved from Yerevan, and my brother had needed me to pick them up and drive them to their new apartment.

We had then lost touch.

Turns out he's since moved to Calgary.

We joke about the weather and topographical similarities between Alberta and Armenia. Someone who gets it, far more than me, frankly.

IT'S 2015.

The third time I'm visiting Armenia. On this occasion it's with family and friends.

In a handful of days my brother and his fiancée are getting married. They've chosen to do it here, in a three-hundred-year-old church. They'll be exchanging vows in a building that's practically been around since Europeans came to Canada, give or take a few decades.

Again, family is reunited from all over the world.

It's also the one hundredth anniversary of the genocide. But I've somehow managed to avoid thinking about that for most of the trip.

My brother and I are visiting one of our few relatives who lives in Yerevan.

We sit down in her leafy, cool backyard.

Turns out it's also a haunt for a couple of adorable neighborhood stray kittens as well as a group of teenagers who enjoy our cousin's company.

As we banter, some of the youth explain that they're about to hit adulthood. This also means their mandatory military service is coming up.

That's two years in Armenia.

It could very well include getting placed along the Turkish-Armenian border.

Or the Azerbaijani-Armenian border, with its fatal clashes from a never-resolved territorial conflict of the early 1990s over Nagorno-Karabakh, or the Republic of Artsakh, as Armenians call it.

These teens who have barely lived could die in the next year.

As much as our families have had to endure a reset and restart in foreign lands, being a member of the diaspora also means the privilege of awareness on these issues, but from a safe distance, at least in times of peace.

IT'S 2012.

Reversing my ancestors' century-old journey of forced exile, I enter Turkey.

They had left in secret, smuggled out to escape the genocide.

There's not much that's secret about how I'm entering. My name, pretty obviously Armenian, is fully on display on my passport when I present myself at the airport in Istanbul.

There is no unpleasantness whatsoever with security, who simply let me buy a tourist visa and allow me in.

Istanbul is one of the foremost tourist attractions in the world, and I spend around forty-eight hours taking it in while meeting with some members of the Armenian community.

At the risk of generalizing, I'll say that unlike most Armenians who live outside of Armenia, those in Turkey may not necessarily feel as if they're part of a diaspora.

After all, many have not been exiled from their homeland. Istanbul was one of the few places spared the worst excesses of the genocide.

Farther east, in what Armenian Genocide recognition protesters often refer to as "western Armenia," there are no real communities to speak of, just scattered pockets of Armenians, often living with changed names, infrequently broadcasting their ethnicity.

You won't find many Facebook videos posted in those parts, but they, too, feel at home.

While dropping by the Turkish-Armenian biweekly newspaper *Agos*, I meet a young man who does not speak Armenian but is fluent in Turkish.

I find it shocking, but it is completely normal, at least from a utilitarian perspective.

Our mother tongue does not have much use in Turkey.

In fact, once I'm out farther east, in Kharpert, I worry about speaking Armenian too loud with my translator. The latter laughs it off. They point out that the language is so unfamiliar around here that we may as well be speaking English.

This is a part of the world that Armenians had lived in for thousands of years. Their voices are now so silenced the hard "r"s and "kh"s and slower rhythms are indistinguishable from the lingua franca of much of the world.

I am reminded of what an English teacher once jokingly said years ago in high school: that it is the language of storytelling, simply because it is so easy to learn.

How ironic that here it's the language of story erasure, too.

2018.

A bright evening falls on Armenian Day, bringing the event to a close.

Most of us have moved outside to a field next to the community center. Children are running around. The music is now on outdoor loudspeakers, but there are no neighbors nearby or anywhere to be seen. There is some improvised circle dancing going on, and, obviously, someone's brought an Armenian flag. I watch my brother's friend wave it around, setting sun beams illuminating the red, blue, and orange lines.

I'm still not a big fan of overt displays of patriotism, but it's been so long since I've seen the tricolor fly freely that I do not mind at all.

Վերջ

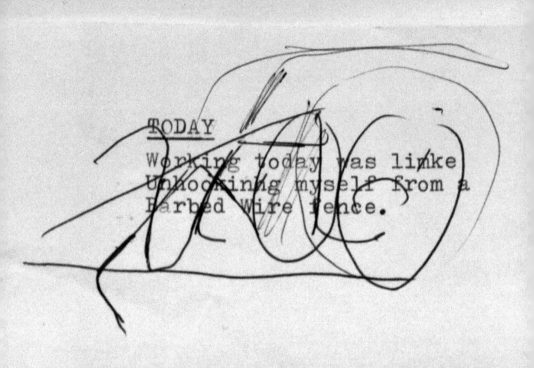

TODAY

Working today was linke
Unhocking myself from a
Barbed Wire fence.

The Story of My Body

HRAG VARTANIAN

I AM UNCOMFORTABLE IN MY BODY.—JANUARY 8, 2003

WHAT YOU'RE ABOUT TO READ was fished out of a memory hole I dug when I handed a US Homeland Security agent in Toronto's Pearson Airport a little slip of paper that I had guarded with my life for as long as I was in the surveillance program, knowing if I lost it, it would be a hassle, perhaps even impossible, to wrestle a replacement from a bureaucracy that would rather erase me than remember my past.

I've always had anxiety. A feeling that sticks to my bones, heightened at borders, particularly international ones, often resulting in me fighting with loved ones during preparations, enacting the hurt I could never express to border agents, engaged in a pantomime of anger, imagining I might not see them again.

This is my story of Armenian America, a parable of belonging that sprung out of the imagination of people with no place to go, who found shelter with those who saw us as children with so much to learn.

To live in America you need to forget. Not only about what came before but also regarding what or who will supplant you next. I can't forget, as these stories are in my bones; they radiate from my head and warm my thighs but chill my extremities until sometimes they feel separated.

I'm not sure which part of my body this story lives in. Is it my fingertips, which have been scanned so many times that they don't retain the memory of how many, where, or who? Perhaps it's my ears, which listen to the world around me, editing out the worst parts so I can function in my day without the soundtrack of sadness that keeps me from living in the present. Is it in my eyes? They've gone blank so many times, lingering on the sterile walls, nondescript corridors, sometimes spotting the CCTV and other times imagining them gone, if only to calm my nerves and feel powerful during the most vulnerable times.

In these liminal nonspaces, passages push into blank plains, seemingly waiting to be filled by bodies for short periods of time, then squeezed through, beyond here, to somewhere, far away, if only in time. Bodies that are separated, broken apart, and reconfigured, categorized into the needs of empire and then drowned in the macaronic aurality that adapts to such pain and discombobulation.

Our bodies are maps of imperial geography, topographies of nowhere and everywhere, roads and rivers that snake through history, sometimes doubling back, crossing bridges, stranded on gorges, cliffs, and canyons. Each line recording our past journeys through layers of skin, bumpy roads of folded epidermis that contain multitudes, packed in so tightly that they drag and droop, revealing the heavy weight they carry within. My body tells me to remember, even when those who love me forget.

WHEN I WAS APPROXIMATELY SIX, I was being sexually abused by my downstairs neighbor. He was a short Brazilian man married to a taller woman, and they had two children, one of whom I was enamored with because he was a teen with small muscles that poked out from his lean arms. I would often ask him to flex as I fantasized about being around him, slowly realizing I was most certainly gay.

My first childhood crush was on Mighty Mouse, that cartoon figure whose muscles bulged all over, but this early teen was the first real human being I added to my burgeoning sex fantasies.

I would go downstairs to play with him, even though that amounted to me doing nothing but standing about. Eventually, his father would be around us. I don't remember when he started raping me, but he did. And he would offer me ice cream to eat before he used me. I normally eat very fast, but with ice cream I consume it very slowly, often being the last to finish in a group of friends. I learned to take my time as a way to delay the inevitable.

He would eventually bring in others, some of whom paid him to use me. One of the grisliest incidents was in the backseat of an abandoned Volkswagen bug in the parking lot behind our building on Lawrence Avenue West. The man, who I don't remember well except that his body was hairy, spoke almost exclusively Brazilian Portuguese, but by then I had started to understand words and phrases, as I was at the age when children absorbed languages like a sponge. The man he was speaking to looked at me with confusion. "He's from Syria," my primary abuser said. "Don't worry," he continued, "he's Muslim, not Christian." "Christian," I screamed in Portuguese, simply mimicking the sounds like he had said them, knowing what it meant even if imperfectly, and not realizing what was happening to me. He looked perplexed and said some things to the other man to quell doubts. It wouldn't stop them from raping me anyway.

AROUND THE AGE OF SEVEN OR EIGHT, my mom enrolled me in an Armenian Canadian Boy Scout troop at our city's Armenian General Benevolent Union (AGBU), a philanthropic organization my mother had felt a sense of belonging to since her own childhood in Aleppo. As a Cub Scout, I learned to camp, which meant igniting fires from birch bark and tying knots with enough speed that the other scouts would joke I was a knotty boy.

Once, we attended a Canadian national scouting jamboree where all the scouts gathered from across the country to feel camaraderie and compete. There was another Armenian scout troop there, this one from the other (as we called it), or Tashnag, side, our term for the nationalist Armenian political party that dominates many aspects of life in the Armenian diaspora, and they wouldn't interact with us because we were considered the կորուսած (lost or assimilated) side. We didn't speak Armenian as well and felt more at ease in odar culture than they did. They often spoke English or French with a slight accent, particularly if they were from Montreal. They ignored us mostly, so we kept to ourselves and they listened to Armenian music at gatherings while we often sang old English-language Scouting songs, none of which I remember any more.

During an evening when we were free to wander, I was hanging out with my friend Ed, an awkward, pale, blond kid who acted differently than everyone else, and his inadvertent uniqueness somehow felt reassuring. It's rare among Armenians to actually be blond, and not the chestnut hair that often passed for it. I liked to hide behind his social awkwardness, as it allowed me to hide while mirroring my own discomfort in the world. We were alike, even if my disconnect with everything around me was buried deeper inside.

We met a group of WASPy kids from another troop one night. One of the kids looked at us as if to examine our physiognomy, which is not a word I would've known at the time, but one that in retrospect describes the scene's weird scrutiny.

"Where are you from?" one asked. "Rexdale," I offered, though I don't remember if I anticipated the follow-up "No, really," at the time.

"I'm from Syria, and he's from Egypt," I said. That seemed like the wrong thing to say, as I could feel the other group of boys well up with emotions, even if I couldn't recognize what they were. They whispered to themselves and then started. "Sand N*****s!" they screamed as they pointed. The words lingered in the air and in my brain decades later, even if it feels shrouded in a mist that soon appeared all around the memory, like a protective foam to shelter me from the lick of flames.

We went back to our campsite, and our leader, who was also my dentist, realized what had happened and left to go talk about it with his fellow scout leader. I overheard what they said, as our leader told them we were not Muslim, but Christian, and we were subjected to genocide by Muslims. I saw him performing the Islamophobia many West Asian Christians turn to in North America to ingratiate themselves to white Christians. It wasn't the last time I'd encounter this performative Islamophobia. That evening I shut my eyes tighter than most nights in an attempt to mentally purge the whole thing from my mind.

WHEN I WAS AT THE UNIVERSITY OF TORONTO studying art history, I thought I lived a charmed life. Removed from the daily stress I felt in Rexdale, living in the Annex felt like the life I dreamed about in my comic book–plastered, cheap-wood-paneled basement bedroom. Walking on the streets of a city filled with other exiles and drifters like me, I felt safer than where I grew up, which I assumed for a long time was the same thing as feeling safe.

My walk through campus usually involved a sylvan passage along Spadina Avenue, one of my favorite thoroughfares because it encompassed the city's manic energy and multicultural pastiche from beginning to end. My classes were almost always in Sidney Smith Hall, a modernist slab of a building that reminded me of the structures I saw in 1985, when my parents sent me to Soviet Armenia for summer camp.

I used to arrive and take the elevator up just before my class started. There were few inviting spaces in the complex to linger and meet others, so the elevator became one place you could encounter other students in your department. One day, I went up with an older white woman who was looking at me with a particular, uncomfortable interest.

Later that day, I heard through the department secretary that someone was thinking of filing a complaint because they felt unsafe with me in the elevator. "Why?" I asked. "You were wearing a terrorist scarf," she said.

That scarf was a black and white keffiyeh, which is a traditional Palestinian garment. It was the early 1990s, and the first Intifada had just ended, offering the dispossessed people of Palestine a deal that would mount the misery, rather than assuage it.

She was Jewish Canadian with a connection to Israel, though what the exact connection was I have no idea, even if I remember it being mentioned, and she heard that I was born in Syria, which fired up her fears. It was clear the department administrator, Elsa, who had known me for a few years at that point, was confused by this irrational response. The woman didn't calm down when she was told I was Armenian, since many Torontonians still remembered the threat a few years before when the Armenian Secret Army for the Liberation of Our Homeland threatened to blow up the city's subway system.

Eventually, Elsa would tell her I'm gay, offering up that point without first asking me, during a time when it still felt dangerous for people to openly know. Even though I wore bright metal pride rings on a chain around my neck, I always thought I could hide them away in precarious situations, particularly on subways or buses.

At that time, AIDS raged around me, and my generation learned to fear our bodies in ways the generation before us never did. Sex wasn't our salvation but a minefield. Telling someone you were gay could push them away, like the young Jamaican Canadian woman in my high school who aspired to be the new Oprah Winfrey—her words, not mine—and stuck to me throughout high school until she realized I was gay and said, "That's disgusting." A few years later, I ran into her at a downtown pharmacy and she chided me for looking sick. She meant from AIDS, because I had shed eighty pounds from my teen years, when I was quite obese. She wasn't the only one to remark on my weight loss that way.

"He's gay," Elsa told the elevator bigot. That seemed to work, and the next time I saw her she smiled the way people often do when they're trying to comfort you during an illness. She even mouthed "Hi" when she saw me, and the anger inside me was so intense that it built tombs deep in my chest, amid a brittle cavity of hurt. I could feel myself digging a plot to bury this memory too. It would take me decades to understand why I carried a cemetery inside of me, where memories that were long inanimate and robbed of life were placed to decompose while feeling largely inaccessible, even to me.

IN THE LATE 1990S, when I lived in Beirut, my aunt would warn me that she was scared for my safety. "Why?" I asked. "You're too light," she said in her most serious Armenian, using the word "բաց" meaning "open" or "uncovered," but also "lighter skinned." "I'm scared people are going to think you're Israeli."

I took her caution seriously because she lived through patches of the Lebanese civil war, including the time around the Israeli invasion of 1982. One of the most curious stories she shared from that period was of the female Israeli soldiers who would shower in a rather public back alley, which shocked the conservative religious types who dotted the area, as they found it vulgar.

BEING ARMENIAN has felt like a heavy burden, and more so at borders, where the lines that transverse the world, dividing us into imaginary teams, also disrupt our families, severing parts for decades—or forever—into fantastic and complicated schemes that rip apart and reconstruct our more intimate lives into something unrecognizable. Those borders transverse our bodies as well.

I remember when the kids in school would routinely wonder where my hair came from with its tight black curls, poking up from my light-colored body into what they'd call an Afro, thinking that would discourage me from growing it.

When the teasing got too bad and the names cut deeper and deeper to the point I couldn't feel their sting anymore, I learned to control my locks with cheap hair gel bought in pails at the dollar store. It would stiffen my unruly appendages, like quills, and defang the sting and my pride, turning it into a shadow so that the other kids and adults would simply look at me with pity, unsettled by my mane. This felt safer, as it made others feel superior and discouraged violence.

My dad cut his hair so regularly I don't think I ever saw his curls until he had resigned himself to the old age home he picked for himself. In that place, on the edge of Toronto, he sat in his room looking onto a highway and later a garden courtyard that would grow, as his curls sprouted for the first time in decades. I imagined Claude Monet's atmospheric effects blending with moody candor, like my father, like the seascape that hung on his wall. That cheap painting, he proudly told me, cost him fifty dollars at a flea market, which he thought was a lot. He sat in his favorite cushy chair by the window, regardless of the time of day, bathing in the outdoor light, imagining his summer-kissed olive skin somewhere else, though he never said where. He had resigned himself to a quiet life tending to his weeds without ever pulling them out completely.

THE PART OF THE STORY that most Americans just can't believe about the first so-called Muslim registry is that it actually existed. I rarely have this same problem with non-Americans, who are always less surprised when I tell them about the registry, called by its bureaucratic name, the National Security Entry-Exit Registration System (NSEERS). They've heard similar things before, though mostly when enforced by other governments or during different eras.

I've been shy about telling the story of the registry to many people because most ask too many personal questions. They try to rip my words apart like an experiment to test my reliability, often looking for details that don't feel right to them. I get tired of trying to explain what happened, why they may not have heard about it, and being confronted with insinuations that I may have done something wrong. At first, they're perplexed at the fact that over eighty thousand men could be forced to register with little pushback or notice in the press. They don't get how over thirteen thousand of us were placed into deportation hearings without protesters chaining themselves to doors or rushing to airports or government offices with placards in hand. They act as if the inability of the news to reach them was the root of the problem, as if it was a problem of circulation rather than blindness.

When I tell people I wasn't allowed to use LaGuardia Airport and numerous other points of entry (a beautifully bureaucratic term) to travel to Canada or Mexico, that's usually what gets their attention. It's at that moment people realize this was very serious because, I assume, most think of a registry as a paper annoyance—which it also was—but their imaginations don't allow them to grasp where those documents were collected and sent, and why.

Then I tell them I had to arrive at least three hours before each trip out of the country and go through a special immigration office, where I was fingerprinted and photographed, then asked a slew of questions by an immigration officer who was constantly trying to classify and explain me away.

After I returned from my journey, I had to spend a whole day at the INS office near City Hall, a bleak and inscrutable building. An immigration lawyer taught me a trick to bypass the immigration line that would form out front on the sidewalk, even in the snow and cold. She told me I could dress up in a suit, which I rarely did, and downplay any hint of an accent while conjuring up the confidence to pass through a side door, explaining that I was venturing up to the social security office. It worked: once you were in the building, no one monitored which office you were going to, even in a building that served as a hub of surveillance.

I registered in the fall of 2002. I was combing over press reports for work, and one day I remember fixating on a story in a California newspaper that profiled an Iranian Canadian who was forced to be part of this new surveillance program. It mentioned the man was born in Iran and moved to Canada at a young age. I stopped. It mentioned the first wave of aliens, all men, that had to register, and it read, "Group 1: Iran, Iraq, Libya, Sudan or Syria."

The year before, I had watched the Twin Towers burn and collapse from my rooftop in Bushwick, Brooklyn, and I sunk into an all-encompassing depression like half the city shortly thereafter. By mid-2002 the drumbeats of war were loud and deafening. I can't even remember the date I registered. It's a bit of a blur, but yes, I also can't forget it.

The day I arrived at the blank-looking INS building I remember in parts. It felt as claustrophobic as driving through a heavy rainstorm with the windshield wipers, only offering glimpses of what lay ahead. I wish I could say I let it wash over me, but it was a heavy rain that seemed to pound the car. I didn't dare open the door.

I was with my lawyer, named Rakhi, pronounced Rocky, "as in Rocky Balboa," she told me the first time we met. She was aggressive: not simply assertive but a fighter. She told me her husband normally doesn't like it when she goes to the immigration building because he fears she may never come back out. "He thinks I'll get deported," she explained, which was a very awkward thing to say to someone in my situation, but her honesty felt reassuring in the moment.

Rakhi watched me as she steeled her nerves in the overcrowded waiting room. She realized how uneasy I looked at one point and stopped speaking to me for a while as I collected my thoughts and mentally traveled elsewhere. One man told me he thought Rakhi and I were married, which made me laugh as she instantly corrected him.

I naively asked Rahki what I should and should not say to the agent. She quickly stopped me and pointed out that there were most certainly listening devices all around and reminded me that I could be detained. There was little any lawyer could do, particularly because I was an impermanent resident alien. That feeling of helplessness never went away.

The room itself was filled almost exclusively with men. I pegged the man who sat across from me as a Maronite or Assyrian with his black shirt and leather jacket punctuated by a large gold Latin cross. Looking around the room I saw Hasidic Jews, other Christians dangling crosses like talismans against bureaucratic evil, an unshaven man in a galabieh under a thick coat, a Kurd with worry beads, and a friendly Coptic man who spoke broken English and tried unsuccessfully to get free legal advice from Rakhi. There were light-skinned people, dark-skinned people, but most of us were somewhere in the middle. It was a diverse crowd that roughly approximated the city with its myriad of types, but part of me felt like I was in a casting room for *Aladdin* or *Lawrence of Arabia*, as we were all about to act out someone else's fantasy of who we should be.

When I was a teen, I asked my dad if I could get a Syrian passport. He refused. "Nothing good will come of that place," he would insist in his shrill, emotional voice that disrupted his attempts to seem stoic so that his traumas didn't peek through.

The day I registered, part of me collapsed. The silence around me felt dangerous, and it followed me home.

My neighbors, Amy and Jae, knew what was going on, but they seemed removed emotionally, perhaps perplexed. They never saw my struggle on a daily basis and the emotional weeds that I would pull out from the most unlikely places. I'm not sure how we decided to create a secret sign among ourselves, but we eventually did.

If I was ever contacted by the authorities, or if I suspected anything off, perhaps a constantly clicking call, arriving home to see things out of place, or a knock from someone who seemed strange and disconcerting, we would have a sign that would alert Amy, though we never figured out what we'd do next.

If I sensed anything wrong, Amy and I agreed, one of us would take an ice cube in our right hand, look straight into the other person's eyes and place it in their right hand. It was sufficiently strange to cause alarm, we must've thought, but not odd enough to stir suspicion.

ON THE DAY OF 9/11, I saw the second plane go into the Twin Towers after my radio channel was disrupted. I somehow knew to rush to the roof to figure out why, before going downstairs and waking all my neighbors up, telling them they had to see this. I rushed back to see the first building collapse. As we stood there in disbelief, I made a tasteless joke, the kind you do to pat down the horror you don't want to feel, and the morose, traumatized Middle Easterner in me wanted to dismiss this as something that felt so much smaller than what my family endured. I went downstairs to see the second tower disintegrate live on a television screen. I almost couldn't believe it was real, but it also felt more real than anything else had for a while.

I was the only person in the whole loft building to receive a phone call on my cell soon after. No one else's mobile phone worked for hours. Just mine, and the call was from Carmen in Beirut who called to see if I was all right. It was the first time I heard clicking on my phone while I talked to someone, but not the last. It wasn't until later that afternoon that our phones started to work again and I could call my parents in Toronto or friends around the world.

After a few hours of waiting around, staring at my neighbor's potted plants and trying to figure out what had just happened, we heard that the hospitals needed blood donations, so we went over to Woodhull Hospital, which was nearby. After waiting for an hour, a nurse came out perplexed, and then said anyone with a tattoo couldn't donate blood. It was unclear why, and so half of us just left, including me.

ON AUGUST 8, 2003, I wrote:

> *My anger continues to well up. I'm unable to halt it and it is becoming increasingly difficult to put it in check. I worked out and it did little to focus my anger so it was no longer generalized but it is now concentrated. I have spoken to many of my friends and it did little except make me feel I have justification for my anger. I am drinking margaritas and smoking now and hoping that recording this rage will ease the anger itself into something more constructive. I called Dr. B. and I got her cell phone answering machine, I left a message (at roughly 10:30 p.m.) but she has not returned my call. I hope my anger does not consume me. I know it has something to do with the abuse, but I can't put my finger on it.*
>
> *For the first time in a while (almost the first time ever!!) I feel violent.*

IN 2002, a Syrian Canadian named Maher Arar passed through JFK on his way to Montreal from a vacation in Tunis. US authorities stopped him and rerouted him to Assad's Syria for torture and questioning.

Arar had moved to Canada, like me, when he was a kid. There was no logic for his detention, or his torture.

I refused to take a plane after that and even canceled my holiday plans to visit my family. In spring, when I eventually visited my parents in Toronto, I took a train, which meant I had to devote a whole day to travel each way, twelve plus hours through upstate New York, across Niagara Falls, up the Golden Horseshoe to the capital of Ontario. I knew there was almost no risk of deportation to Syria that way.

The journey there wasn't particularly eventful, even if I had to get a stamp from the US side before easily passing by Canadian customs by waving my Canadian passport. It was the return that scared me.

I took the Maple Leaf Express back to New York, which meant when we crossed the border I had to disembark accompanied by a border agent to a small immigration building surrounded by snow at the side of the tracks. I don't remember my interaction in the room, as I closed off my mind to the stares of my fellow passengers who never had to endure the humiliation of this immigration perp walk, and it delayed the train by at least an hour, though I think it was much more. They did my paperwork in a room that felt far smaller than it should've been. I walked back smirking, as if I was trying to convey that it was all a mistake.

After I sat down, a young woman in her twenties joined me. She reminded me of Anne O'Neill, who grew up next door to me. Anne's parents were Catholics from Northern Ireland who quickly became my surrogate parents. My years as Anne's best friend were formative and taught me so much about being in the world, even as her parents used to joke that I was an "Aye-rab." "You're from the Syrian Arab Republic," Mrs. O'Neill would tease me, "so you're an aye-rab." It confused me and stung, even though I didn't necessarily feel it was a threat at the time.

The woman who sat next to me clearly felt a jolt of attraction, or so it seemed. At the time, I was working out regularly, having taken up jogging, and partying even more frequently, ensuring I had an appropriate release from my working life in a Midtown office.

She asked me about my life, in a gentle way that didn't alert me to anything except a gesture of bored friendship, but it did eventually make me aware we were certainly past the comfort level of most conversations I had with strangers on trains or planes. We spoke about Beirut, and that was the first time I saw her lean in with interest, not the kind of exotic thrill others had demonstrated but a more focused attention that was my first sign that something was perhaps awry.

She asked me if I knew any communists. I told her about Lori, who was the only woman I had fooled around with because she was attracted to gay men, which I later realized meant she liked men she could dominate. When we tried to have sex, it went nowhere because I hated to be dominated, and I pushed back until we both grew cold and just moved in together.

Lori was an academic and a devout communist, and our friendship would disintegrate when both her parents were diagnosed with lung cancer a few months apart and then died soon after. She expected too much from me, a man in his early twenties who didn't even know himself. She wanted me to comfort her all the time, and she returned to our apartment expecting me to be her emotional caretaker through a crisis. I was uninterested. I told the story to my train companion, who seemed pleased with my words. She later asked if I read any Graham Greene, which I hadn't, associating him with a type of dusty old book that I never found refuge in.

At one point, she left her seat for a long time, returning a few hours later as if nothing had happened. "Do you know the man over there?" She pointed to a nervous Middle Eastern–looking man in the back, who strangely looked like a younger version of my dad. I recognized him as someone who also had to leave the train with me at the border. "No," I said, still unclear why she asked. Perhaps she saw us both leave the train together at the border and assumed we knew one another, I thought.

We continued our conversation, and I told her about my year in Beirut. I was so used to sharing this story that I slipped into automatic, but I'm unsure why. Eventually we finished talking for what felt like hours at a time. I kept imagining her as Anne, which put me at ease, even though she had none of my friend's innocence or warmth, and what we discussed felt transactional.

Near the end of our journey, she offered her phone number on a slip of paper, suggesting I call her if I wanted to hang out. She then clearly stated, "You probably already figured this out, but I am with the border and I think you would make a good immigrant. I'll make sure to put a note in your file."

I felt violated. I pretended nothing had happened.

She added that she had stepped away because immigration officials—I can't remember if we called it Homeland Security at that point—had jurisdiction only within one hundred miles of the border, which meant our whole journey, including New York City, was under their jurisdiction except for one patch in Upstate New York, which, she hazily explained, was still gray according to the courts.

I kept that slip of paper with me for years. I may have pasted it into a book but have forgotten where, as I often kept odd scraps of paper around even if I never clearly labeled them.

That fall, my close friend Scott passed away while volunteering in Namibia. He was encouraged by my own stint in Beirut, which made him realize he was far too rooted in one country and wanted to see the world. And while all his friends, including me, knew he had survived a house fire as a kid, we didn't realize it had damaged his heart to such a degree that he continued to face lifelong issues. He died in his thirties helping others after a few happy years in Vancouver as a programmer for a porn site. He would complain about that city on our phone calls but didn't want to go back to Toronto, and I had a feeling he secretly wanted to end up with me in New York.

I had no time to take a train to his funeral in Canada, so I chose to fly, finding the only somewhat affordable ticket out of Philadelphia. The night before I left, I had a one-night stand with a sensitive, tall, light-skinned, hairy man from Mexico City. Halfway through the night I panicked that I would miss my plane, knowing I'd have to take a train out of Penn Station at 6:00 a.m. I asked him to leave at 3:00 a.m. He looked defeated and sad. It wasn't about him but me, and I was afraid to be vulnerable with someone so quickly. I fucked him that night without enough lube, so we eventually gave up, as we were mostly wasted anyway and fell into each other's arms, looking for comfort. I barely slept that night, waking up every half hour afraid I would miss my flight.

The plane left at noon, but I had to arrive very early, as I had no idea where the NSEERS office was and they were often in unusual places.

The man inside the makeshift office, which was indeed in an odd location in the airport, seemed surprised to see me but angry at the same time. He looked like a white, middle-aged high school football player: pale, with the sheen of too many hard liquor drinks at the strip club with old friends.

When he realized why I was there, he turned grumpy, grabbing my papers while his colleague looked on slightly horrified at his change of face. I wasn't sure where his emotions began and my rights ended, but I knew there was a line in his mind.

I got on my flight and made it to Toronto for the funeral. I was picked up by Bruce, who was driving to the funeral that day in Grimsby, Ontario, where Scott hailed from.

Years before, Bruce had looked at me once and said, "I know you were sexually abused too." I hadn't yet known I was. I wouldn't know until eight years later, when I was in bed with a young, short, white Midwestern doctor with a hairy chest who lived up at the northern tip of Manhattan. Running my fingers through his chest surfaced a body memory that made me realize that what I thought were nightmares for so long were buried memories I had pushed away because they felt suffocating.

I gave a speech about Scott at the event, and it was perhaps too elaborate for the occasion, but I knew he would've liked that. I quoted Allen Ginsberg on Nina Simone, in a room evenly divided between multi-culti Toronto club kids and small-town white Ontarians who didn't understand any of my references. Their loss.

Scott's mom mentioned at one time during the event that when he told her there was someone he was thinking about in New York, she assumed it was a woman.

Bruce dropped me off at the airport after the funeral—at least that's how I remember that difficult day—and I headed back home. The whole terminal was empty, and I walked to the front of the line immediately. After the agent inspected my papers, he quickly shooed me off to an office that was largely obscured from the rest of the airport, and soon enough I was in front of a South Asian American NSEERS agent in record time. He looked me up and down, and waited a few minutes, tapping his disposable plastic pen on his lips.

It was during that trip I waited for over an hour—was it two or more?—in a stern-looking room, mostly by myself. Occasionally, the same man showed up to prod me with pointed questions that I have mostly forgotten. One of those questions asked about the makeup of my family, which was the first time someone had asked me about that. I didn't consider it strange at the time, even though I retain a shadowy recollection of it being posed.

This was before the age of smartphones, so I sat quietly with only a wristwatch to keep me busy. Mine had stylized Arabic on the face, which I hid under my sleeve so it wouldn't attract attention. Eventually, the agent returned with that little slip of paper I was told to guard with my life by everyone who handed it back to me. This man said I was out of NSEERS, and I was free to go.

He asked me if I wanted the slip of paper. "No, thanks," I said, even though I secretly wanted it, if only to prove it existed, that I existed in this system with passages to nowhere. I acted as if I wanted to prove to him, to them, one last time that I was unaffected by this. All of it. The daily unease that turned into rashes on the sweaty patches around my body, or the spot behind my ear I would scratch under my hair until it bled. I let him take that from me too. No other paper said NSEERS. I let it slip inside me to join the rocks in my stomach that formed a quarry of pain.

"I feel like Scott helped me, my friend who died, who I came up here for his funeral, I mean," I said.

"He didn't do it; I did," the agent insisted in a way that made me stop.

I got back to Brooklyn and called that Mexican guy to make another date and apologize. His roommate picked up and she seemed confused. "Oh, he seemed upset and left suddenly, back to Mexico City. I'd wondered why. He didn't say," she replied.

I never saw him again, and a decade later Bruce killed himself.

I DON'T HAVE many ruminations from those years, as the paranoia of surveillance wormed their way into my most quotidian activities and some days I experimented by figuring out new routes home, pretending—and sometimes wondering—if I was being followed.

At that time I had no television, a habit I picked up in college, which saved me from the daily barrage of media-induced anxiety that would've made my life unlivable. I regularly read a stack of magazines and newspapers from around the world, as well as articles I found through my work in a press office. I drowned my thoughts in drugs, alcohol, cigarettes, and exercise to varying degrees, allowing myself to float in the ambrosia of forgetfulness that dulled my suffering. I was both the healthiest I had ever been and the most on edge and sickly.

My body would eventually collapse in 2003, when I was hospitalized one last time before I was diagnosed with severe allergies to birch, tree nuts, and other things. I woke up at 7:00 a.m. in Woodhull Hospital after seeing two nurses in a slap fight the night before. I hailed a livery cab home. I felt like my body had rejected everything. It was the only thing I hadn't felt besieged by, until then.

I knew in that moment that I didn't want to be alone anymore.

IN 2015, I visited Israel/Palestine for the first time as part of a work trip. A US-based art nonprofit devoted to promoting Israeli artists reached out with the offer, and I took them up on it, thinking this would be an easy way to visit a place I had written papers about in my Crusader Art class in college. I took the course partly as an excuse to study Armenian art, the only way I could figure out to do that in U of T's art department, though I later found out I could do Armenian art in Islamic art classes, too, which was a better fit anyway.

The passport control agent at Ben Gurion Airport immediately sent me to a small waiting room with others. A Palestinian man, looking ten years older than me, joined me soon after. He sat across from me, while there were a few others on the far side of the room, mostly people who looked Southeast Asian or Arab. At one point, a nervous Black American sat beside me. He was clearly losing it, and then his shaky white wife joined him, and she looked absolutely terrified. "We didn't do anything," she offered out of nowhere as she sat down a few seats from me. "We didn't either," I said as I looked around the beige and metal roomette with walls that only went high enough to stop you from seeing out or others from looking in.

They left after only thirty minutes, and when they did, they acted like they were fleeing an infectious disease ward. I'm not sure why I felt there was an "us" so quickly with the people in the room, but these Americans felt like invaders.

Maybe it was after two hours (was it three?) that I was first called in. A middle-aged Israeli woman asked me questions in such a rote manner that I wasn't immediately sure if she was talking to me.

She asked about my family. But then she asked me the name of my grandfather. I knew which one she meant, but I didn't want to play along so quickly, as if I was OK and accustomed to this.

"Which one?" I asked.

"Father's," she said.

"I don't remember," and I didn't. I hadn't thought about his name in over a decade. I knew it when I was younger, but it slipped away most of the time into the shoebox full of slips of paper, old tapes, physical photos, and thumb drives, so I said, "I'm not sure, but I can call someone."

She didn't know what to do. She made me draw my family tree. She was clearly looking for Arabs, but she asked about the wrong parts. I couldn't believe I was doing this. It only went back to my grandparents because I know nothing about my great grandparents since only a few on my mom's side were able to escape the Armenian Genocide alive. There was no way I knew their names.

I went back outside to wait. I would go back in an hour later, I think—I can't remember anymore—for more questions with another agent in a different room.

While I was seated outside, I pulled out my laptop and logged into the Wi-Fi. The man across from me looked horrified, gesturing with his face that they were probably searching my laptop. I was so used to being under scrutiny that I expected my devices to be searched. For a long time, I wrote my inner thoughts on paper, never on a screen.

I smiled at this new amo seated a few meters away, and when I said it was fine, he resolved himself not to care anymore.

After I sat down, I posted a status update on a social media site. The invisibility of NSEERS had pushed me to be more public about my profile so that over a decade later I could tweet my way through customs, knowing there would be a trace. I'd constantly be reminded of the benefits of visibility: digital breadcrumbs so that someone could find you in case something went wrong.

In this second interrogation room, a man a few years older than me sat behind a desk. He looked like an Upper East Side hipster, and he asked me if I knew why I was there.

"I'm guessing it's my Lebanese or UAE visa? And the fact I'm born in Syria."

"Yes, the Lebanese, and, yes, Syria," he said. "Why were you in Lebanon?" he asked, referring to my visa from a few months before.

"To visit family."

"Who do you have there?"

"My husband's uncles."

"Your husband."

"Yes."

"Do the uncles have families? Are they married?"

"Yes, they're married."

"With kids?"

"No, they're married to one another. So, one is his mom's brother, and his partner."

"Is he Arab?"

"Yes. Maronite," knowing very well what was coming next and trying to appear cooperative. I couldn't honestly remember if Henri identified as Arab or not, but I didn't know what else to say. I certainly wasn't going to offer this man a free lesson in post-national identity and the fictions of Orientalism in this power dynamic.

"I hear Beirut is a beautiful city," he said. It confused me for a second.

"Yes, it's beautiful. One of my favorite cities in the world. You should visit."

He stopped to do some paper and computer work. I looked at him when he wasn't looking. He was confident, attractive, wearing pants that were just a little tight, perhaps something from a few pounds before that he stuffed himself into nowadays. He looked like he was on his way to an afternoon drink at a Tel Aviv cocktail bar and decided to stop in to do some paperwork. He asked me for my email, and I gave one of them away. He asked if I had Gmail and I said no. He asked if I had another phone for Lebanon or another chip. I said no. I had an iPhone and it was locked, but I didn't like the hassle, so I rarely used my phone when I went except out of necessity, like for maps and important messages.

He asked to look at my phone, but he wanted me to unlock it. I hesitated but I did it, and he looked at my contacts. I didn't keep an up-to-date address book anyway, I thought to myself. What he did ask for was the name of my close relatives in Syria, which I had to give, he said, if I wanted to enter Israel. I did, begrudgingly. He asked if I wanted to call them now. I said no. "Are you sure?"

He took down my husband's name and phone number too. I felt drained by the time I returned to the maddeningly bad waiting room. Someone came out with some water and a sandwich. My friend Nancy Kricorian, who has a long history of social justice activism, told me in the comments of one of my regular status updates that it was a good sign if you got a sandwich. I may have wondered why I was getting something like this at first, even questioning when it wasn't fully packaged, like on a plane, after it was handed to me, but I was anxious, and food often helped me push down that heavy load.

I had booked my room in an affordable hotel in East Jerusalem, and if I got in on time, I figured I could wander the Old City before things closed. I knew it wasn't possible anymore.

It was definitely past the five-hour mark when someone came over to tell me I was free to go. I already hated it here, or this part of it, anyway.

I got into a taxi in front of the terminal. I told him where I was going and he seemed scared. "Do you know it?" "No." He was reassured when I showed him a map, and we drove off. We started to talk, as his broken but clear English made it possible. He refused to go down one street because it was Sukkot, he said, and the Hasidic residents would stone his car. He said it in a dramatic way that reminded me of my dad. It was getting dark, and he told me he was a supporter of Benjamin Netanyahu, the right-wing Israeli politician. He then tried to find the hotel, and I realized he spoke some Arabic when he asked a local Palestinian for directions.

"You speak Arabic?"

"Yes, my parents are from Iraq."

"I was born in Syria, Aleppo."

"What are you doing here?"

"I'm here for work."

"You are allowed?"

I didn't know how to respond, or if I should, so I didn't. The reception at the airport made more sense, even if it didn't make me feel better, but tracked, measured, quantified. Though in retrospect I realized how incompetent the Israeli authorities seemed, I had recognized the same thing in NSEERS years before.

This taxi driver spoke Arabic with uncertainty, like he was going to be unveiled as an imposter. He had heavy brows, leathery skin, and the baritone of a person who smoked and drank regularly. No one he asked seemed to know where my hotel was. After he drove around erratically in what eventually felt like going in circles, he got frustrated and left me near a roundabout in a city I'd never been to before. Alone, but feeling less lonely than I had before, in the airport or the car, I knew it was possible to get lost here to find myself.

I was eager to jump out after I realized he was noticeably scared. He told me that after sundown it was dangerous for him to be in this neighborhood, maybe for me, too, he added. I didn't see any signs of danger, so I shrugged, but I'd seen how panicked he appeared and knew what it meant.

I thanked him half coldly, paid, and took my cheap broken luggage on a journey eight blocks away with my smartphone as a guide.

I slept for the next two days and spent most of it in my room, shaken. I didn't want to leave and I was pounding my anger into stones, using the all-you-can-eat buffet on the roof as fuel, until the calcified hurt sunk deep into my stomach. For years these all gathered on the grave of my wound, which felt bottomless. Later I learned how to turn this pain into pearls, to give form to the formless so its edges don't choke out all the light.

A TAXI DRIVER in Morocco was looking at me for a while in his rearview mirror as we drove toward Casablanca from Marrakech. I could tell he was trying to figure me out. He eventually built up the confidence to ask, "Where are you from?" "I'm originally from Aleppo, and Armenian, but I live in New York," I said. "Ah, he replied. I could tell you were Arab by your hair," he said. "I'm Berber."

WHEN I WAS YOUNGER, I would shed the world by trying to exist without leaving a trace. In cub scouts, I was taught that a good scout entered and left a campsite the exact way they found it. I adopted that philosophy, only to realize years later that it had been developed by British imperialists who never did any such thing, so it was all a lie.

Sometimes I dress in bright clothes, and I wonder whether it's an attempt to ensure I don't disappear. So my body isn't reduced to parts and sold into a system that destroys us when we resist.

I used to grow angry when I saw my husband, Veken, perplexed at my anger, maybe recognizing the problems with his own. It took me years to realize his response was numbness of another type, pushing away his feelings until he imagined himself a machine, acting out his own belonging in ways that others tolerated.

You, dear reader, may think the story is over. American stories often thrive on the celebration of conquest, reinvention, and rebirth, but this story just ends. The silence is your own, as you now carry this burden with me, knowing that it may never find a place to settle, rest, multiply; traveling the universe in search of a home that may have never existed.

Valley View

An Armenian Diasporic Account in Lieu of a Glendale Biennial Review

MASHINKA FIRUNTS HAKOPIAN

1

"No" was the only word my grandmother, Lida Khatchatrian, knew in English. She declined to learn any others. The only relation she wanted to the English language was one of radical unintelligibility. After immigrating at seventy, my grandmother launched a sixteen-year performance of linguistic refusal. It was staged for a private audience of émigré intimates. No recordings were made.

We relocated from Yerevan to Glendale in 1991, like so many. By 2017, approximately 40 percent of the city's residents were of Armenian descent, marking it the largest diasporic population of Armenians in the West. In Glendale, it was still possible to live in Armenian dialects. On East Acacia Avenue, we gathered with neighbors to hear the Soviet Socialist Republic collapsing at the end of a long-distance telephone call we could not afford.

I am telling you this because I recognize that there are no views outside of embodied viewers and historically contingent practices of looking.

When I was fifteen, we moved to a street in the Glendale foothills from which you could see the mountains. It was called Valley View.

2

The Pit Gallery opened in Glendale in 2014, and four years later it announced the launch of *Vision Valley: The Glendale Biennial*, slated for May 5, 2018. The exhibition would be curated by the Pit, an artist-run commercial gallery, and hosted at the Brand Library & Art Center, a publicly funded municipal space. I volunteered there as a teenager, enticed by the gleaming white architecture of the library building originally called the Miradero (the Overlook or Vantage Point).

Among the thirty-two, majority white artists selected for the *Glendale Biennial*, none were Armenian.

The Pit launched in Glendale amid a precipitous influx of finance capital and real estate development in the city, a period whose economic violence is obliquely hinted at in the widely used description; this was "the Boom." "Violence," as David Harvey puts it, "is required to build the new urban world on the wreckage of the old." In 2006, the Glendale City Council adopted the Downtown Specific Plan, offering developers incentives for large-scale building projects within municipal limits. Two years later, Caruso Affiliated opened the long-planned Americana at Brand, a $400 million luxury residential and retail complex. Its Tiffany & Co. and Tesla storefronts peer out onto impeccably manicured lawns, animated fountains, and audio kiosks piping Frank Sinatra into a lavish open-air "lifestyle center." When the Onyx Glendale Apartments finished construction in 2017, they were advertised as a testament to "Downtown Glendale's spectacular urban renaissance" and its "newly found sense of cutting-edge style, eclectic culture and bountiful energy." The complex offers one-bedroom lofts at $3,270 per month. One effect of redevelopment was a surge of new residents who wanted, as the Onyx invites, to "explore like a traveler. Enjoy like a Resident." Another was rendering working-class and immigrant communities a surplus population.

Against the backdrop of the city's "spectacular urban renaissance," the Pit announced the *Glendale Biennial* in 2018. The curatorial statement for *Vision Valley* described the show as follows:

- "a celebration of artists working in a specific community"
- "a nod to Glendale's long-standing artist community"
- "a dynamic multilogue between artists living or working in a specific geographical area" that
- "showcases the many coincidental visions at work in the valley known as Glendale."

Its title presents a set of fairly straightforward queries: Whose visions of the valley do we get to see? Whose are withheld? Who decides?

While *Vision Valley* includes no members of the Armenian community among its thirty-two contributors, it does include all three directors of the Pit, as well as its gallery associate.

Vision seems an ill-fitting rubric for an exhibition that insists on the invisibility of a vast diasporic population. Practices of looking, we know, are also practices of world-making embedded in fields of power. This is why, historically, the right to look was denied to the dispossessed. Avetik Isahakian, a poet and Armenian Revolutionary Federation activist, wrote in 1897, "be fearful of dark eyes."

There is another vision spotlighted in *Vision Valley*, that of American photographer Edward Weston, who established a studio in Glendale in 1910 and whose photographs are featured in the exhibition. His inclusion, the curators suggest, "enriches the exhibition with a significant bit of Glendale history." The nostalgic longing to glance back at the city's golden yesteryear poses a problem. In the first half of the twentieth century, Glendale was a "sundown town," with ordinances that prohibited people of color from being within municipal limits after dark. Glendale was also a national stronghold for white supremacists: a hub for the KKK in the 1920s (a decade after Weston's relocation) and home to the Western Division headquarters of the Nazi Party in the 1960s. While Weston indeed suffuses the exhibition with "a significant bit of Glendale history," it remains unclear whose history of Glendale his inclusion conjures. The curators never specify.

WHAT WESTON'S INCLUSION TACITLY SUGGESTS is that the region's cultural chronology is bookended by his 1910 arrival, on one end, and the founding of the Pit Gallery in 2014 on the other. In the temporal valley that separates these two discoveries of Glendale lies a century of diasporic cultural production. To posit Edward Weston as the punctual origin of artistic activity in the city is to unapologetically whitewash its historical narrative. It is to erase the practices of the Indigenous Tongva people, who preceded Weston's appearance by millennia, and those of the Armenian, Filipinx, Korean, and Latinx communities who have been living and working in the city in the one hundred years since. One Pit director recently spoke to the *Glendale News-Press* with the hauteur of someone who had just carried out a civilizing mission, benevolently importing culture to a newly occupied territory. He explained that the idea for the show had started as a joke, about "how people act so surprised that there's a contemporary art gallery in Glendale."

Glendale is host to at least five Armenian-owned or Armenian-inclusive art galleries. These include Tufenkian Fine Arts, Roslin Art Gallery, Mkrtchyan Art Gallery, Silvana Gallery, and Armenian Arts.

To perform this erasure in an exhibition that celebrates "artists working in a specific community" while also featuring a majority of white artists is a dazzling instance of what Aruna D'Souza calls whitewalling. "Whitewalling" refers to racialized exclusions that operate by "covering over that which we prefer to ignore or suppress; the idea of putting a wall around whiteness, of fencing it off, of defending it against incursions." Framing the *Glendale Biennial* through Weston's vision without acknowledging that vision's historical milieu suppresses the racialized violence of the city's past and enables the exclusion of its current diasporic residents.

When Edward Weston first visited Tropico, as the city of Glendale was then called, he described it with delight as a "little village." At the time of his arrival, the city was home to 155 acres of strawberry fields, farmed through the exploited labor of migrant workers from Mexico and China. Maybe this is also what the Pit and affiliated artists saw when they settled in Glendale in the last half decade. Perhaps when they established studio outposts en masse on San Fernando Road, they believed they were entering a rural idyll devoid of what appeared, to them, as official culture. Perhaps they thought they had stumbled upon a blank, pastoral canvas waiting to be injected with cultural content. Perhaps it did not seem germane to ask, to borrow from Tara J. Yosso, "*Whose* culture has capital?" Perhaps they were surprised to discover that there were already cultural producers here, some engaged in gallery work and others in the communal reproduction of social life.

Some of the thirty-two contributors neither live nor work in Glendale. Edward Weston neither lives nor works in Glendale because he has been deceased since 1958.

What Weston's inclusion also tacitly suggests is that the curators were more willing to feature a dead, white male artist in the exhibition than an Armenian one. This is perplexing considering the exhibition's one criterion is that contributors must be artists residing or working in the region today. Despite being dead for sixty-odd years, Weston is apparently more legible as a contemporary Glendalian artist than any Armenian artist now living in the city of Glendale.

I imagine telling my grandmother about this. I can guess at her one-word response: "No."

1

My mother, Sona Hakopian, was a linguist trained in Russian philology at the Academy of the Pedagogical Sciences of the USSR. In Glendale, she worked as a paralegal specializing in political asylum cases. For over twenty years, she advocated for Armenian asylum seekers who traveled along extended routes of dislocation, fleeing the Lebanese Civil War (1975–1990), the Iranian Revolution (1978–1979), the Iran-Iraq War (1980–1988), the dissolution of the Soviet Union (1991), the subsequent collapse of Armenia's economy (1992), and the Syrian Civil War (2011–present).

Theories circulate about why the diasporic community crystallized in Glendale. My mother would say it's because the valley views approximate the mountainous topographies of Armenia. The valley, as she said, visually softens the losses of territorial dispossession.

2 (A Selected Chronology of Recent Cultural Activity in Glendale, California)

Fifty-three days before the biennial opened, Glendale City Council voted to begin renaming a stretch of Maryland Avenue as "Artsakh Street." My mother maintained an office on that block for a decade, holding court in smart black suit dresses at Urartu Cafe, where she would meet clients to fill out political asylum applications over delicate cups of Armenian coffee. My mother is gone two years but still lives in Glendale, among the residents who may not otherwise be in the city but for those afternoons on Artsakh.

Twenty-two days before the biennial opened, the Glendale Tenants Union rallied with a coalition of renters in Los Angeles.

Eighteen days before the biennial opened, Glendale City Council voted to approve the construction of a 59,800-square-foot Armenian-American Museum downtown.

Eighteen and nine days before the biennial opened, two Armenian cultural workers contacted the Brand Art Center and the Pit curatorial team, respectively, to address the exhibition's lack of cultural and racial diversity. The second, artist Gilda Davidian, described the biennial as a "colonizing" enterprise. She asked for the exhibition's name to be changed or its scope to be broadened. The Pit explained that it never claimed to represent the diverse histories or cultures of Glendale and encouraged her to direct further queries to the Brand. Gilda called the Brand exhibitions supervisor, but her call was never returned.

Thirteen days before the biennial opened, five thousand marched in Glendale in solidarity with protesters in Yerevan, who were organizing against the decade-long rule of president and then–prime minister Serzh Sargsyan and Armenia's Republican Party. Their signs read, "The Armenian Diaspora of Los Angeles Stands with Armenia."

Twelve days before the biennial opened, residents gathered at Glendale City Hall to celebrate the success of Armenia's Velvet Revolution and the possibility of Armenian self-determination. Yerevanian grocery stores reported champagne shortages.

Eleven days before the biennial opened, tens of thousands gathered in Los Angeles to march for global recognition of the Armenian Genocide, for divestment from Turkey, for reparations and the repatriation of land, and for the one and a half million lost in 1915. They held signs that read "I Remember and I Demand."

Eight days before the biennial opened at the Brand Art Center, the same venue closed the show *Continuity and Rupture: An Armenian Family Odyssey*. The photography exhibition charted the violent dislocation of the Dildilian family from Ottoman Turkey during the genocide. The irony plainly speaks for itself: one show documented the attempted erasure of a population; the next enacted a symbolic erasure, excising the visual traces of that population's diasporic community.

1

The Armenian diaspora resists monolithic cohesion. It encompasses, instead, manifold cultural identifications and discrete migratory trajectories. Racialization operates differently across these varied communities. In 1909, the US government refused the naturalization petitions of four Armenians on the basis that they were not "free white persons." A court later ruled that the Armenians were "white by law" because they could be "readily adaptable to European standards." In other words, they could convincingly perform whiteness. Legal scholar John Tehranian calls this "white performance as a proxy for white racial belonging." As Tehranian notes, the juridical classification of whiteness doesn't immunize against the experience of racial injustice. In the realm of daily encounter, bodies marked as Middle Eastern remain vulnerable.

In Glendale, this dynamic often manifests in volatile community response to Armenian-American political participation, which ranges from xenophobic epithets to death threats. In 1999, after Rafi Manoukian's election to the city council, one resident dutifully attended the council's meetings every week to "tell Armenians to go back where they came from." In 2016, when Ardy Kassakhian ran for the Forty-Third District Assembly, his campaign headquarters were evacuated after a caller phoned to say, "You fucking Armenian scum. You're going to get your head flushed. . . . You are not safe in that office."

2 (A Selected Chronology of Recent Cultural Activity in Glendale, California, Continued)

Days before the biennial opened, the city requested that the curators change the exhibition title. Multiple community members had voiced concern about a Glendale biennial in a partially publicly funded space that omits 40 percent of Glendalians. "Glendale Biennial" was officially redacted from the title. All promotional materials and wall text for the exhibition were reprinted to reflect the change and read, simply, "Vision Valley." No public acknowledgment, announcement, or apology was made.

The Pit continues, today, to use #theglendalebiennial to tag its social media posts. It asserts its inalienable right to claim the city of Glendale over and against the protests of its residents.

Vision Valley, the curators contend, was never "an actual biennial." Rather, the term "biennial" was deployed in a tongue-in-cheek fashion, a droll commentary on the art field and its blue-chip exhibitions. If the *Glendale Biennial* is mere jest, it's a gag they are unwilling to relinquish, disregarding the city's and community's objections. If the *Glendale Biennial* is mere jest, it lampoons the art field's exclusionary mechanisms while unapologetically excluding 40 percent of the city's population. If the *Glendale Biennial* is mere jest, its comedic value lies in the suggestion that there could be an internationally legible cultural community in the formerly barren badlands of Glendale. The titles *New York Biennial* or *Paris Biennial* could not possibly conjure the same drollery. In other words, "Glendale Biennial" works as a joke only because the city's perceived cultural deficit is the butt of that joke.

It did not, perhaps, occur to the curators that Glendale might be more than a joke to the tens of thousands who escaped genocide, civil wars, the collapse of a republic, and extreme economic deprivation to assemble a community here.

To be clear, it is not merely the word "biennial" that is at issue. Its absence does not authorize gathering thirty-two artists in a publicly funded municipal space, purporting to represent a geographic region, and subsequently excluding nearly half of that region's population.

During the exhibition opening, two Armenian-American attendees approached the curators to inquire about the absence of Armenian artists. One, Ani Tatintsyan, is a filmmaker and artist who has lived in Glendale since 2001. The other, Araik Sinanyan, is a clinical researcher who recently graduated from Humboldt State University, where he founded the Armenian Student Association (ASA). They were told that the organizers didn't reach out to any specific communities but that all arts professionals in the area had been consulted. As with Gilda, they were encouraged to address further queries to representatives of the Brand Art Center.

This chronology attests to astonishing feats of selective vision. With unwavering conviction in the virtues of its exclusionary gaze, the exhibition proceeded apace.

One day after the exhibition opening, I received a note from a city representative writing on behalf of the mayor and Glendale City Council members. It stated that the Brand Art Center hoped that "in the future when they work with other curators, that the artistic representation be more inclusive."

Today, only two discussion posts appear on *Vision Valley*'s social media event page. One reads: "A biennial about art in Glendale with no Armenian artists? hm." The other, simply: "Armenian artists?"

1

When the Pit calls for an exhibition of "contemporary fine artists," it's impossible to miss echoes of "the fine art of gentrification." In an eponymous essay by Rosalyn Deutsche and Cara Gendel Ryan, the authors entreat the art field to recognize its role as a gentrifying agent, one that actively participates in "systematically destroying the material conditions for the survival" of neighborhoods and localities. This essay was written twenty-four years ago.

In 2017, as the Pit was conceiving of a biennial to celebrate a newly formed art community of recent transplants, city residents established the Glendale Tenants Union. The formation of the union responds to a state of economic violence and pervasive crisis in Glendale and across Los Angeles. Nearly two-thirds of Glendale's seventy-three thousand renters are classified as rent burdened, allocating more than 30 percent of their household income toward rent.

On the day of the biennial opening, the Glendale Tenants Union (GTU) collected signatures outside Jons Marketplace for a proposed Community Stabilization and Fair Rent Act.

One GTU housing advocate, Hayk Makhmuryan, is an Armenian-American artist, community activist, and longtime resident of Glendale. He works as the program coordinator of the Studio 526 Arts Program in Downtown Los Angeles, providing studio and exhibition space to members of the Skid Row community. On the subject of *Vision Valley* being staged against the backdrop of Glendale's recent transformations, he observes that economic injustice and cultural exclusion often work hand in hand. One systematically eliminates the material conditions necessary for a community to survive; the other eliminates the conditions necessary for a community to make its narratives visible.

2

When they were asked about the curatorial process, the organizers said:

> The criteria were simple: any contemporary fine artist who lives, works, or maintains a studio in Glendale would be considered. We had in-person discussions and sent emails . . . asking for suggestions of contemporary artists who fit the criteria. . . . The resulting exhibition showcases some of the many contemporary artists who live or work in Glendale and whose work is part of a larger conversation around contemporary art in the region and beyond.

"Contemporary" appears four times in this paragraph. Its appearances suggest a temporal incompatibility between the present moment and the cultural activities of Armenian Americans. It's difficult not to read its ubiquity as an injunction that no duduk players, khachkar carvers, or provincials need apply. The insistence on the "contemporary" as a stable category that explains the exclusion of diasporic artists frames Armenians as non-contemporary producers of non-art. It resurfaces Edward Said's postcolonial commonplace: the other is a figure whose cultural products are frozen in amber, outside of time, suspended in the tense of the "timeless eternal."

When they were asked which art spaces and professionals were consulted in the curatorial process, the organizers said they reached out to all galleries in the city. The owner of the Armenian Arts Gallery in Glendale, a venue that hosted the 2017 exhibition *Los Angeles—Our Eyes*, tells me he has never heard of, or from, a place called the Pit.

When they were asked why no Armenian visions were included in *Vision Valley*, the organizers said they "did not seek out any artist based on background, ethnicity, race or gender." This implies a wholly bias-free curatorial process. It implies that when the organizers approached MOCA, the Hammer, LACMA, their friends, and their associates—and emerged with a majority white roster absent any Armenian Americans—they were not consulting a specific community but rather a set of individuals regarded as the neutral, regulatory body of contemporary art practice.

When they were asked by Araik Sinanyan why there are no Armenian Americans in the exhibition, the organizers inquired whether he was an artist, coding "the artist" as a privileged category of citizenship requisite to civic participation. Araik wondered, "Why does it matter [if I'm an artist]? What if I'm just a community member who wants to be represented?"

When they were asked online why they continue to use the name "Glendale Biennial" on social media after agreeing with the city to remove the title, the organizers blocked the inquiring party.

When they were asked about the curatorial process, the organizers quoted a line from the press copy: *Vision Valley* does not turn on any "conceptual, political, or philosophical themes, . . . [and] it does not claim to distill a particular trend, aesthetic, or idea." The exhibition, they insist, is devoid of any specific conceptual, political, or philosophical content.

The conceptual, political, and philosophical content of this exhibition is the fine art of gentrification and its economic violence.

The conceptual, political, and philosophical content of this exhibition is whitewalling and its racialized exclusions.

The conceptual, political, and philosophical content of this exhibition is the refusal to ask, *Whose culture has capital?*

The conceptual, political, and philosophical content of this exhibition is the practice of imputing a cultural deficit to a diasporic community.

The conceptual, political, and philosophical content of this exhibition is the use of a community's fictive cultural deficit as the pretext for claiming ownership of a city, its histories, and its geographies.

The conceptual, political, and philosophical content of this exhibition is a vision of the valley that renders the people who live there invisible.

1

The promotional imagery for *Vision Valley* features photographs of Glendale intersections from which you can see the mountains. They are bathed in hyper-saturated, technicolor magenta hues. These valley vistas are absent any human agents: a depopulated visual field from which the bodies of the city's residents have been evacuated. A pink monochrome awaiting figurative content. They picture a place where nobody lives.

At the onset of my engagement with *Vision Valley*, I set out to write a standard exhibition review. I began thinking about my grandmother. About her sixteen-year performance of linguistic refusal. About the tactical repetition of the word "no."

Acknowledgments

I am grateful to the many interlocutors whose vision directly and indirectly informs this text: Sona Hakopian, Lida Khatchatrian, Danny Snelson, David Arzumanyan, Naira Harutyunyan, Gilda Davidian, Iggy Cortez, Patricia Kim, Meldia Yesayan, Jacob Halajian, Nathalie Halajian, and Hayk Makhmuryan.

Bibliography

Adamian, Flora. "Xenophobia and Death Threats Plague Glendale Politics." *Asbarez*, November 3, 2016. http://asbarez.com/156656/xenophobia-and-death-threats -plague-glendale-politics.

Chernick, Brian. "Glendale Tenants Union Formed." *Crescenta Valley Weekly*, July 6, 2017. http://www.crescentavalleyweekly.com/news/07/06/2017/glendale -tenants-union-formed.

Deutsche, Rosalyn, and Cara Gendel Ryan. "The Fine Art of Gentrification." *October* 31 (Winter 1984): 91–111.

Dillingham, William Paul. *Reports of the Immigration Commission: Immigrants in Industries*. Washington, DC: Washington Government Printing Office, 1911.

Dreier, Peter. "A California Suburb Reckons with Its Nazi Past—and Present-Day Controversy Follows." *Salon*, August 19, 2017. https://www.salon.com/2017 /08/19/a-california-suburb-reckons-with-its-nazi-past-and-present-day -controversy-follows.

D'Souza, Aruna. *Whitewalling: Art, Race & Protest in 3 Acts*. New York: Badlands Unlimited, 2018.

Fittante, Daniel. "But Why Glendale? A History of Armenian Immigration to Southern California." *California History* 94, no. 3 (Fall 2017): 2–19.

Harvey, David. "The Right to the City." *New Left Review* 53 (September–October 2008): 23–40.

Housing Is a Human Right. "Resist Gentrification Action Summit: We Shall Not Be Moved We Will Improve." http://www.housinghumanright.org/summit.

Isahakian, Avetik. "Untitled (October 25, 1897)." House-Museum Avetik Isahakian. http://www.isahakyanmuseum.am/htmls_eng/banastercutyunner_2.html.

Loewen, James. *Sundown Towns: A Hidden Dimension of American Racism*. New York: New Press, 2005.

Mellen, Greg. "Glendale Approves Armenian-American Museum as Its 'Forward-Looking Legacy.'" *LA Weekly*, April 24, 2018. http://www.laweekly.com/news/glendale-approves-armenian-american-museum-as-its-forward-looking-legacy-9391021.

Mikailian, Arin. "Glendale's Recent Growth Built on a Foundation of Years-Old Decisions." *Glendale News-Press*, November 14, 2015. http://www.latimes.com/socal/glendale-news-press/news/tn-gnp-glendales-recent-growth-built-on-a-foundation-of-years-old-decisions-20151114-story.html.

Onyx Glendale Apartments. "Features and Amenities." https://onyxglendale.com/features-and-amenities.

Reyes-Velarde, Alejandra. "The Brand Library and Art Center to Showcase Glendale Artists." *Glendale News-Press*, May 8, 2018. http://www.latimes.com/socal/glendale-news-press/news/tn-gnp-me-vision-valley-art-exhibit20180507-story.html.

Said, Edward W. *Orientalism*. New York: Vintage Books, 1979.

Sturken, Marita, and Lisa Cartwright. *Practices of Looking: An Introduction to Visual Culture*. Oxford: Oxford University Press, 2018.

Tehranian, John. "Compulsory Whiteness: Towards a Middle Eastern Legal Scholarship." *Indiana Law Journal* 82, no. 1 (Winter 2007): 1–47.

Vaule, Rosamond B. *As We Were: American Photographic Postcards, 1905–1930*. Boston: David R. Godine, 2014.

"Vision Valley." *Artillery*. https://artillerymag.com/events/vision-valley.

"Vision Valley: The Glendale Biennial." Facebook, accessed April 21, 2008. https://www.facebook.com/events/1763997570333203.

Yosso, Tara J. "Whose Culture Has Capital? A Critical Race Theory Discussion of Community Cultural Wealth." *Race, Ethnicity and Education* 8, no. 1 (March 2005): 69–91.

Zurcher, Anthony. "Glendale Armenians in Shadows of the Past." BBC, October 1, 2016. http://www.bbc.com/news/election-us-2016-37455372.

Perspectives on Artsakh from a Black Armenian Angeleno

CARENE ROSE MEKERTICHYAN

MY FATHER AND HIS FAMILY immigrated to the United States in 1991, in the chaos of the collapse of the Soviet Union and the last major war between Armenia and Azerbaijan.

If my father had been drafted before our family's immigration paper-work was finalized, I would not be here. By the same token, if Armenia had been in a state of prosperous peace at the time, my family may never have emigrated.

My mom had moved to Los Angeles a few years prior from Chicago for a job opportunity. She met my dad when they were working at what is now the Intercontinental Hotel in Century City. As the old Armenian proverb says, "Chakatagrits ches karogh khusapel," or "You cannot escape destiny." So here I am, after the stars aligned, allowing my passage into this world.

I am a proud Angeleno. I grew up in Silverlake, back when it was vibrant and diverse. Before I started kindergarten, I could speak basic Armenian because I spent my days at my tatik and papik's (grandparents') apartment while my parents were working. Once I started school, however, I lost the words I had known, and my understanding of the Armenian language is still remedial at best.

Here in L.A., I'm surrounded by the largest diasporic Armenian population and yet I've struggled to feel connected to this community in which I felt I wasn't seen or wanted. I remember walking through the Glendale Galleria holding hands with my parents and seeing the stares from other Armenians as they turned to whisper with each other.

"But I'm Both!"

This was not the case with the Black community. I remember my first day at Ivanhoe Elementary School, when my soon-to-be friend Aliya came over to me and said, "We are the Black girls. We have to stick together." This unconditional acceptance has remained true throughout my life.

When we would visit my mom's side of the family on the South Side of Chicago, my light skin resulted in some hurtful taunts. There were girls on the playground who said they didn't want to play with a "vanilla ice cream girl." My cousin Ayanna set them straight as I left the park crying. I was called everything from "yellow" to "Lite-Brite." Family members would playfully joke about my last name, calling me "McKetchup" because they couldn't handle the pronunciation.

All those otherizing experiences aside, I navigated Black spaces with an ease I still don't feel anywhere else.

Both my parents ensured I understood the history and the suffering of my ancestors. I remember my mother sitting me down one day when I must have been five years old or so and explaining the history of slavery in the United States and our continued struggle for justice. While I don't remember what sparked that conversation, I remember it knocked me right out of my California bubble. The idea of someone hating me because of my skin and features was foreign to me.

I first became aware of my Blackness around the same age. My Armenian cousin said, "Even if you have just one little drop of Black, the people, like at your school, will only see you as Black."

"But I'm both!" I remember saying, upset because I had no understanding of the "one-drop rule." Although he didn't fully understand the implications of what he had said, it still hurt.

It has always been a strange paradox to acknowledge the fact that the United States, a nation built by Black slaves on stolen Indigenous land, has given my Armenian family freedoms and opportunities they never could have imagined under the Soviet Union. I accept this truth while also understanding this country is steeped in systemic white supremacy.

Even with my light-skinned privilege, I myself have been subjected to racial slurs, followed in stores, unjustifiably pulled over by the police and forced to endure countless microaggressions. The dismissal of these disparities by some Armenians, who boast that our community is "self-made," is inherently racist and feeds into the flawed "pull yourself up by your bootstraps" mentality glorified by so many immigrant communities.

I believe it is hard for many Armenians to understand that they, too, benefit from white supremacy, despite our indigeneity, the genocide, and the uniqueness of ethnic SWANA identity.

Legacy of the Genocide

I don't know when I first learned about the Armenian Genocide, as it was always a topic of conversation among my family. I just knew the "Turks killed a lot of Armenians." I remember studying World War I in high school and feeling my heart skip a beat when I saw Armenia mentioned in my textbook.

I quickly deflated, reading the "massacre of Armenians by Ottoman forces." Our ethnicity, our genocide, was just one sentence in my history textbook. As the years went on, I learned more about my own family's survival and the atrocities that occurred, so I pushed for genocide recognition by means of constituent letters, protests, and organizing the first Armenian Genocide vigil in Dartmouth College's history.

Now, before I explain the current conflict, it is critical that I provide the full historical context that so much of today's journalism sorely lacks. The Ancient Kingdom of Armenia (Urartu) has existed since about 900 BCE. Armenia was the first nation in the world to adopt Christianity, and the full scope of ancient Armenia's territory can be found on numerous maps. Over time, Armenia was conquered and ruled by the Ottoman Turks, Persians, and Russians, losing territory in the process.

For Armenians, we don't have to go very far back into our family trees for evidence of our historical displacement and genocide. My great-grandparents come from Van, Nakhichevan, and Ghars, all Armenian regions that are now part of Turkey and Azerbaijan. While the Armenian Genocide is perhaps Turkey's most well-known atrocity, in which it is estimated that one and a half million Armenians were killed under the cover of WWI, it is important to understand the full scope of terror caused by the Ottoman Empire at the time.

These atrocities include the Hakkari massacres (1843), the Massacre of Aleppo (1850), the Batak Massacre (1876), the Hamidian Massacres (1894), the Diyarbakır Massacres (1895), the Adana Massacre (1909), the Greek Genocide (1913), the Assyrian Genocide (1914), and the famine of Mount Lebanon (1915). I believe that it is this genocidal legacy that Turkish President Erdogan emulates in his own quest for a fascist pan-Turkic state.

I am the direct descendant of Armenian Genocide survivors. We were lucky enough to have my grandtatik Nvart with us until 2017, and she helped keep our family history alive. Her husband, Garegin, my tatik's father, was born in Van and survived the genocide. Garegin didn't say much about that time, but there are some details our family has remembered and carried with us.

When Garegin was eight or nine, he was chased into a river along with his little brother by Turkish soldiers and survived by holding on to the tail of an ox to get across safely. The last he saw of his little brother, he was carried away by a Turkish officer on horseback. At some point, Garegin made his way to the Echmiadzin Church. At the church wall, he found what remained of his family. There is uncertainty as to who was left, but he did see his mother, father, and at least one sister. Apparently, upon first seeing his mother, he went to get her food, and when he returned, she had died. His father and sister died soon after, all stricken with cholera. Before or after this encounter, Garegin was placed in an American orphanage in Jerusalem.

My papik's mother, Ashken Mayasyan, who also survived the genocide, never knew her true age. One story from the genocide that she recounted with my papik and his brothers has stuck with me over the years. Her mother, Tamar, was nicknamed "Sirun Tamar" because she was known for her beauty. When Turkish soldiers came looking for her, she smeared her face with dirt, tattered her clothes, and told them, "They took her already and went that way."

At some point, Ashken lost her father, mother, and two other siblings, but those details have never been discussed in my family. Ashken, her sister Arus, and her brother Gurgen ended up in an American orphanage in Gyumri.

They were lucky to have each other. At that time, many surviving Armenian girls were converted to Islam and forced into sex slavery and marriages. Some were tattooed on their faces and hands as a mark of their ownership. It is this understanding of my family history and our shared intergenerational trauma that tethers my spirit to my ancestors and our Armenian community.

The Conflict

Following the Russian Revolution in 1918, Armenia (along with many other countries at the time) established the first Republic of Armenia, which existed briefly before being incorporated into what would become the USSR in 1920. It was then that Azerbaijan formed a republic for the first time for their ethnic group descended primarily from Albanian and Turkic ancestry (undoubtedly Armenian ancestry as well).

Between 1918 and 1920, the Azeris perpetrated massacres of Armenians in Baku and Shushi. These were the first of many pogroms to push ethnic Armenians out of the region. When what would be the USSR was formed in 1921, Joseph Stalin, at the time a high-ranking government official, gave Artsakh (Nagorno-Karabakh) to Azerbaijan, despite its predominantly Armenian population, to appease Turkey and incentivize its allyship.

In 1988, the people of Artsakh voted to reunite with the Armenian Soviet Socialist Republic. As a result, the pogrom of Sumgait occurred, in which hundreds of Armenians were murdered. There were gang rapes of Armenian women in the streets. Azeri allies hid their Armenian neighbors as they waited to leave the town safely. This pogrom was well documented by the Soviet government officials who escorted surviving Armenians to safety. There was another pogrom in Kirovabad that year and a well-known pogrom in Baku in 1990 and Maragha in 1992.

These tensions escalated into the Artsakh Liberation War, or Nagorno-Karabakh War, which resulted in an estimated thirty thousand deaths on both sides. Armenia won the war and a ceasefire was declared. Artsakh has remained an autonomous republic under de facto Armenian control within Azerbaijan since 1994. There have been numerous violent clashes since.

Azerbaijan destroyed Armenian churches, gravestones, and khachkars in what has been called the worst cultural genocide in history. In 2004, Ramil Safarov, an Azerbaijani Army officer, murdered the Armenian officer Gurgen Margayarian with an ax while Margayarian was sleeping. Both men had been sent to a NATO training program by their respective governments. In 2005, the mayor of Baku, Hajibala Abutalibov, said the following to a municipal delegation from Bavaria, Germany: "Our goal is the complete elimination of Armenians. You, Nazis, already eliminated the Jews in the 1930s and '40s, right? You should be able to understand us."

In 2016 there was the brutal Four-Days War between Azerbaijan and Armenia, in which there were cases of Armenian civilians executed and mutilated, like the remaining residents of Talish. A number of Armenian soldiers were also beheaded.

In July 2020,[1] Azerbaijan bombed the Tavush region of Armenia, shelling a PPE factory and schools, and threatening to bomb Armenia's nuclear power plant. This was a clear violation of the UN pandemic ceasefire, which

Armenia had signed but Azerbaijan had not. Since the attack on Tavush, the Azeri and Turkish governments have been stirring up anti-Armenian sentiments and there has been a spike in hate crimes across our diaspora. Thousands of Azeris protested in Baku, demanding war with Armenia.

A few days before the fighting began on September 27, a number of Armenians were engaging in a ridiculous and hurtful debate online about Armenian identity. Some argued that marrying and having children with non-Armenians will lead to the loss of our culture and identity.

Having to argue the validity of my existence was frustrating, but I found that most people engaging in the discussion were overwhelmingly supportive of multiracial Armenians. We carry our ancestors in our souls; no amount of cultural gatekeeping and adherence to "blood quantum" can ever take that away from us. Whenever Armenia is under attack, we stand united, no matter what our differences are. It is my sincere wish that this unity remains once we make it through this crisis.

We see this genocidal war on Artsakh as an existential threat to the Armenian diaspora. Armenians have been indigenous to Artsakh for thousands of years and had no incentive to start a war over the small bit of land we already have. Why would Armenia, a nation of three million, start a war with Azerbaijan, a nation of ten million, backed by Turkey, a nation of eighty-five million? President Erdogan of Turkey has cited Adolf Hitler's Germany as an effective government and stated he planned to "fulfill the mission our grandfathers have carried out for centuries," alluding to the Armenian Genocide.

Azerbaijan and Turkey had been holding military exercises on Armenia's border as a means of intimidation since August; the conflict that was sparked on September 27 should have come as no surprise to anyone paying attention. The Turkish government has paid and misled mercenaries from Syria, who are being pushed to the front lines and are losing their lives. There are reports of refugees and jihadist rebels being conscripted into a fight that is not theirs, many of whom have requested to return home.

Why We Are Protesting

The way Western media has been reporting this crisis is dangerous because there is no neutrality here. The focus of Azerbaijan's and Turkey's strikes has been civilian territory with the goal of exterminating as many Armenians as possible. They have targeted Armenia proper by shelling Vardenis and Artsvanik. They have shelled our iconic Ghazanchetsots Cathedral twice, killing civilians and injuring reporters. This conflict is bigger than Azerbaijan, with foreign superpowers involved on all sides. In addition to military support from Turkey, Israel supplies about 60 percent of Azerbaijan's weapons. The Azeri military is currently using Israeli kamikaze drones to strike Armenia. Russia brokered a ceasefire for the purpose of recovering bodies that was immediately violated.

As those of us in the Armenian diaspora continue to collect donations and protest, we are also engaged in an information war on social media. Azerbaijan's troll farm was recently exposed, and the Azeri government continues to ban social media and foreign journalists from the region while questioning and arresting citizens who are calling for peace. The government of Azerbaijan has a well-documented history of money laundering and lobbying of journalists. A number of celebrities who have come out in support of Armenia have also been bullied into silence by Azeri bots.

Armenians are shutting down your freeways and marching in your streets because *we want your attention*. We want as much coverage and visibility as possible. We know what happens when governments choose neutrality over people, and we refuse to allow this attempt at ethnic cleansing to go unnoticed.

Now, it doesn't come as a surprise to me that people have no interest in engaging with what is happening in Armenia. The conflict seems distant and confusing, and it's so much easier to focus on the election and pandemic instead.

When the movement for Black lives was reignited in June following the murders of George Floyd, Breonna Taylor, and Ahmaud Arbery, I was amazed at the sheer number of "allies" who emerged among friends and communities that had stayed silent for so long.

I attended my first Black Lives Matter protest in 2014 after the killing of Michael Brown, and, in the years since, we have lost and continue to lose countless Black lives to law enforcement and lynching. It hurt to see this sudden mobilization of allies because I understood that you all had the ability to fight alongside us this entire time, yet you chose the comfort of your privilege instead.

Whether it's a selfie at a protest, an empty black square, or the continued meme-ification of Breonna Taylor, these actions are meaningless without substantive direct action to back them up. Performative activism is useless and often harmful. It is safe to say that the spike in activism we saw at the start of the summer has died down, and people are returning to their natural state of apathy and privileged ignorance.

I am here to tell you that it is possible and necessary to care about more than one issue at a time. Your taxpayer dollars are funding Azerbaijan, and President Trump has business interests in both Turkey and Azerbaijan, so this is your fight as well.

Just as I called on the Armenian community to stand in solidarity with the Black Lives Matter movement, I am now pleading with everyone who takes the time to read this to fight for your Armenian friends while we are still here. At least one hundred thousand of your fellow Angelenos marched in the streets in one weekend demanding you listen to us. Like all Armenians, I had been a mess since the attack, alternating between frantic action and catatonic anxiety. It filled my spirit to see Black, Assyrian, Filipino, and Mexican allies standing with us in solidarity. It is my sincere hope that you, my fellow Angelenos, join us in condemning this continued attempt to erase Armenians from this earth.

The Armenian diaspora is so vast, rich, and diverse, in spite of the loss of much of our indigenous land and our continued struggle for survival. Like Garegin and Ashken, we persevere and thrive in the face of adversity. I always say that, as a Black Armenian woman, I am the proud legacy of two failed genocides. The failure of these genocides is dependent on our commitment to speaking truth and ensuring that history doesn't repeat itself. Our existence is resistance, and we aren't going anywhere.

Note

1. Author's note: This piece was originally published by *LAist* on October 16, 2020. In this call to action, Carene Rose Mekertichyan reflected on her identity as a Black Armenian Angelena and the legacy of the Armenian Genocide in the midst of Azerbaijan's genocidal attack on Indigenous Armenians in Artsakh that occurred from September 27 to November 10, 2020. The conflict ended in a tenuous ceasefire that continues to be violated at the time of this publication.

We Are All Armenian

SCOUT TUFANKJIAN

I GREW UP in a small Massachusetts town a couple of hours away from the main Armenian enclave of Watertown. We had some access to the community. We could make the drive to get lahmajun or braided cheese or the little black seeds you need to make choereg, but it wasn't like growing up in Glendale or Bourj Hammoud or Alfortville. For me, seeing other Armenians—even in a book—was a special occasion. There were a few Armenian families that spent summers in my town, and we would get together on the weekends for kebabs and dolma, and there was one other Armenian girl at my school, but beyond that, my main exposure to the Armenian community was through weekends with my grandparents.

There are few people as colorful as a colorful Armenian, and my grandfather was a colorful Armenian. Despite being born in the United States, he continued to live like he was back in the village, including filling their all-American suburban backyard with goats, sheep, and horses that would inevitably get loose and run around town with my humiliated father and uncles in hot pursuit. My days with them were spent in the backseat of their car as they visited a seemingly inexhaustible network of other Armenians. They would catch up on some gossip, have some sourj, and then go on to the next friends' houses, the goodbyes lasting longer than the supposed visit. I found the whole routine unbelievably boring. I didn't know the people they were gossiping about. I didn't care about the people they were gossiping about. They spoke in two languages I could barely understand. They wouldn't let me have any coffee. It was terrible.

Luckily for me, all of these houses had giant piles of Armenian newspapers and magazines stacked in front of the fireplace or on the coffee table. I would sit flipping through the pages, my sulks dissipating in the face of the ancient script that always triggered something deep in my imagination, something that felt like it belonged to me, no matter how impenetrable it was in reality. I don't know whose house we were in or which publication it was, but I remember opening up one of the magazines and seeing a giant map of the world covered in little dots. I still don't remember whether the dots stood for AGBUs or agumps, churches or schools, but I remember seeing them and realizing that where there were dots, there were Armenians.

And I found it totally mind-blowing.

There were Armenians in Brazil, Armenians in Hong Kong, Armenians in Argentina, the Soviet Union, India, Ethiopia. To a six- or seven-year-old kid, these were places inconceivably far away, places that I never imagined I could or would go to.

This map and its little dots took up permanent residence in my brain. Everywhere I went, I looked for stories about these people. What were their lives like? What was it like to be Armenian in Addis Ababa? Or Sao Paulo? I went to libraries and church bazaars, poured through books, and watched every single one of the PBS documentaries, all the time looking for glimpses of these people's lives, wondering what it was like to be a soccer-playing Armenian teenager in Buenos Aires or an Armenian jeweler in Lebanon or an Armenian schoolkid in Moscow. And I could never find it. The only stories I could find were stories about the genocide. And, like any Armenian kid, I already knew what happened during the genocide. I had listened to my grandparents' stories, read the books, and even argued with a denialist history teacher after turning in a middle-school paper. What I didn't know was what happened to us *after* the genocide.

This infuriated me. We did not disappear into the desert of Deir ez-Zor. This was not our entire story. There was so much more to be written and to be shown.

Looking back on my outrage, my drift toward photojournalism now seems inevitable. I channeled my child's fury at my denialist history teacher into a career where I demanded that others see the things that I have seen. They might refuse to look beyond the genocide when it comes to my people's story, but I could try to make them see that there was more to other peoples' stories. No matter who I was following, whether it was members of the Salafi community trying to navigate their way through postrevolutionary and pre-coup Egypt or the grassroots movement sur- rounding the future president Barack Obama, there was always a slight tug, a sneaking suspicion that there was another story I was supposed to be telling.

There was only one problem. I felt like a fraud around Armenians. Is it possible to have imposter syndrome for your own culture? Don't get me wrong, my favorite foods as a kid were kheyma and choereg. I was roundly mocked by all of my peers for drinking tahn in elementary school (and called the Commie for my imagined history in the Armenian SSR, no matter how much I pointed out that my family was from Anatolia and Syria). I look so much like my Armenian dad that I am recognized on the street by the resemblance alone. It didn't matter that I had to affirm my Armenian-ness every time I told someone my name ("What IS that?"); at the end of the day I had only been to Armenian churches for weddings, my language skills were rudimentary at best, my family did not belong to any of the organizations, and—worst of all—my mother was not Armenian. Whenever I was around Armenians, I secretly worried that I did not count. It didn't matter that my mom is a very lovely woman (who do you think made all the choereg and kheyma?) and that I had begged my parents to send me to Saturday school (too far away) or had tried to learn Armenian through books purchased at church bazaars (not possible). I was definitely not a Good Armenian. And for years, I told myself that this might make me the wrong person to tell our story. While my love for Armenia was sincere and lifelong (I mean, seriously, what kid begs to go to Saturday school), was it an outsider's fascination?

Looking back, yes, I was absolutely being a coward. I was a photojour- nalist. I had spent my entire career working and building relationships in countries where I did not speak the language. At the end of the day, even if I wasn't the right person to tell the story, even if no one cared about this other than me, I knew that if I began working, I would at the very least be able to set my own mind at rest and know that I had tried. I just needed to figure out how to get started.

The first part ended up being easy. In the wake of the first Obama campaign, I went on an extended book tour, doing interviews and giving talks. At every single one, people asked me what my plans were, and at all of them I said that I was working on a project about the Armenian dias- pora. Boom. Done. I had to do it now.

The second part proved a little harder, but it seemed to make the most sense to start by trying to answer my earliest questions. As a kid growing up with my face pressed against the glass of the Armenian community, I really wanted to know about belonging and connectedness. Was there a global Armenian community? Were we all connected in some way? Did kids in Moscow have the same experience of being Armenian as kids in Hollywood? Did being Armenian connect us if we were growing up in Hong Kong or in Hayastan? Did the Homenetmen scouts in DC and the scouts in Cyprus think of themselves as being part of one community? Was there a connection between dancers in Anjar and dancers in Yerevan? Or had the different paths taken by our refugee grandparents and great-grandparents separated us in some way? What did it mean that one could feel Armenian in America but American in Armenia? Or that many of us secretly felt more at home in Turkey than in Hayastan? And if we were all still one people, why? One hundred years after we had been scattered across the world, were we even connected at all?

I began looking for answers in Anjar.

Anjar is a village in Lebanon's Bekaa Valley, where almost all of the residents are Armenian. Not only are they Armenian, but they are the descendants of the survivors of the Musa Ler/Musa Dagh resistance, where villagers were able to resist deportation and massacre during the Armenian Genocide for fifty-three days before they were eventually res- cued and evacuated by a French warship. A long, winding road took the survivors to Anjar in 1939, where they established a community divided into districts, each named after one of the six villages of Musa Ler. And they have thrived, fighting off threats ranging from the physical ones of the civil war to the less visible ones of assimilation and cultural amnesia. It is an amazing place, and one I had been hearing about for my entire life, as my own family has some of its roots in Musa Ler.

When an Anjartsi friend invited me to a family friend's henna night, I jumped at the opportunity.

There was, of course, a catch. Anjartsis are tough. You don't hold off a seemingly unstoppable wave of cultural imperialism by being wishy- washy. But if I was worried about being the wrong person to tell this story, what was I doing starting off in Anjar, where people have been known to call less traditional Beiruti Armenians odars (or "yabanjos" in the local dialect)? What on earth were they going to think of this non-Armenian- speaking half-Armenian showing up in town with her camera? Anjar, or rather the idea of Anjar, was important to me, and I was incredibly, laugh- ably afraid that I was going to screw it up. But a funny thing happened when I arrived. Something about the village felt like home to me. My friend's family felt like my family. The unmistakable sound of the davul zurna brought me back to the backseat of my grandparents' car, those long afternoons remapping their old villages onto the highways and towns of Massachusetts. By the time the local priest was telling me stories about meeting my Musa Lertsi great-grandmother, I had a whole new sense of my family and my history.

While Anjar showed me one continuation of our story, I knew there were more, and I chased them across the globe. Far from being dis-appeared, it was clear that our community was vast, vibrant, and diverse. Over the next few years, I swam with resettled Syrian-Armenian refugees in one of the world's oldest plain forests in Artsakh. I attended candlelight vigils for the victims of the genocide in Glendale. I celebrated Vartavar, the most Armenian of Armenian holidays, where at the hottest time of year we dump water on each other (it's a religious holiday, obviously), with Istanbul Armenians on the island of Kinali Ada the morning after a concert by the Armenian/Turkish/French band Collectif Medz Bazar. I attended perfectly silent meals and the occasional khorovats party with the monks on San Lazzaro Island in Venice and rooftop summer soirees in New York City. I ate home-cooked manti in the light-filled Kessab kitchen of the wonderful Atamian/Honsorian family, and I watched the 2010 World Cup at the Homenmen Club in Damascus. I drank tea with migrant workers in Moscow and attended Easter Mass at the newly restored (and sadly now destroyed) Surp Giragos in Diyarbakir. I made paper flowers at a pre-wedding feast in Paris and listened to jazz sung by the Ethiopian-Armenian musician Vahe Tilbian in Addis Ababa. I sat for an hour watching kingfishers swoop around the Armenian church in Singapore, watched Armenian dancers rehearse in Australia, and saw the great Charles Aznavour perform in Sao Paulo. I marched in the New York Pride Parade with the Armenian Gay and Lesbian Association the day after New York became a marriage equality state, and I played tavla everywhere from the basement of a police station in what was once Hadjin to the club at Sourp Hagop in Montreal. I learned how to box at the Union of Russian Armenians' Sporting Club in Moscow, and I cheered on Indian-Armenian rugby players in Kolkata. I even learned that we are locally famous for our rugby playing, and if you are Armenian and you ever go to Kolkata, every-one will ask you if you play rugby. Even me.

As I moved across the map, I began to realize that I was documenting an extremely important time in our history, not only because we were approaching the centennial of the genocide but also because of what was happening to us now. The girl I photographed running through Surp Sarkis Church in Damascus now lives in a completely different world than she did when I met her. The Syrian Armenian community, which was the heart of the Middle Eastern Armenian community, and arguably the heart of the entire diaspora, has been decimated by the brutality of the Syrian Civil War. Most of my Syrian Armenian friends now live in Yerevan or Beirut or Los Angeles. The once powerful Ethiopian Armenian community (who wrote the national anthem and built the queen's palace) is down to a few remaining families. Everyone I photographed in Egypt now lives in Los Angeles, having fled postrevolutionary upheaval. In Armenia, entire villages are emptied of working-age men as they travel to Moscow or Turkey to find work. Even Anjar, right on the border of Syria, has been rocked by both the nearness of the Syrian Civil War and the collapse of the Lebanese economy. In more secure communities, like Los Angeles, Brazil, Buenos Aires, and Paris, people worry that our physical survival might be at the cost of our culture.

So, after all, what does it even mean to be an Armenian? Is it only villages like Anjar that are keeping our community alive? Is it the church? The dances? The organizations? The food? Or is it something more nebulous? A woman in Argentina described it to me as a membership in a secret club, invisible to nonmembers but instantly recognizable to other Armenians. I myself frequently say it's like having eleven million cousins—not quite brothers and sisters, but definitely close family. Kevin Dubois of Nice, France, told me, "You know, when I meet an Armenian, it's like we have been friends forever. The connection is there right away due to our ancestors and history."

But what is this history? Is it solely the genocide or something more? Midway through the project, I was losing focus and having a hard time figuring out what story—and, frankly, whose story—I was trying to tell. I decided to join a friend on what she called a "vision quest" to what my grandparents had always called the Old Country. We didn't go on an organized tour; we just met in Adana with a guidebook, a smattering of Turkish between us, Google translate, and a rough understanding of the shared taxi industry.

It didn't always go smoothly. No matter what the bus schedule says, my friend's ancestral village of Hadjin is considerably more than two hours away from Kozan (formerly Sis, the capital of Cilicia). After many hours of driving through nationalist towns and past MHP (Turkey's far-right ultranationalist party) offices, we hopped off the bus, bleary eyed, into a snowy evening, and were promptly taken to the police station after inquiring in my beyond broken Turkish if there was a place we could spend the night. But even that ended well, with my friend thrashing the local constabulary in tavla and one officer—the giant, gentle, soft-spoken Mehmet—haltingly telling us stories that his grandmother had told him about the time when the Armenians had been there, stories she had told him to make sure that there was at least one person in town who knew the real history.

It was here that I started to understand what I was getting wrong, what I was missing. I had been trying to figure out what connected our people one hundred years after we had been scattered across the globe, but I had been thinking about it all wrong.

I thought of a hundred years as being a long time, but Anatolia had been our home for over four thousand years. Compared to that, one hundred years was nothing. The trees that we had planted were still alive. The rivers ran along their same paths. The grooves in Kharpert's hillside that once held our homes stood in testament to the thousands of Armenians, including my great-grandfather, who once called that city of thirty thousand—now a tiny village—home.

All of us were raised by families forged in this or other nearby lands, and this connection is impossible to erase in a mere one hundred years, no matter how far we have been scattered across the globe and no matter how different our lives might seem today. The history that ties us together is so much more than just the genocide. While it is the defining trauma that runs through our past and understandably reverberates throughout our present, we are not a disappeared people, and it does not define us. Our story began thousands of years before 1915, and by no means did it end there. The strength of our survival ties us together far more than the genocide's horror. The history that we reflect is so much more than our shared trauma.

In 2014, four years after beginning my diaspora project, I returned to Anjar for Surp Khatch, or Holy Cross Day, which commemorates the survival and rescue of the Musa Ler villagers. In normal years, Armenians from Syria, Lebanon, and beyond come to Anjar for the festivities, which include davit zurna, dancing, food, and, most important, an all-night vigil next to the massive vats of harissa, the wheat and meat porridge that kept the villagers alive as they fled the genocide. That year was quieter. The reverberations from the Syrian Civil War had hit Lebanon hard, and the road to Anjar and Anjar itself were no longer considered 100 percent safe. Worried about the possibility of kidnapping or worse, many people stayed away, making the commemoration more local in spirit, although no less fervent. A month earlier, I myself had lost friends to the Syrian Civil War, and that loss hung in the shadows as the evening grew long. As I danced with my friends and sat up all night, mesmerized by the stirring of the harissa, I couldn't help but think of my great-grandmother. What would she have thought of this? Of me, almost one hundred years later, sitting surrounded by the descendants of her old neighbors, dancing to the songs she had loved? I kept seeing her face reflected in the older women of the village, my grandfather in some of the rowdier men—many of whom set up patrols to protect the village from possible dangers—and my cousins in the young men and women flirting and laughing as they danced.

If our collective history is reflected within us, it was my specific history that brought me here. In a way, I was merely echoing a journey that my great-grandmother had herself made. Midway through my project, while chasing down the story the priest had told me of her return to Anjar, I found an old, red leather photo album in the bottom drawer of my grand-mother's dresser. Apparently, in the sixties, she and my great-grandfather decided to make their own return to both the Old Country and the rela-tives they had been separated from in the rush to flee the slaughter. I have the photographs: visits with family in Paris and Lyon, outdoor dinners with cousins in Beirut and Aleppo. There is even a single frame labeled "Harpoot," showing the empty hillside that had once been my great-grandfather's home.

I'm not sure why I was so surprised. If I had learned anything across twenty-two countries, through encounters, both chance and planned, with my fellow Armenians across the globe, it was that we are all in some way reflections of our past.

Just as the echoes of my great-grandmother's life reverberates within me, the mothers I met in Paris and in Armenia are each the reflections of those women who were the hearts of their Old Country communities and who gave everything to ensure the survival of their children. They led the charge to rebuild their communities after reaching safety. The father I met who moved his family from Qamishlii in Syria to Berdzor in Artsakh left out of the same desperate need to keep his family safe that moved so many of our ancestors. The men I met playing cards in the agump in Bourj Hammoud share the same laughter as the men I shared tea with in Vakifli who never left the Old Country. Young men of the church, whether they are acolyte monks from Armenia or half-Black altar boys in Ethiopia, keep alive the same two-thousand-year-old church.

And all of our kids—whether they are young girls in India experiencing monsoon season for the first time or kids playing in a Lebanese refugee camp or my own three-year-old son—share the same spirit of all of those village kids who were too full of life to ever give up, no matter how insane the world grew around them.

Yes, every community has been influenced in one way or another by their adoptive cities. The fact that the Lebanese Armenian community is one of the few where Armenian is still the lingua franca is almost certainly connected to the insularity born out of the Lebanese Civil War. But this does not mean that the culture is being lost.

Just as there was no fixed way of being Armenian before April 23, 1915, there is no fixed way of being Armenian now. Armenian culture changed and evolved in the four thousand years before the genocide, and it continues to change and evolve today. A man sitting suited in his Hong Kong office tower is as Armenian as a woman in Taraz preparing to dance in Freedom Square. The self-proclaimed keepers of the culture may sneer at girls in miniskirts at a Moscow party or L.A. guys lounging on the hoods of their cars in Hollywood (I don't know how many times I've been told that some of the people in my photographs are "not real Armenians"), but those are real Armenians.

I had grown up thinking that there was a tiny box you needed to squeeze into to be a good Armenian, a box that I did not fit in, but my travels showed me that there is a place for all of us within this huge Armenian family, whether we are half Armenians, gay Armenians, Black Armenians, arty Armenians, atheist Armenians, non-Armenian-speaking Armenians, or good old-fashioned 100 percent Armenian AYF/AGBU-belonging/churchgoing/future-engineer Armenians. We are all Armenian. All of us have a role to play in the future of our community. Even me. What I had thought was my lack of belonging was in fact my way of belonging. While my sense of this belonging may have been fractured, I did, despite it all, still belong. Each of us has our own ways of being Armenian and relating to the community at large, but when we meet, the connection is clear.

The great William Saroyan tells the story of one of these meetings between two Armenians in the world's most misquoted short story, "The Armenian and the Armenian." In the story the protagonist is walking through Rostov-on-Don when he catches a glimpse of a waiter through a restaurant window and immediately recognizes the man as being Armenian. The connection is immediate despite all their differences, and they quickly begin to talk over terrible Russian beers. While they are talking, Saroyan reflects on the things that matter:

> The Armenian gestures, meaning so much. The slapping of the knee and roaring with laughter. The cursing. The subtle mockery of the world and its big ideas. The word in Armenian, the glance, the gesture, the smile, and through these things the swift rebirth of the race, timeless and again strong, though years have passed, though cities have been destroyed, fathers and brothers and sons killed, places forgotten, dreams violated, living hearts blackened with hate.

These are the things that cannot be erased, not by massacre, migration, or assimilation. Saroyan ends the story by challenging the world to try to destroy what he called "this small tribe of unimportant people."

"See if you can do it," he wrote.

> Send them from their homes into the desert. Let them have neither bread nor water. . . . See if they will not live again. See if they will not laugh again. See if the race will not live again when two of them meet in a beer parlor, twenty years after, and laugh, and speak in their tongue. Go ahead, see if you can do anything about it. See if you can stop them from mocking the big ideas of the world, you sons of bitches, a couple of Armenians talking in the world, go ahead and try to destroy them.

Acknowledgments

First and foremost, an enormous thank you to the University of Texas Press for believing in the project and to the contributors for making it possible. I am grateful to these writers for their patience, compassion, and generosity. In particular, thank you to the Kuzmich family, who enthusiastically welcomed the republication of Naira Kuzmich's essay that served as a significant source of inspiration for this collection. Thank you to Leila Emery and Lisa Gulesserian for reading the early manuscript with a critical eye and offering thorough and necessary recommendations for revision. Thank you to my sponsoring editor, Jim Burr, for seeing the vision of this project from the get-go.

Thank you to my wife, Kelsey, for never allowing me to give up on my many projects, even when I am convinced I have nothing to offer. Most important, thank you to my parents, who have always believed in me and taught me to be proud of who I am. Mom and Dad, your unflagging support means everything.

My sincere gratitude also goes to the authors and publications that granted permission to include previously published material: "How Armenian Funeral Halva Helped My Family Find Home in America," originally published in *Food 52* (October 23, 2018); "Hava Nagila," originally published in *Michigan Quarterly Review* (summer 2017); "Language Lessons," originally published in *Los Angeles Review of Books Quarterly* (no. 30, Trending issue, May 2021); "Valley View: An Armenian Diasporic Account in Lieu of a Glendale Biennial Review," originally published in *Los Angeles Review of Books* (May 27, 2018); "Going Home Again," originally published in *The Boston Globe* (December 26, 2015); "Perspectives on Artsakh from a Black Armenian Angeleno" originally published in *LAist* (October 26, 2020). A portion of "Where Are You From? No, Where Are You *Really* From?" was published in *MuslimGirl*.

Reading List

Fiction

Leonardo Alishan, *Free Fall*
Michael Arlen, *May Fair*
Adam Bagdasarian, *Forgotten Fire*
Michael Barakiva, *One Man Guy*
David-Matthew Barnes, *Swimming to Chicago*
Chris Bohjalian, *The Sandcastle Girls*
Carol Edgarian, *Rise the Euphrates*
Nonny Hogrogian, *One Fine Day*
Nancy Kricorian, *All the Light There Was*
Nancy Kricorian, *Dreams of Bread and Fire*
Nancy Kricorian, *Zabelle*
Micheline Aharonian Marcom, *Draining the Sea*
Micheline Aharonian Marcom, *The Daydreaming Boy*
Micheline Aharonian Marcom, *Three Apples Fell from Heaven*
Armistead Maupin, *Maybe the Moon*
Chris McCormick, *Desert Boys*
Chris McCormick, *The Gimmicks*
Mark T. Mustian, *The Gendarme*
Aline Ohanesian, *Orhan's Inheritance*
Nigoghos Sarafian, *The Bois de Vincennes*
William Saroyan, *My Name Is Aram*
William Saroyan, *The Armenian Trilogy*
Elif Shafak, *The Bastard of Instanbul*
Aleksandr Shaginyan, *Pogrom*
Leon Zaven Surmelian, *Daredevils of Sassoun*
Virginia A. Tashjian, *Three Apples Fell from Heaven: Armenian Tales Retold*
Hovhannes Tumanyan, *David of Sassoun*
Andranik Tzarukian, *Letter to Yerevan*
Varujan Vosganian, *The Book of Whispers*
Dana Walrath, *Like Water on Stone*
Franz Werfel, *The Forty Days of Musa Dagh*
Zabel Yesayan, *My Soul in Exile*

Nonfiction

Levon Abrahamian, *Armenian Identity in a Changing World*

Nancy Agabian, *Me as Her Again: True Stories of an Armenian Daughter*

Taner Akçam, *A Shameful Act: The Armenian Genocide and the Question of Turkish Responsibility*

Taner Akçam, *Killing Orders: Talat Pasha's Telegrams and the Armenian Genocide*

Taner Akçam, *The Young Turks' Crime against Humanity: The Armenian Genocide and Ethnic Cleansing in the Ottoman Empire*

Mark Arax, *In My Father's Name*

Michael J. Arlen, *Passage to Ararat*

Arlene Voski Avakian, *Lion Woman's Legacy: An Armenian-American Memoir*

Armen Avanessian, *Overwrite: Ethics of Knowledge—Poetics of Existence*

Bob Avian, *Dancing Man: A Broadway Choreographer's Journey*

Grigoris Balakian, *Armenian Golgatha*

Peter Balakian, *Black Dog of Fate: A Memoir*

Peter Balakian, *The Burning Tigris: The Armenian Genocide and America's Response*

Kerop Bedoukian, *Some of Us Survived: The Story of an Armenian Boy*

Eric Bogosian, *Operation Nemesis: The Assassination Plot That Avenged the Armenian Genocide*

Raffy Boudjikanian, *Journey through Genocide: Stories of Survivors and the Dead*

Chris Edwards, *Balls: It Takes Some to Get Some*

Lerna Ekmekcioglu, *Recovering Armenia: The Limits of Belonging in Post-genocide Turkey*

John M. Evans, *Truth Held Hostage: America and the Armenian Genocide—What Then? What Now?*

Joseph Kassabian, *The Hooligans of Kandahar: Not All War Stories Are Heroic*

Dawn Anahid MacKeen, *The Hundred-Year Walk: An Armenian Odyssey*

Aurora Mardiganian, *Ravished Armenia: The Story of Aurora Mardiganian, the Christian Girl, Who Survived the Great Massacres*

Markar Melkonian, *My Brother's Road: An American's Fateful Journey to Armenia*

Sato Moughalian, *Feast of Ashes: The Life and Art of David Ohannessian*

Joanne Randa Nucho, *Everyday Sectarianism in Urban Lebanon: Infrastructures, Public Services, and Power*

Karnig Panian, *Goodbye, Antoura: A Memoir of the Armenian Genocide*

Rubina Peroomian, *The Armenian Genocide in Literature*

Henry H. Riggs, *Days of Tragedy in Armenia: Personal Experiences in Harpoot, 1915–1917*

Aram Saroyan, *Last Rites: The Death of William Saroyan*

Scout Tufankjian, *There Is Only the Earth: Images from the Armenian Diaspora Project*

Leon Z. Surmelian, *I Ask You Ladies and Gentlemen*

Meline Toumani, *There Was and There Was Not*

Heghnar Zeitlian Watenpaugh, *The Missing Pages: The Modern Life of a Medieval Manuscript from Genocide to Justice*

Zabel Yesayan, *In the Ruins: The 1909 Massacres of Armenians in Adana, Turkey*

Poetry

Nancy Agabian, *Princess Freak: Poetry and Performance Texts*
Christopher Atamian, *A Poet in Washington Heights*
Peter Balakian, *Ozone Journal*
Susan Barba, *Fair Sun*
Armen Davoudian, *Swan Song*
Gregory Djanikian, *So I Will Till the Ground*
Diana Der Hovanessian, *How to Choose Your Past*
Armine Iknadossian, *All That Wasted Fruit*
Lola Koundakjian, *The Accidental Observer*
Lola Koundakjian, *Advice to a Poet*
Shahé Mankerian, *History of Forgetfulness*
Aram Saroyan, *Complete Minimal Poems*
Alan Semerdjian, *In the Architecture of Bone*

Anthologies

Levon Abrahamian, Nancy Sweezy, and Sam Sweezy, eds., *Armenian Folk Arts, Culture, and Identity*
Gourgen Arzoumanian, ed., *Birthmark: A Bilingual Anthology of Armenian-American Poetry*
Violet Grigoryan and Vahan Ishkhanyan, eds., *Deviation: Anthology of Contemporary Armenian Literature*
Agop J. Hacikyan, Gabriel Basmajian, Edward S. Franchuk, and Nourhan Ouzounian, eds., *The Heritage of Armenian Literature*, volumes 1–3
Diana Der Hovanessian, ed., *Anthology of Armenian Poetry*
David Kherdian, ed., *Forgotten Bread: First-Generation Armenian American Writers*
Artur Mkrtichyan, ed., *Armenians around the World: Migration and Transnationality*
Marc Nichanian, ed., *Writers of Disaster: Armenian Literature in the Twentieth Century*
Marc Nichanian, ed., *Yeghishe Charents: Poet of the Revolution*
QY Collective, lusine talalyan, Shushan Avagyan, and Arpi Adamyan, eds., *Queered: What's to Be Done with XCentric Art*
George Stambolian, ed., *Men on Men: Best New Gay Fiction*, volumes 1–4

Notes on the Contributors

Nancy Agabian is a writer, teacher, and literary organizer, working in the spaces between race, ethnicity, cultural identity, feminism, and queer identity. Her recent work of auto-fiction, *The Fear of Large and Small Nations*, was a finalist for the PEN/Bellwether Prize for Socially Engaged Fiction. She is the author of *Me as Her Again: True Stories of an Armenian Daughter* (Aunt Lute Books, 2008), a memoir that was honored as a Lambda Literary Award finalist for LGBT nonfiction and shortlisted for a William Saroyan International Writing Prize, and *Princess Freak* (Beyond Baroque Books, 2000), a collection of poetry and performance texts. Her personal essays that explore liminal spaces of identity have been published in *The Margins*, *The Brooklyn Rail*, *Hyperallergic*, *Kweli Journal*, and the Nauset Press anthology *Fierce: Essays by and about Dauntless Women*. She teaches creative writing at universities and art centers, most recently at NYU and the Leslie-Lohman Museum of Gay and Lesbian Art in SoHo. From 2002 to 2010, she coordinated Gartal, an Armenian literary reading series in NYC. She is currently a caregiver to her elderly parents in East Walpole, Massachusetts, in the house where she grew up.

Born in Iran, **Liana Aghajanian** is a journalist based between Detroit and Los Angeles whose work has appeared in the *New York Times*, the *Guardian*, the *Atlantic*, and the BBC, among other publications. She is the winner of the Write A House residency program, which awarded homes to writers in Detroit, and is currently at work on a project tracing the legacy of Armenian cuisine in America and beyond. Her writing can be found at www.lianaaghajanian.com.

Sophia Armen is an organizer, scholar, and writer from Los Angeles, California.

Kohar Avakian is an Armenian, Black, and Nipmuc scholar from Worcester, Massachusetts. She is currently pursuing a PhD in American studies at

Yale University. She graduated from Dartmouth College in 2017 with a BA in history, modified with Native American studies, where she completed a senior thesis on the history of legal whiteness in the United States, focusing on the case study of Armenian immigrants in Worcester—the first Armenian community in America. For her doctoral research, Kohar is interested in situating the history of Armenian racial formation within a wider framework of settler colonialism, slavery, and Asian exclusion. While she primarily draws from historical photography and oral history research methods, she also seeks to interrogate archival silences and create space for alternative modes of knowledge in the face of such absences. Her work strives to explore the palimpsestic histories of her Armenian, Black, and Native ancestors in order to illuminate the intersections of race, migration, and genocide in the United States and beyond.

John Parker Der Boghossian founded and curates the Queer Armenian Library (queerarmenianlibrary.com), the first ever library of queer Armenian literature and media. He works in higher education as an equity and inclusion officer. His book chapter "The Minnesota LGBTQ Standards of Inclusion" was published in *The Routledge Handbook of LGBTQIA Administration and Policy*. He is working on essays about Soghomon Tehlirian's epilepsy, the day he saw Matthew Shepard's mom cry, and how a Ouija board led him to investigate the death of his youth pastor. To address the dearth of queer Armenian voices in fiction, he is writing a novel about the intertwined fates of an Armenian widow and Armenian graduate student at a family reunion. He lives in Minnesota with his two partners, Jim and Gordy.

Chris Bohjalian is a number one *New York Times* best-selling author of twenty-three books, including *The Lioness*, *Hour of the Witch*, *Midwives*, and *The Flight Attendant*, which is an HBO Max limited series starring Kaley Cuoco. His other books include *The Guest Room*, *The Red Lotus*, *Skeletons at the Feast*, *The Double Bind*, and *The Sandcastle Girls*, his love story set amid the Armenian Genocide. His novels *Secrets of Eden*, *Midwives*, and *Past the Bleachers* were made into movies, and his work has been translated into more than thirty-five languages. He is also a playwright (*Wingspan* and *Midwives*). He lives in Vermont and can be found at chrisbohjalian.com or on Facebook, Instagram, Twitter, Litsy, and Goodreads @chrisbohjalian.

Raffy Boudjikanian is a Canadian-Armenian journalist and author. He has reported from a number of places around the world, including Nicaragua, France, and Canada. He currently lives in Ottawa, Ontario, where he works for the Canadian Broadcasting Corporation's national news service. Raffy's first book, *Journey through Genocide: Stories of Survivors and the Dead* (Dundurn Press, 2018) is a personal exploration of three modern crimes against humanity as the writer visits Darfuri refugees in Chad and survivors of the Tutsi Genocide in Rwanda and reflects on his own ancestors' fate in Kharpert, modern Turkey during the Armenian Genocide of 1915.

Anna Gazmarian lives and writes in Durham, North Carolina, where she works for the *Sun* magazine. She received an MFA from Bennington Writing Seminars. Her work has been featured by the *Rumpus*, *Longreads*, and *Quarterly West*. Her memoir about mental illness and faith will be published by Simon & Schuster in October 2023.

Mashinka Firunts Hakopian is a writer, researcher, and artist born in Yerevan and residing in Glendale, California. She is a senior researcher at the Berggruen Institute and held a teaching appointment in UCLA's Department of English from 2017 to 2019. She holds a PhD from the University of Pennsylvania in the history of art. She is an associate editor at *Noema* magazine and a contributing editor at the *Los Angeles Review of Books*. Her writing and reviews have appeared in *Performance Research Journal*, *Art in America*, the *Journal of Cinema and Media Studies*, and the *Los Angeles Review of Books*. She is a cofounder of the media performance collective Research Service, with Avi Alpert and Danny Snelson, with whom she has presented projects for the New Museum, Palais de Tokyo, LA MOCA, ICA Philadelphia, and elsewhere. Her book *Algorithmic Bias: Lectures for Intelligent Machines* is forthcoming from X Artists' Books.

Olivia Katrandjian is a writer and journalist whose work has been published by the *New York Times*, the *Los Angeles Times*, the BBC, PBS, ABC News, and *Quartz*, among other outlets. In 2016, she moved to Luxembourg to write *The Ghost Soldier*, a historical novel about two Armenian Americans in the Ghost Army, a top-secret group of artists who used inflatable tanks, sound effects, and fake radio transmissions to deceive the Germans in World War II. The manuscript was awarded second place in the National Literary Prize of Luxembourg in 2019. Olivia is currently pursuing a master's degree in creative writing at Oxford University and is the founder and president of the International Armenian Literary Alliance.

Nancy Kricorian is a writer and organizer based in New York. She is the author of the novels *Zabelle*, *Dreams of Bread and Fire*, and *All the Light There Was*. She has taught at Barnard, Columbia, Rutgers, Yale, and New York University, as well as in the New York City public schools with Teachers and Writers Collaborative and in Birzeit for the Palestine Writing Workshop. She is currently at work on a novel about Armenians in Beirut during the Lebanese Civil War.

Naira Kuzmich was born in Armenia and raised in the Los Angeles enclave of Little Armenia. Her nonfiction has appeared in *Ecotone, Threepenny Review, Michigan Quarterly Review, Cincinnati Review, Massachusetts Review, Guernica, Southern Review, Shenandoah*, and elsewhere. Naira passed away from lung cancer in 2017 at the age of twenty-nine.

Chris McCormick is the author of a novel, *The Gimmicks* (Harper, 2020), and a short story collection, *Desert Boys*, winner of the 2017 Stonewall Book Award–Barbara Gittings Literature Award. His essays and stories have appeared in the *Atlantic*, the *Los Angeles Times, Tin House*, and *Plough-shares*. He grew up in the Antelope Valley on the California side of the Mojave Desert before earning a BA from the University of California, Berkeley, and an MFA from the University of Michigan. He is an assistant professor in the creative writing program at Minnesota State University, Mankato, and is at work on his next novel.

Carene Rose Mekertichyan is an actress, writer, singer, educator, and proud Angelena. She received her training from Dartmouth College and the London Academy of Music and Dramatic Art (LAMDA). As a Black Armenian woman, she is drawn to storytelling that centers marginalized narratives and firmly believes that true art exists to create empathy and social change. Her identity and upbringing in Los Angeles informs both her art and intersectional activism. She serves as the artistic associate for social justice at Independent Shakespeare Co. and is also a teaching artist who has worked with the Unusual Suspects, Harlem School of the Arts, Creative Acts, Star Education, and Bresee Academy. She has most recently performed with Independent Shakespeare Co., Rogue Artists Ensemble, Palos Verdes Performing Arts, and Hero Theatre, and at the Getty Villa. Her plays have been produced at the Edinburgh Fringe Festival, MeetCute LA, and Sacred Fools' "We the People Theater Action." She is a Hero Theatre Company member and associate member of Sacred Fools.

Aram Mrjoian is a writer, editor, critic, and educator. He earned a PhD in creative writing at Florida State University and an MFA at Northwestern University. Aram has also served as a creative writing mentor or instructor at the Adroit Journal, 826, Hugo House, StoryStudio, and Open Books Chicago. His writing has appeared or is forthcoming in *Electric Literature*,

Barrelhouse, Gulf Coast, the *Millions,* the *Rumpus, Boulevard, Longreads,* and many other publications. He is currently a visiting assistant professor in English at Pacific Lutheran University.

Aline Ohanesian is the author of the critically acclaimed novel *Orhan's Inheritance* (Algonquin Books, 2015). She is currently working on her second novel, a reimagining of Homer's Odyssey. She lives and writes in San Juan Capistrano, California.

Although she has spent the bulk of her career working in the Middle East, **Scout Tufankjian** is best known for her work documenting both of Barack Obama's presidential campaigns. Her book on the 2007–2008 campaign, *Yes We Can: Barack Obama's History-Making Presidential Campaign,* was a *New York Times* and *LA Times* best seller. Her second book, *There Is Only the Earth: Images from the Armenian Diaspora Project,* is the culmination of six years documenting Armenian communities in over twenty different countries. More recently, she has worked for the HALO Trust in Nagorno-Karabakh and Angola, and has served as a temporary acting director of the Committee to Protect Journalists' Emergency Response Team. She is a two-time TUMO Workshop leader, in Yerevan and Stepanakert, and continues to work as a freelance photographer and as a consultant for both RISC Training and the Committee to Protect Journalists. While she still feels guilty about her extremely poor Armenian language skills, she has recently started taking classes again and is using this bio to make sure she sticks to it. More of her work can be seen at www.scouttufankjian.com.

The editor in chief and cofounder of Hyperallergic, **Hrag Vartanian** is an editor, art critic, curator, and lecturer on contemporary art with an expertise on the intersection of art and politics.

Raffi Joe Wartanian is a writer, musician, and educator who currently teaches writing at UCLA. His essays have appeared in the *New York Times, Los Angeles Review of Books, Miami Herald, Baltimore Sun, Outside* magazine, and beyond; his poetry has appeared in *No, Dear* magazine, *Ararat* magazine, and elsewhere. Raffi has taught writing to veterans at the Manhattan VA, incarcerated writers at Rikers Island jail, youth in Armenia, and undergraduates at Columbia University, where he earned an MFA in writing. He is the recipient of grants and fellowships from the Fulbright Program, Humanity in Action, and Eurasia Partnership Foundation. As a musician, Raffi has released two albums of original compositions: *Critical Distance* (2019) and *Pushkin Street* (2013).